Southeast Asian Chinese and China

The Politico-Economic Dimension

Edited by

Leo Suryadinata

TIMES ACADEMIC PRESS

First published 1995 by

Times Academic Press
An imprint of Federal Publications (S) Pte Ltd
(A member of the Times Publishing Group)
Times Centre
1 New Industrial Road
Singapore 536196

Reprinted 1997

ISBN 981 210 066 0

Printed by JBW Printers & Binders Pte Ltd, Singapore

Contents

List of Tables

List of Figures

List of Appendices

Preface

The papers included in this volume were originally presented at the *International Conference on Southeast Asian Chinese: Culture, Economy and Society*, held on 21–23 January 1994 in Singapore. They have been revised and edited for this publication. The conference was jointly organized by the Singapore Society of Asian Studies, the Association of Nanyang University Graduates and the Singapore Federation of Chinese Clan Associations.

I would like to take this opportunity to thank the writers for their contribution and Times Academic Press for publishing this book.

Chia Ban Seng
Chairman
Organizing Committee
January 1995

A Note from the Editor

Hanyu Pinyin has been used to transliterate Chinese terms, except in Yen Ching-hwang and Huang Jiangli's papers which use the Wade system as they are historical studies. (For instance, Ch'ing is used instead of Qing.)

Please also note that the terms "Overseas Chinese" and "Chinese overseas" in various articles in this volume have not been changed to "ethnic Chinese" as I do not want to impose my view on the paper contributors.

Leo Suryadinata
January 1995

Part 1: Overview

The Southeast Asian Chinese and China: An Introduction

Leo Suryadinata

The opening of China in recent years and the increase in ethnic Chinese investment there have drawn attention to the so-called overseas Chinese again. Many observers are of the view that there is a direct link between China and the "overseas Chinese". This is based on the assumption that the ethnic bond is the most important factor in determining the above relationship. This point is of course debatable.

Many observers tend to use the term "overseas Chinese" to refer to all Chinese outside mainland China. In this category, the Chinese in Hong Kong and Taiwan are also "overseas Chinese".[1] I have difficulty in accepting this category, because Hong Kong and Taiwan are Chinese societies. They are part of China and the Chinese there are not "overseas Chinese". If Hong Kong Chinese and Taiwanese Chinese are not "overseas Chinese", can all the Chinese in Southeast Asia and in other countries be termed "overseas Chinese"? I think this is equally misleading.

The term "overseas Chinese" is often considered as the English version of the Chinese term *Huaqiao*, which means Chinese sojourners.[2] Indeed, prior to the Second World War, all Chinese in Southeast Asia by China's law were considered as Chinese nationals. They were overseas Chinese. However, it is debatable if we should continue to call the 20 million Chinese in Southeast Asia who were born and brought up in Southeast Asia and who have local citizenship, overseas Chinese. Are they still sojourners who will eventually "return" to their ancestral land? Surely they are in their own country and their own homeland. Granted, there are many Chinese who are recent migrants and some are still citizens of China. However, these Chinese tend to form a small minority.

One can argue that in the modern context, the term "overseas Chinese" or "Chinese overseas" does not denote Chinese citizenship. It is merely a geographical expression. Therefore, it is not wrong to call the Chinese outside mainland China, Taiwan and Hong Kong "overseas Chinese" or "Chinese overseas". Even if the term no longer has the connotation of China citizenship, it is still China-centric as it sees things from China's point of view.

If the term overseas Chinese (or Chinese overseas) is improper, what term should be used to refer to the Chinese in Southeast Asia in general? Ethnic Chinese is a more neutral English term as it embraces the Chinese population outside China regardless of their citizenship.[3] The Chinese equivalent of this term is *Huaren*.[4] Mainland Chinese government and scholars have also employed this term to refer to the Chinese population who live in foreign countries. *Huaqiao* can be used when one refers to Southeast Asian Chinese during a certain historical period and to Chinese nationals who reside in Southeast Asia.[5]

The Chinese in Southeast Asia are indeed a heterogeneous group. However, it is a well-known fact that no matter where they reside, they are quite successful in their economic pursuits. Why are they successful? What is their economic position? What is the nature of their economy? Are they an integral part of Southeast Asian society? What are their political and economic links with resurgent China? What has motivated them to invest in mainland China? What is the extent of their investments and what are their prospects? What are the problems faced by the Southeast Asian Chinese? These are some of the questions that the papers in this collection attempt to answer.

The Chinese in Southeast Asia play a crucial economic role. Some observers maintain that they have dominated the economy of each country in this region. Yoshihara Kunio's paper argues that Southeast Asian Chinese, especially those in ASEAN, are economically very successful due to the fact that the ethnic Chinese have a stronger work ethic than the indigenous population. He is also of the view that the ethnic Chinese are rent-seekers rather than genuine capitalists. In fact, he contends that in Southeast Asia, there has been a development of *ersatz* capitalism based on light industry rather than genuine capitalism based on heavy industry and high technology.[6]

Jamie Mackie gives another perspective of the economic role of the ethnic Chinese in Southeast Asia. He points out that there is no such thing as an ethnic Chinese economy but many Southeast Asian economic systems. He analyses the five economic systems in the ASEAN states in which ethnic Chinese are an integral part. Taking issue with Yoshihara, he argues that many Chinese tycoons in Southeast Asia can no longer be described as rent-seekers and *ersatz* capitalists but genuine entrepreneurs. They are making positive contributions to the development of the ASEAN states.

Christianto Wibisono examines the economic role of the ethnic Chinese in Indonesia from the colonial time to the present, arguing that there has been a basic change in the Indonesian economic structure and the growth of Chinese economic share in the country. The emergence of Chinese conglomerates tended to dominate the private sector, giving rise to friction between the indigenous Indonesians and the ethnic Chinese in recent years. There is no solution in sight due to the deep-seated racial prejudice.

Chew Soon Beng and Azlan bin Ghazali, on the other hand, examine entrepreneurs in Singapore. Focusing on the graduates of tertiary education, Chew and Azlan discover that there are two factors which will determine whether the graduate will opt for self-employment. Nevertheless, a large number of the graduates (the majority happens to be ethnic Chinese) in the past tended to seek salaried employment. It is only in recent years, due to an increased supply of graduates, that more may be pushed to opt for self-employment, i.e. to become entrepreneurs. The study is based on the survey sample of six organizations, comprising National University of Singapore, Nanyang Technological University, Canadian Alumni, New Zealand Alumni, Marketing Institute of Singapore and Massachusetts Institute of Technology Club. It is a pity that the graduates of the defunct Nanyang University have been excluded. In fact, many Nanyang graduates are known to have become successful entrepreneurs. A study of this group may contribute to a better understanding of entrepreneurship among the Singapore graduates.

Generally, the economic position of ethnic Chinese in each Southeast Asian country has been strong. They have also established "ethnic networks" in Southeast Asia which have promoted their business. Due to this position, there is a misperception that ethnic Chinese form a homogeneous group which dominate Southeast Asian economy. In recent years, as mentioned earlier, they have also invested in mainland China on a massive scale. Ethnic ties have been mentioned as the major factor for their investment.

Wang Gungwu's article examines the role of ethnic Chinese in China's development from a historical and global perspective. He maintains that the two historical models of ethnic Chinese involvement in China – the Sincere/Wing On model which was profit-oriented but was a prelude to the eventual return of the company to China, and the Tan Kah Kee model which was a form of patriotism – can no longer be applied to the present.

China as a profitable place in which the Chinese abroad are attracted to invest is unique in history. Nevertheless, the present investment in China by Southeast Asian Chinese must not be exaggerated, and must be placed in the perspective of world-wide interest in China's rapid economic development. Like Mackie's, his article argues that many Chinese are Southeast Asians and the bulk of their investment is still in the region. Wang ends his article by offering a few scenarios on ethnic Chinese investment in mainland China, arguing that the profit factor tends to guide the behaviour of ethnic Chinese businessmen.

Yen Ching-hwang also looks at the relations between the ethnic Chinese and China during the early 20th century, using the Chinese Chamber of Commerce in Singapore as a case study. During the late Qing period, there was a triangular contest among the Qing government, the reformists and the revolutionaries for the support of overseas Chinese. Yen argues that the Qing government used the Singapore Chinese Chamber of Commerce as a mechanism for the control of the overseas Chinese and succeeded. Although it is a historical study, it sheds light on China's behaviour during the Kuomintang (KMT) era and even after the Communists came to power in 1949.

Huang Jianli's article deals with the economic relations between ethnic Chinese in Singapore/Malaya and the founding of the People's Republic of China. He argues that in 1949–50, Communist China remained very keen in tapping the resources and skills of overseas Chinese. Beijing was making special efforts to restore family remittances to its normal level. However, Communist insurgencies in Malaya/Singapore and the fear of deportation among the businessmen in the British colonies led to the local orientation of the Chinese. Huang contends that during the Communist takeover, the Chinese in Singapore/Malaya were deeply concerned with three other matters: the foreign exchange clamp-down, the East Indies trade and the Sterling Trade Pact with Japan. They were concerned with their economic interests. And these economic interests eventually pushed the ethnic Chinese here to look beyond China and back to the region and the West.

The triumph of the Communist party in mainland China caused a temporary break between the relations of many Southeast Asian states and China. Ethnic Chinese remittances and investment in China also declined significantly. However, China did not abandon the overseas Chinese completely. But because of the Cold War, it was difficult for China to gain a lot of benefits from the Southeast Asian Chinese.

The situation changed only after the end of the Cold War. The disappearance of the threat of communism served as an impetus for ethnic Chinese investment in the mainland. More important is the economic opportunity provided by mainland China to the ethnic Chinese, especially to those who are still first generation migrants or those who are still culturally

Chinese. Leo Suryadinata's paper examines China's policy towards the ethnic Chinese after the re-emergence of Deng Xiaoping which attempted to stop the exodus of the domestic overseas Chinese. It also wanted to tap the skills and capital of the ethnic Chinese from all over the world.

To a certain extent, Beijing has been quite successful in attracting Chinese capital. However, the largest amount has come from Taiwan and Hong Kong rather than Southeast Asia. Nevertheless, since some Southeast Asian Chinese capital has also been invested in Hong Kong, it is quite difficult to know for sure the proportion of Southeast Asian Chinese investment in China. However, from available information, most scholars are of the view that the bulk of ethnic Chinese capital is still in the region rather than in the mainland.

Some scholars have exaggerated the influx of "overseas Chinese" capital into mainland China and considered all Chinese outside China as "overseas Chinese". Hence Taiwanese Chinese and Hong Kong Chinese became "overseas Chinese". This tends to confuse the problem and does not add real understanding to the relationship between the Southeast Asian Chinese and China.

Nevertheless, it is true that during the post-Cold War period, trade and investment from Southeast Asia increased remarkably. The ASEAN states which had not been too friendly with China in the past began to pay attention to the economic opportunities provided by China. Ho Khai Leong's paper analyses the increased economic interactions between Malaysia and China. The role of the ethnic Chinese in these relationships is important. Nevertheless, foreign investments in China from Malaysia, especially by the Chinese, has still been quite limited.

Foreign investment in China from the Philippines has also been quite limited. Many, in fact, have invested in Taiwan. Nevertheless, in the last couple of years, there is indication that the Philippine Chinese have begun to invest in the mainland. President Ramos appealed to the Philippine Chinese tycoons to invest in the national projects first before going overseas. As the ethnic Chinese play significant economic roles in their countries of residence, their investment in China often caused concern, if not dissatisfaction, among the indigenous population. The ethnic Chinese in Indonesia, Malaysia and the Philippines often face criticism because they have invested in China. Their political loyalty has sometimes been questioned. Opposition politicians often use this sensitive issue to embarrass the government.

Since the Chinese population forms the majority in Singapore, investment in the mainland does not create a domestic problem. Not surprisingly the largest investment in China by Southeast Asian states came from Singapore. In 1990 Singapore also constituted 2% of the total overseas investment in China. However, in the last couple of years, the amount has drastically increased. Yong Pow Ang's paper traces the investment of the city-state in China, providing some interesting figures. There is a form of joint venture between Singapore government companies and the Chinese government, which is absent in other ASEAN states. Since Singapore is surrounded by the "Malay seas", the government is also careful in having balanced investment in other countries.

It is also interesting to note that not all ethnic Chinese tycoons have invested in China. Many have shied away due to political and other reasons. In fact, many Chinese investors from the ASEAN states belong to the category of small or medium businesses. More studies have to be done in order to know the actual economic relations between the Southeast Asian Chinese and China.

Endnotes

1 See for instance, S. Gordon Redding, *The Spirit of Chinese Capitalism*, New York: Walter de Gruyter, 1993.

2 For an excellent study on the term *Huaqiao*, see Wang Gungwu, "A Note on the Origins of Huaqiao", in his *Community and Nation in Southeast Asia*, Kuala Lumpur: Heinemann, 1985, pp. 118–127.

3 In some cases, the term Chinese descent may be more appropriate when we refer to Southeast Asians who have largely lost their Chinese cultural identity. The equivalent Chinese term is *Huayi*.

4 Zhou Nanjing (ed.), *Shijie Huaqiao Huaren Cidian* (*Dictionary of Overseas Chinese*), Beijing: Peking University, 1993, pp. 267.

5 *Ibid.*, p. 277.

6 Yoshihara first developed his idea of *ersatz* capitalism in his book entitled *The Rise of Ersatz Capitalism in Southeast Asia*, Kuala Lumpur: Oxford University Press, 1988.

1

The Ethnic Chinese in Southeast Asia and China

*Wong Kan Seng**

There are about 20 million ethnic Chinese in Southeast Asia which is only 5% of Southeast Asia's total population. But Southeast Asian Chinese make up about 80% of the ethnic Chinese outside China, Taiwan and Hong Kong. Most have been here for many generations. They are citizens and an integral part of the countries they live in. Yet all too often, Southeast Asian Chinese are still perceived by the public and scholar alike as a mirror reflecting the observer's broader concerns about China. In the process, their real place in their respective countries of residence has been overlooked.

During the Cold War, for instance, they were sometimes regarded with suspicion as possible agents of communist ideology. Such a perception ignored the fact that many, if not most, were private businessmen and traders who had the most to lose if communism ever triumphed in Southeast Asia.

China's present economic reforms have again focused attention on the Southeast Asian Chinese. Competition for investments from China has drawn attention to their role in China's economic development, thereby occasioning some questioning of their loyalties.

Some press commentary in the region has suggested that the decline of investments in their countries is due to the ethnic attraction of China to Chinese businessmen. Such ideas are not shared by governments. But they are deeply ingrained and could well catch popular imaginations. Of course, such ideas are false. Businessman everywhere are motivated only by the hard-headed calculation of profits. If they do not believe that they can make money, nothing will induce them to invest in China or anywhere else. And all countries are now facing a more competitive environment. Nobody is compelled to invest in Southeast Asia. If not China, businessmen will put their money in India, Vietnam, Myanmar, Cambodia, Mexico, or anywhere they can make money.

In fact, it would be foolish for any businessman or country to depend solely on China for a livelihood. The Asia-Pacific as a whole is one of the most vibrant and dynamic markets in the global economy. China is of course of growing significance in the Asia-Pacific market. But Japan and North America are still and will remain the largest components for some time to come. The lesson is obvious. We all need wider linkages to continue to prosper. Hence, the importance that most countries in the region place on APEC. And we must also work for closer individual and collective ties between the ASEAN economies and the vast North American market.

When Southeast Asian Chinese invest in China, they do, of course, have an advantage in understanding the language and cultural mores. But they are acting primarily as businessmen and citizens of their own countries and not as Chinese. Businessmen invest where they can make profits. This would be true even if there were no China.

Misunderstanding over the role of Chinese businessmen in China's economic development is only one facet of a wider problem. The distinct and often complex cultural, social and economic roles that Southeast Asian Chinese play in their own countries and in their interactions with China, Taiwan and Hong Kong need to be better appreciated. They should be studied not through the prism of the Cold War or some other external framework, but as intrinsic parts of their own societies and the region. The Southeast Asian Chinese are no longer just sojourners. They have no intention of returning to China. They have chosen to make their homes and raise their children in the countries where they now live. Their future is inextricably linked to that of their countries of residence.

This conference is therefore an important occasion. I understand it is the largest bilingual international conference on Southeast Asian Chinese. The Singapore Society of Asian Studies, the Association of Nanyang University Graduates and the Singapore Federation of Chinese Clan Associations are to be congratulated on their initiative.

I am told that the conference will cover a wide spectrum of subjects: economic relations between the ethnic Chinese in China, Hong Kong and Taiwan, continuity and change in the ASEAN Chinese societies, ethnic Chinese literature in Southeast Asia and their religions and beliefs, among others. I hope that it will lead to a deeper and broader understanding of the unique role of the Southeast Asian Chinese and the contribution they have made to their countries.

Such an understanding is all the more important because it cannot be denied that China's rise has aroused anxieties, not just in the region but further afield, even in the West. An unemotional and scholarly re-examination of the Southeast Asian Chinese is thus critical. China's rise to great power status – in reality and not just by diplomatic courtesy – is the central strategic fact of the 1990s. It will exert a profound influence on the international relations of the 21st century.

It is a fact of life that small countries living on the periphery of a large and powerful country will always cast a wary eye at their neighbour. This is a geo-political reality that has nothing to do with the intentions of the big country. Ethnic differences are also a fact of life that will not be erased by wishful thinking. In some Southeast Asian countries, the role of the ethnic Chinese will therefore always be sensitive. We should recognize this as a fact and learn to deal with it. In such countries, the Chinese community will always have to do more to prove themselves as good citizens. But a better understanding of their real role can ameliorate the problems even if they will never be completely erased. Hence, the importance of this conference.

I have also been told by the organisers that prominent scholars from the ASEAN countries, Australia, Japan, France, China, Hong Kong and Taiwan are participating. Let me welcome you to Singapore. Your research and discussions will not be just of academic interest. It can have a real impact on the lives of Southeast Asian Chinese. I wish you every success.

Note

* Mr Wong Kan Seng is Singapore's Minister for Home Affairs. This is his opening address (with title provided by the editor) at the *International Conference on Southeast Asian Chinese: Culture, Economy and Society*, delivered on 21 January 1994.

2

The Southeast Asian Chinese and the Development of China

Wang Gungwu

There has been growing international interest in investments in businesses in China by those of Chinese descent, especially those from Southeast Asia. Reports in the press include stories of a few spectacular investments with overtones of pride in the success of China in developing itself after many years with a closed economy. There have also been wild exaggerations about the extent of Southeast Asian Chinese investments in China. Many of these reports are unable to distinguish between investment monies from ethnic Chinese in Southeast Asia investing in China and investments emanating from Hong Kong and Taiwan. And this can indeed be very confusing.

Other reports emphasize the pace and size of the China economic boom and the way that has attracted a great deal of international attention. China has attracted foreign investment from all over the world. And it is important to see the whole thing in context. Yet other reports concentrate on the reactions of various peoples in the Southeast Asian region, especially in ASEAN countries, where local ethnic Chinese have been particularly successful during the past two decades. In particular, much interest has been shown in North America and Europe, as well as elsewhere in Asia, in how people in Southeast Asia react to the idea that there are 25 to 30 million ethnic Chinese outside of China. And when these Chinese are mixed up with the Chinese of Hong Kong and Taiwan, thus making a total of over 50 million, their seeming economic power is regarded as somewhat alarming.[1]

All this attention and concern form part of the same reaction to a rapidly developing Chinese economy. One must understand why this concern is there and how we can explain the circumstances that have led to the present set of developments. It is important to note that many of the contemporary comments reflect past reactions to the political and economic activities of Southeast Asian Chinese, especially those during the first half of the century. We need, therefore, to ask the question, what is new about ethnic Chinese investment in China today? And how significant is it? I shall argue that what is happening now is unique, meaning that it comes from a unique combination of factors which deserves careful study.

The best way to appreciate what is significant or unique about recent investment decisions is to compare them with the developments of the past hundred years. You may not be surprised to hear this from a historian. But I do think that making these comparisons would greatly help us understand the major differences between what happened in the past and what is happening today.

Some Definitions

Let me begin with a few definitions about who we refer to as the Southeast Asian Chinese and what we mean by business investments that support the development of China. It is important to remind ourselves that when we talk about the ethnic Chinese, or *Huaren*, the term refers to those of Chinese descent who live *outside* the territories of China, that is, outside mainland China, Taiwan and Hong Kong-Macao.[2] Of course, for centuries, most of these Chinese were sojourners, but the process of turning these sojourners into citizens in the second half of this century is itself a new and most important historical phenomenon.

I might add a footnote about a word that is coming into regular use in other parts of the world which many apply to the Chinese, a term which may also be extremely misleading. This is the word 'diaspora', meaning dispersal. I note that in North America and Europe, it is a word that is used frequently for all kinds of people who live outside their home country. The Jewish diaspora is the one most frequently referred to, but there are also the Arab diaspora and the African diaspora.[3] And almost all non-native minorities in the United States and Canada are often referred to as such and such a diaspora, and, of course, that includes the Chinese diaspora. So you can imagine that word spreading elsewhere eventually. I do not agree to the word being used for the Chinese because it has implications which may have applied to some aspects of the sojourners in the past but do not apply to ethnic Chinese today. In many ways, diaspora is a word that has the kind of political content comparable to the term *Huaqiao*, which also has many political overtones. It has been difficult to remove some of the political connotations from that latter term. It is one of the reasons why we do not use the word *Huaqiao* in Southeast Asia today. But it is still used in China and it is still widely used in other parts of the world, most notably in North America. We must be very careful about its exact meaning and the proper context when it can be correctly used. In particular, we should try to make sure that the political content of the term is not misused, abused and misunderstood.

Let me return to the sojourners before they became citizens. The word sojourner originally referred to the traders, artisans and their relatives and clansmen who were peripheral to the economy of a great imperial power, who sought profits in overseas trade, and brought home exotic merchandise. They were in and out of China from the Song to the Qing dynasties, and most of them did not settle abroad. They went out to do business, many of them remaining outside, especially in Southeast Asia, for generations. Some of them did eventually settle but, as traders, they did not normally need to. Later on, by the middle of the 19th century, there came the labourers, men who left China as coolies with no intention or hope of becoming traders. They had gone out as indentured labour or on contracts, and most of them returned to China. Again, some of them did stay behind and, like the traders, became something like sojourners themselves.

We do not know whether these Southeast Asian traders invested their profits in China, if we understand investment to mean making business investments for the sake of profit. We know that the merchants came out of the ports of Southern China, particularly from Fujian and Guangdong, and that many of them went back, presumably with their profits. But what did they do with their profits? Did they re-invest in their trading ventures and go out to Southeast Asia again? Did they use their profits to support the larger imperial economy in China, or did they spread the profits around their villages and home towns, purchasing land and property and enriching their families and their local institutions? We must assume that some proportion of their wealth went to assist economic development in their native countries.

As for the large numbers of labourers who set off in search of a livelihood during the 19th century, they worked hard, sending some money home, and returning with savings to help their families, many simply relieved to be alive. Some of them did stay abroad to become traders and artisans, but most of them returned after a few years. However much they may have helped in the development of their home districts, there is no evidence to suggest that their impact on the larger economy, either of their province or their region, was ever significant.

After the 1890s, we know a great deal more about the Chinese outside China. There had evolved the concept of *Huaqiao*, translated as overseas

Chinese, an all-embracing term which emphasized the status of all Chinese as sojourners who, however long they had been outside China, had always intended to return to China. The term, in fact, more accurately describes those sojourners who were prepared to be associated with patriotism, and with Chinese nationalism. This was the period when China was much weakened through wars with the Western Powers and with Japan. In that context, the political significance of the term became greatly enhanced, and it became more difficult for *Huaqiao* to talk of investing in China for business profit alone. It was increasingly expected of them that their remittances to China were for patriotic, if not for philanthropic, reasons. That is to say, it was patriotic for them to remit their monies back for investment, even if that was not profitable.

The concept of patriotic overseas Chinese was further highlighted by the participation of some of the Chinese sojourners in the overthrow of the Qing dynasty and the support of the revolutionary movement of Sun Yat-sen. After that, for over four decades, the same patriotism led to their involvement in the struggle for power between the Guomindang and the Chinese Communist Party and also in the patriotic wars against Japan. In Southeast Asia and elsewhere, the concept was further articulated and strengthened by the growing numbers of the better educated sojourners, notably school teachers and journalists who joined the traders and workers in most territories and helped to make them more committed to politics in China.

The experiences of these years added to the political content of the concept of *Huaqiao*. As I have written much about this elsewhere, I shall not say any more here.[4] I shall turn to the next stage, the transition from the intensely political concept of *Huaqiao* to the new one of *Huaren* used to describe the citizens of the new nation states of Southeast Asia after the Second World War. This transition was not an easy one for most ethnic Chinese. Most of us who have lived through it know how difficult it was and how painful it was for the people of that generation. It was, of course, much easier for the children of the next generation. And by the time of the grandchildren, it would be very much easier. Nevertheless, we cannot ignore the fact that changing from alien sojourner to loyal citizen was a difficult transition and one that is not yet complete in some parts of the region.

We can now safely talk about *Huaren*, the common term since the 1960s for the ethnic Chinese who have become the new citizens of the nation states. In China, the term used is often *Waiji Huaren* (Chinese of foreign nationality). Very clearly, this reflects the fact that the majority of Chinese sojourners have settled down and sought local nationality. Also clearly, the fact that they settled down in different countries, and that these countries have different languages, cultures, histories and political and economic policies mean that we are now talking about a greater variety of ethnic Chinese. Each group of ethnic Chinese would be moulded by the different influences and conditions of the new nation states of which they are citizens. Also important is the fact that there has grown among them an educated middle class of professionals, including new generations of modern businessmen with an international outlook. There has thus been a natural transition from the era of patriotic and philanthropic remittances to one which emphasizes investments for business profit in a global capitalist environment.

This leads me to two other important definitions. We must distinguish cross-border business investment from remittances sent home for domestic, patriotic and philanthropic purposes. In the context of the development of China, the former is solely in search of profitable ventures. Business investment is not directly concerned with whether it contributes to the economy or not, although in fact it does if the investments are successful. Remittances, on the other hand, bring much needed foreign exchange into China's economy and create much temporary wealth for family, community or country. Unless they are invested profitably, however, they may not in fact do much to advance economic development and strengthen the national economy.

The ethnic Chinese entrepreneurs and business executives in each Southeast Asian country today naturally invest in local industry and development. They have been encouraged to do so for at least three decades. The more successful they are with their local invesments, the more they have surplus capital for further investment, most of which they have re-invested in their countries of adoption. But as surplus capital accumulates, there is also a natural drift of this capital as they look for new places and more profitable enterprises to invest in. And crossing borders for that kind of investment is totally natural in the world of business. All businessmen and their governments know that a certain amount of these investment funds have crossed from one country to another, especially within ASEAN, but also to Hong Kong and elsewhere, and more recently, via Hong Kong, to coastal China. In open capitalistic economies, the principle of investing where profits can be made is the norm. When investments across national boundaries are successful, it is expected that they would also strengthen the home bases of the entrepreneurs. In that case, they are actions which need not unduly trouble the home governments.

Huaqiao Investments: The Last Years of the Qing Dynasty

Let me turn to my main subject, the role of the Southeast Asian Chinese in the development of modern China. Prior to the 19th century, it would never have occurred to the imperial governments of China that sojourners originating from the southern provinces of Guangdong and Fujian, whether merchants or labourers, could help China by investing in its economic development. But when, from the 1870s onwards, Chinese diplomats regularly reported back to the Qing government about the large numbers of wealthy and successful Chinese living abroad, particularly those in Southeast Asia, attitudes began to change. Interest was shown in these successful Chinese and they were invited to invest in China. This was particularly true after the efforts to modernize the Chinese government following the Hundred Days Reform in 1898. The consulate officials of China in Singapore, Tokyo and San Francisco appealed to the local Chinese businessmen to increase trade with China and invest both capital and skills in China. Those merchants who responded were conferred titles that raised their status to that of "official merchants" (*shang-shen*). In this way, the Qing government was able to draw support from the wealthy and respectable community leaders (*qiaoling*), or the local Chinese establishment.

The wealth of the *Huaqiao*, as the term began to be commonly used, the modern skills the Qing officials recognized that the *Huaqiao* had acquired, and the fact that the *Huaqiao* longed to be recognized for their achievements by the Chinese government, were taken into account when officials began to contact *Huaqiao* businessmen overseas and tried to interest them in investing in China. Many of them needed little encouragement. They were already going back and forth between China and their businesses in Southeast Asia and some of them were looking for places in which to invest. At that time, however, good investment opportunities in China were limited. Furthermore, there were many obstacles to investing beyond one's own home town or village, and very little protection for one's investments. The easiest thing to do, and indeed that was what most *Huaqiao* did, was to send their remittances to the districts or counties nearest their own homes and look for safe investment opportunities there.

It is not easy to separate funds that were sent to China for these local investments from the money the *Huaqiao* were sending home to their families. Remittances of the latter kind went to build homes for their parents and other close relatives, to buy land and make sure that the future of their clans would be assured, to build schools and other community facilities and services and generally to improve the standard of living of the people who lived in their neighbourhood. There is little evidence of large-scale business investments. Even the few exceptions, which have become famous stories commemorated in various parts of Guangdong and Fujian, were mostly local ventures.

For example, Chen Qiyuan who had been in Southeast Asia, introduced the silk reeling factory to his home town of Foshan (near Guangzhou) and helped to enhance the quality of silk produced in his district.[5] Zhang Yunan pioneered railway transportation between Chaoan and Shantou in eastern Guangdong,[6] and there was the even better known Xinning (Taishan)-Jiangmen railway southwest of Guangzhou constructed through the efforts of Chen Yixi. The great pioneers of entrepreneurial investments for this period were Zhang Bishi, the Hakka capitalist who made his fortune in the Netherlands East Indies and invested in many parts of the Qing empire, and the Jian brothers whose business reached from Japan to the Malay Archipelago and who started the famous Nanyang Tobacco Company.[7]

The above examples can clearly be identified as modern investments, the first examples of technology transfers by Chinese living outside China. Those who chose to build railways had been impressed with what these could do for economic development. The case of Chen Yixi is specially noteworthy.[8] He had been a railway worker in the western United States. Many others in the United States and Canada had had similar experiences and shared his enthusiaism. He therefore had little difficulty in collecting funds from his friends and fellow natives of the Four Counties (including Taishan) to invest in the railway that joined Taishan to the major town of Jiangmen.

The railway is no longer there unfortunately, but I recently had the chance to visit Taishan and Jiangmen and read the public memorials to Chen Yixi. Clearly, his enterprise was greatly appreciated. Many writings suggest that he invested in the railway for patriotic reasons, to improve transportation and help develop China's economy. There was certainly an element of that. But no less important was the service he was performing for his home district. We will never know whether he had embarked on the project for profit alone because it was not proper to speak of such motives at the time. The railway cost him and his friends a great deal of money because there was local opposition to the railway passing through peasant farms and ancestral lands. If, over the decades, he and his friends made any profit from the whole investment, that would have been seen as just reward for their patriotism.

We do not have reliable figures for the overseas remittances to China during the Qing dynasty, not even for the first decade of the 20th century. We do know, however, that the investment projects mentioned above were few and exceptional. It is thus unlikely that similar investments would add up to more than a small proportion of the large sums sent back by the Chinese overseas to support family incomes, build new homes, new schools, new community halls and used to improve local services.

At the same time, there was the new phenomenon of anti-Manchu or anti-Qing activities among the Chinese overseas, especially after the defeat by Japan in 1895. Both reformists and revolutionaries sought funds for armed uprisings in China. Strong appeals were made for funds to support patriotic causes, including calls to invest in China's technological and commercial modernization. Sun Yat-sen and his revolutionary friends were the first to try and tap overseas Chinese sources. They had particular appeal among southern Chinese who wanted to see the Manchus overthrown, but the funds they received for arms and patriotic recruits came mostly from the poorer classes and the secret societies.

Kang Youwei, Liang Qichao and other reformists followed and appealed to the better educated and the middling rich, and had some impact among the wealthy commercial establishment, notably in Japan, Southeast Asia and North America. But the funds received were given for patriotic reasons. Investments in newspapers and modern schools supporting the reformists were certainly not made for profit. Again, like the examples of exceptional commercial and industrial investments for profit mentioned earlier, funding for the much publicized political causes received by both reformists and revolutionaries is likely to have been only a fraction of the total volume of remittances sent back by the overseas Chinese.

Huaqiao Investments: 1911–1980s

The next period from 1911 to the 1980s may be divided into two. During the first period, from the establishment of the Republic of China to 1949, there were numerous reports about politicians who continued to go among the Chinese overseas to compete for support and for funds. Some of them received considerable publicity, others were clandestine efforts and were unknown until party archives and other records surfaced in more recent times to document the amounts received.[9]

More dramatic were the various appeals to save China from imperialists of one kind or another, especially the angry responses to the Treaty of Versailles that culminated in the May Fourth movement in 1919; the nation-wide demonstrations associated with the May Thirtieth movement in 1925; the Japanese advances in Shandong province that led to the Jinan Incident in 1928; the outrage at the invasion of Manchuria in 1931–32; and the eight-year Sino-Japanese War that started after 7 July 1937. After the end of the War in 1945, there were also calls to reconstruct the postwar economy which led to a brief period of optimism when much money was remitted to China.

In addition, there were numerous calls for relief donations in aid of natural disasters, like floods, famines and epidemics; and for the financial support of education, infrastructural projects to boost the national economy, other patriotic movements to buy national products to assist Chinese manufacturing industries, and so on. Added to the normal flood of remittances to meet family, locality and other economic and domestic needs in the home towns and villages of the overseas Chinese, estimates of some three and a half billion US dollars from all over the world being sent to China between 1911 and 1949 would not seem unlikely.[10]

For this period, we also know a great deal more about the remittances. They provided the Chinese economy with a large part of its foreign exchange and, in this way, the *Huaqiao* contributed some badly needed capital for the development of the country. Direct business investment for profit by overseas Chinese, however, was another story. The research done by various scholars over the past decades has enabled us to gather usable data about the size of the total remittances during those 38 years as well as of the industrial and commercial investments recorded for provinces like Guangdong and Fujian and the municipality of Shanghai. I am indebted to the careful work of Professor Lin Jinzhi and his colleagues in calculating the figures for this period.[11] Of the figures recorded for investment, they suggest that about 60% of the investments went to Guangdong and slightly more than 20% to Fujian and the remainder, slightly less than 20%, to Shanghai.

Also of interest is that, for Guangdong, more than 50% of the investments was in real estate, and nearly 50% of all investment in Fujian was also in real estate. In contrast, about 80% of the capital sent to Shanghai was invested in industry (nearly 50%) and commerce (about 30%). Very little went into industry in Guangdong: of the remaining 45% or so of investments, they were, in order of importance, in commerce, transport and finance. Fujian did a little better where industry was concerned: industrial investment was slightly ahead of commerce and transport.

According to Lin Jinzhi, the most significant indicator of the scale of known business investment as compared with the total amount of remittances to China from the Chinese abroad is that investment was about 3–4%, and at most 5%, of the total remittances. The figures suggest that overseas Chinese were overwhelmingly concerned with helping their family and trying to meet local social, cultural and economic needs, and with being patriotic and philanthropic. This is not an unreasonable conclusion. Any survey of the conditions of China during these years would confirm that China did not provide the environment for safe and profitable investments. It was simply much easier to make money outside China than within. Most Chinese overseas knew by the 1920s, if not earlier, that they could help China more by sending home some of the money made abroad than by investing in businesses inside China.

We can now point to two kinds of overseas Chinese response to China's appeals which emerged during this period. The first might be described as the Sincere-Wing On model, and is drawn from the successful example of Chinese in Australia investing in department stores and a variety of light industries, first in Hong Kong and then in Shanghai.[12] The investment decisions were modern and rational. There was no sentimentality behind them. The money was not invested in one's home town. It was not seen as investing to help the national economy or to save China from imperialism. While not being the first of its kind, it represented the most successful example of capitalist investment for profit. The Sincere and Wing On companies were so profitable that they were copied by companies like Daxin and Xinxin which followed the earlier two into Shanghai. It was a model that did attract imitators, but the numbers were few and the amounts invested relative to total remittances from overseas were small. A distinctive feature of this model was that the Chinese entrepreneurs who invested in this way in Hong Kong and Shanghai did so as a prelude to, or as preparation for, their eventual return to China.[13]

The second had an earlier history and had become quite common by the beginning of this century. The most outstanding example of the model, however, was Chen Jiageng (Tan Kah Kee) who started his spectacular career as benefactor to his home and family, to his village and district, to the neighbouring city of Xiamen and the counties of southern Fujian, and finally to the nation.[14] His example was so influential that it would be proper to call it the Tan Kah Kee model. By this model, philanthropy was extended to cover investments in local industry, but mainly to support the philanthropic projects that had been started. Some of the investments did lead to involvement in the development of the national economy, and even to a role in national politics in the People's Republic of China, but these latter were peculiar to the personality of Tan Kah Kee rather than a necessary part of the model.

Both models were prominent in the literature of overseas Chinese contributions to the development of China during the 1911–1949 period. But neither can be applied to the present for reasons that shall be dealt with in the final part of this paper dealing with the reform years of the 1980s.

The second part of this period covers the years from the founding of the People's Republic in 1949 to about 1980. During these 30 years, capitalist families and their investments were generally unwelcome, certainly suspect and eventually penalized. Three periods might be distinguished.[15] Between 1949 and 1957, there was a period when overseas Chinese who returned to China were considered patriotic. Although the remittances sent back to the families of *Huaqiao* (*Qiaojuan*) were important, and the money brought back by returned sojourners (*Guiqiao*) was welcome, this was mainly politically motivated, and partly to deny support and legitimacy for the regime in Taiwan.

Between 1957 and 1966, most Southeast Asian Chinese turned their attention to becoming loyal nationals of the new states of the region, investing in local nation-building projects and taking advantage of the many new opportunities to assist in national development.[16] This was particularly true in Thailand, Malaysia and Singapore, but also in the Philippines, Indonesia and Burma, and even in the increasingly complex situation in the Indo-Chinese states. This was necessary at a time when local nationalist leaders had grave suspicions about the loyalty of their ethnic Chinese. This turning away from China invited suspicion and resentment in China towards those who rejected identification with the Beijing government. On the other hand, what was perceived as virulently anti-capitalist policies by Beijing idealogues had further persuaded Southeast Asian Chinese businessmen to concentrate on local economic development. This trend was further encouraged by the Cultural Revolution in China during the period 1966–1976. The reaction in China towards the returned overseas Chinese and to the families of all overseas Chinese within China confirmed that there was no future for any kind of investment in the development of China.

The reforms launched by Deng Xiaoping marked a new era in economic policies, but it is important to note that, for the period from 1978 to 1989, there was still considerable caution among the Southeast Asian Chinese about sending remittances to China, and even more so about investing there. The opening of China was indeed welcome and traditional responses like remitting funds to families and home towns were greatly encouraged. But there were no serious investments in commerce and industry until after 1989.

In short, throughout history and including the most recent period up to the 1980s, most Chinese overseas remitted money home to augment family incomes, to buy land and build homes in their home towns and villages; and also for charities, education, and contributions to local welfare and community projects. Beyond that, there were appeals to them all to help China on issues of national salvation, whether against western imperialists, Japanese invaders, greedy and quarrelsome warlords, or anti-Guomindang communists and other rivals for supreme power. Where appeals concerned investment in industry and commerce, they were usually made in terms of patriotic support for national development, of buying Chinese-made manufactures, and of resisting the encroachments of western and Japanese capitalism.

But never were the appeals *primarily* or *credibly* focused on investment for profit. Had they tried to do so, such appeals would not have been very credible. Given that China was continually under threat from external or internal enemies and often in dire peril of disorder and collapse throughout this period, there were severe limitations on profit-making and there was indeed very little that could guarantee any investment that was made simply for profit.

Reformist China and Rapid Economic Development since the 1980s

Traditional remittances from ethnic Chinese abroad in the early years of reform must be separated from the question of business investments for profit. The hesitation about investing was understandable. Only after 1987 came a gradual awareness that the market socialism of China was not only growing, but there was a firm commitment to the market mechanism. Eventually, it became clear that profits were legitimate; risk-taking could be rewarding; and most telling, real profits could be made by investing in China, possibly more than in Southeast Asia itself. In addition, there is now the prospect that China is becoming the best investment target in the world.

All this is not to be confused with investments from Hong Kong and Taiwan. Although it is difficult to distinguish Hong Kong investments from Southeast Asian investments made via Hong Kong branch and associated organizations, it is necessary to be clear what we are talking about when we refer to ethnic Chinese investments from Southeast Asia.

It is interesting to compare Southeast Asian Chinese with the ethnic Chinese in the Americas, Australasia and Europe. In fact, these latter regions have the only large concentrations of *Huaqiao* today, the Chinese there being recent immigrants with passports and travelling papers issued by Beijing, Taipei or Hong Kong-Macao. Thus stronger "patriotic" sentiments have survived among them than anywhere else. They also have far less wealth than the Chinese in Southeast Asia. Where there is significant wealth, it is often wealth made through their investments in Hong Kong and Taiwan. On the other hand, the governments in the Americas, Europe and Australasia have been more liberal and tolerant about international investments. In fact, their own local capitalists are themselves interested in investing in China; therefore, there are no serious obstacles to investments by those of their residents of Chinese descent.

At the beginning of this paper, I suggested that what is happening today comes from a unique combination of factors. Let me now explain this unique situation by referring to three major changes which make the present totally different from anything that Southeast Asian Chinese investment in the development of China has ever encountered.

Firstly, the major change following the emergence of the Southeast Asian nation states. Those of Chinese descent are citizens and are expected to behave as national entrepreneurs. Having recently experienced the strong local nationalist sensitivities in the late colonial period, these ethnic Chinese either understand the new realities in their adopted homes well, or are fully committed to being loyal to their respective countries. Investing in China cannot be done without taking national concerns and priorities into account.

Furthermore, modern China has never combined an open economy with a fairly long period of full sovereignty and political stability. Certainly, there has not been any period of rapid economic growth in modern times, except possibly during the years 1928–1937 in some coastal provinces. But those were also the years of the Great Depression and the Japanese invasion of Manchuria and North China just prior to the outbreak of the Sino-Japanese War. Whatever economic gains there were did not survive the eight years of war. In comparison, the reforms initiated by Deng Xiaoping from 1978 to the present (despite the trauma of 4 June 1989) have had sustained effects on the whole economy, and especially the coastal provinces. For most of 15 years, there has been rapid growth in most sectors of an increasingly open economy. Such a long continuous period of growth is itself unique in modern Chinese history.

And then, we should note how much ethnic Chinese in the region and elsewhere have changed their attitudes towards China. They have moved away altogether from being identified with Chinese nationalism, patriotism and national salvation issues. There is no thought of returning to China to live. If Southeast Asian Chinese want to emigrate, they tend to choose immigrant socities like the United States, Canada or Australasia. Wherever they settle, the ethnic Chinese have sought to become middle class and modern professionals. Some are still willing to help relatives back in their home towns in China and perform some philanthropic work, but they are largely dedicated to economic and professional ties that bring mutual benefits. Where trade and investments are concerned, doing business solely for profit is, for the first time, openly acknowledged as being in the forefront of the new relationships being established.

There remain, of course, some similarities with the past, but the differences are much more significant. For example, the two notable models mentioned above, the Tan Kah Kee and the Sincere-Wing On models, would seem, on the surface, to be still discernible. But, when looked at more closely, the differences are crucial.

The Tan Kah Kee model of contributing large and regular sums of money to support family homes, local schools and tertiary institutions and other community amenities has not survived in Southeast Asia except among a few older Chinese, and altogether on a much smaller scale. What is gone, however, is the involvement with China politics and the willingness to bring their fortunes back to China the way Tan Kah Kee did.

As for the Sincere-Wing On model of investing in China's industries and markets for profit, there are superficial examples of those who are doing just that today. But the crucial difference is that the modern ethnic Chinese entrepreneurs retain their bases in their own countries and are only prepared to invest from afar. They are neither ready to move their businesses back to China (or Hong Kong), which was what the Sincere-Wing On companies had done, nor prepared to lose any opportunity to firm up their positions as national capitalists in their adopted countries. Indeed, they continually hope to increase their wealth and status and enhance the roles they can play there.

Let me now try and bring all this to a close. China as a profitable place in which the Chinese abroad are attracted to invest is unique in history. Nevertheless, the present investments in China by ethnic Chinese of Southeast Asia must not be exaggerated, and must be placed in the perspective of world-wide interest in China's rapid economic development. Let me take these two points separately.

Firstly, we need to distinguish between local remittances to family and home towns (including funds for schools, temples, domestic and speculative housing) and extensive trading and industrial investments (including modern professional services). It will then be seen that, while the former is aimed exclusively at the places of origin in China of the ethnic Chinese, the latter comes largely from business developments within respective countries and within the region who are seeking to expand their activities into China. The highly profitable enterprises of the region, not exclusively those of ethnic Chinese, had been investing in Hong Kong, or have been venturing into other continents (including North America, Australasia and Europe). Now they include ambitions to obtain their share of the China market.

Secondly, we need to note the full extent of the total foreign investment in China and compare the portion belonging to Southeast Asian Chinese. This requires much careful study and analysis of Southeast Asian investments in China, Hong Kong and Taiwan respectively. We also need to compare them with the volume of ethnic Chinese investments made elsewhere in Southeast Asia, East Asia, North America, Australasia and Europe. And, not least, we must also compare such investments on the Chinese mainland with the large amounts of capital that each group of ethnic Chinese in Southeast Asia has invested in their respective home countries. We should also not forget to consider the role of ethnic Chinese in attracting capital investments into Southeast Asia from outside the region, including the increasing amounts from Hong Kong, Taiwan, and even China itself. That perspective too has to be brought into the equation.

It is clear that the profit basis of the present investments in China's development is a totally new basis for the relationship between Southeast Asian Chinese and China. That all investments should be placed on a rational and profitable basis is one to be encouraged and one that deserves very special attention. Let me summarize the argument for more detailed studies of the ethnic Chinese investment patterns in each Southeast Asian country for the past 50 years.

For the period 1945–1960, we know that relatively little capital went from Southeast Asia into China, but then ethnic Chinese capital was still a very small portion of the total capital invested within the region. Capital was still predominantly in the hands of Western or colonial organizations or their new multinationals. We need to know more about the exact proportions that were identifiably ethnic Chinese.

For the 1960s and 1970s, ethnic Chinese business activities concentrated on becoming recognized as an essential part of national development. Many were conducted together with prominent indigenous entrepreneurs and were eventually recognized as an essential part of national capital accumulation. We must devise ways of determining what is truly ethnic Chinese capital if we are to make assertions about the extent of ethnic Chinese influence or dominance of the respective local economies. Emotional and misleading statements about ethnic Chinese dominance of local economies merely add to the confusion.

By the 1980s, and down to the present, it is clear that, in each Southeast Asian country, the proportion of recognizably ethnic Chinese capital invested in trade and industry has become higher than ever, reportedly as high as 50% in several ASEAN countries, but often clearly exaggerated and put at absurdly high figures. If this were true, we need to consider whether further re-investing all that capital within each country is more beneficial than investing outside when profits are significantly better and opportunities for economic expansion beyond national borders are great. For example, the following considerations are important:

(a) When ethnic Chinese capital within the country is already large, would it be politically sensible to increase it further as a percentage of local capital? Or would it be better to use the available capital to invest outside and thus extend the range and scope of the national economy as a whole? Surely, to tie in the national economy further with international or regional networks would, in the long run, benefit the country itself.

(b) If this is preferred as a matter of national policy, then the outside investment by ethnic Chinese should go into areas where it is clearly more profitable as well as in the national interest. For ASEAN countries, this could mean investing in neighbouring countries like Vietnam, Cambodia and Myanmar or, further afield, in North America, Western Europe, Australasia, South Asia, or in areas where profits are generally acknowledged to be good and prospects even better, like Hong Kong, Taiwan and China. The key factor remains, that capital invested outside one's own country must be profitable, preferably more profitable than within the country, and must be in the long-term interest of the country.

(c) The extensive economic and financial links that follow from such investments by ethnic Chinese, from the many profitable contacts and new exchanges of goods and personnel, could be the basis for attracting more foreign capital, including Hong Kong, Taiwan and China capital, into the region itself. If that occurs, it would further contribute to the larger modern international networks that form the exciting economic future of the Asia-Pacific region.

Conclusion

In conclusion, let me set forth four propositions for your consideration. Each of them points to fundamental changes to the role of ethnic Chinese in the development of China. The four are as follows:

Firstly, if investment in mainland China, Taiwan and Hong Kong remains profitable over a long period, especially if it is more profitable than investing at home, or elsewhere in the world, then ethnic Chinese participation in the development of China will increase. The profits may even be re-invested in the three areas, but they will also enrich ethnic Chinese in their own countries for both consumption and investment at home, and therefore support the home economy. Such a situation would be unprecedented.

My second proposition is, if such investments in China stop being more profitable than investing at home or elsewhere, then that participation would obviously diminish. Capital will be brought back, if it is retrievable, of course, or invested in other countries where it is more profitable, or in other ways diversified, and that could still bring profit to the ethnic Chinese themselves and, ultimately, also to their respective home economies. A situation in which ethnic Chinese could behave in this way has not happened before.

The third proposition. If, however, China's development falters and slows down, and if turbulence and disorder follows from that, then ethnic Chinese could revert to some of the traditional, sentimental and philanthropic help they gave their family and other institutions in China in the past. But they would concentrate on profitable undertakings at home and in other countries. The traditional kinds of help they would offer in China would be limited, especially as the strength of family ties diminish with time, and the sums involved would be very small compared to the great size of ethnic Chinese capital today. This may seem like a reversion to past practices and attitudes, but the scale would be totally different.

My final proposition is that if, on the other hand, China's economy truly takes off, China would be less interested and reliant on ethnic Chinese investment. Today, the whole world seems to be eager to invest in China. Eventually, China would itself become a major player in the region's development. In that case, the ethnic Chinese in each Southeast Asian country could be a valuable asset for the development of their respective countries by helping each country carve out its share of that growing Chinese economy. If that happens, the role of the Chinese economy in the Asia-Pacific region, ethnic Chinese or no ethnic Chinese, could not be more different than anything in the whole of Chinese history.

Endnotes

1 Leo Suryadinata, "Ethnic Chinese in Southeast Asia: Problems and Prospects", *Journal of International Affairs*, Vol. 41, No. 1, 1987 uses the figures 25–30 million. *The Economist*, 21 November 1992, includes the populations of Taiwan and Hong Kong and speaks of over 50 million.

2 Wang Gungwu, "Greater China and the Chinese Overseas", *The China Quarterly*, No. 136, December 1993, pp. 926–948. I reject the unhelpful view that the term "Greater China" should embrace any of the Chinese overseas.

3 Robin Cohen, "Notions of Diaspora: Classical, Modern and Global", Paper presented at the *Third Conference on Global History*, The University of Hong

Kong, 3–5 January 1994 to be published in *Global History and Migration*, edited by Wang Gungwu, Westview Press, 1995.

4 *China and the Chinese Overseas*, Singapore: Times Academic Press, 1991; and *Community and Nation: China, Southeast and Australia* (New Edition), Sydney: Asian Studies Association of Australia and Allen & Unwin, 1992.

5 Chen Tianjie, "Guangdong Diyijian Zhengqi Jiaosichang Ji Chang Long ji qi chuangbanren Chen Qiyuan", *Guangzhou Wenshi Ziliao*, No. 2, 1963; and Sun Jian, "Zhongguo Diyijia Minzhu Ziben Jindai Gongye di Chuxian", *Xueshu Yanjiu*, No. 3, 1979.

6 Yen Ching-hwang, "Chang Yu-nan and the Ch'ao-Shan Railway, 1904–1908", *Modern Asian Studies*, Vol. 18, No. 1, February 1984. For Chen Yixi, see note 8 below.

7 Michael Godley, *The Mandarin-capitalists from Nanyang: Overseas Chinese Enterprise in the Modernization of China, 1893–1911*, Cambridge: Cambridge University Press, 1981; and Zhongguo Kexueyuan Shanghai Jingji Yanjiuso (eds), *Nanyang Xiongdi Yancao Gongsi Shiliao*, People's Publishing Co., Shanghai, 1958.

8 Liu Yuzun, et al, "Huaqiao, Xinning Tielu yu Taishan", *Zhongshan Daxue Xuebao*, No. 4, 1980.

9 For example, for the Nationalists: *Geming Wenxian*, Vol. 45, *Zhonghua Gemingdang Shiliao*, Taibei, 1969; and *Zhongguo Guomindang zai Haiwai*, edited by Zhongguo Guomindang Zhongyang weiyuanhui Disanzu, Taibei, 1961.

10 I have accepted the figures suggested by Lin Jinzhi, "Jindai huaqiao Touzi Guonei Qiye di jige Wenti", *Jindaishi Yanjiu*, Nos. 1–2, 1980. For the very complex subject of remittances sent to China by the Chinese overseas before 1949, the most useful studies are: C.F. Remer, *Foreign Investments in China*, New York: Macmillan, 1933; and Chen Ta, *Emigrant Communities in South China: A Study of Overseas Migration and Its Influence on Standards of Living and Social Change*, New York: Institute of Pacific Relations, 1940. The valuable studies on remittances from Southeast Asian Chinese prepared by the Japanese before 1945 have been brought together in George L. Hicks (ed.), *Overseas Chinese Remittances from Southeast Asia, 1910–1940*, Singapore: Select Books, 1993.

11 Lin Jinzhi, *Jindai Huaqiao Touzi Guonei Qiye Gailun*, Xiamen University Press, Xiamen, 1988, has been particularly useful. The documentary collections for Fujian and Guangdong are, Lin Jinzhi and Zhuang Weiji, *Jindai Huaqiao Touzi Guonei Qiyeshi Ziliao Xuanji*, in two volumes, both published by Fujian Renmin Publishing Company, Fuzhou: *Fujian Volume* (1985), and *Guangdong Volume* (1989). Also useful is his early collection of essays, *Jindai huaqiao Touzi Guonei Qiye shi Yanjiu*, Fuzhou: Fujian Renmin, 1983.

12 Sincere Company, *Xianshi Gongsi Ershiwu Zhounian Jiniance* (1900–1924), and *Xianggang Xianshi Gongsi* (1900–1975), privately published in Hong Kong; Wing On Company, *Xianggang Yongan Youxian Gongsi Ershiwu Zhounian Jinianlu*, privately published, Hong Kong.

13 Wellington K.K. Chan, *Merchants, Mandarins and Modern Enterprise in Late Ch'ing China*, East Asian Research Center, Cambridge, Mass.: Harvard University, 1977; Sherman Cochran, *Big Business in China: Sino-Foreign Rivalry in the Cigarette Industry, 1890–1930*, Cambridge, Mass.: Harvard University Press, 1980.

14 Yong Chin Fatt, *Tan Kah Kee: The Making of an Overseas Chinese Legend*, Singapore: Oxford University Press, 1987.
15 Stephen Fitzgerald, *China and the Overseas Chinese: A Study of Peking's Changing Policy, 1949–1970*, Cambridge: Cambridge University Press, 1972.
16 Linda Y.C. Lim and L.A. Peter Gosling (eds.), *The Chinese in Southeast Asia: Ethnicity and Economic Activity*, Volume One, Singapore: Maruzen Asia, 1983.

Part 2: The Political Economy of the Ethnic Chinese

3

Economic Systems of the Southeast Asian Chinese

Jamie Mackie

Introduction

The topic suggested to me for this paper was "The Ethnic Chinese Economy in Southeast Asia", but the more I have thought about it, the more uneasy I felt about the misleading implications of that title. Can we really speak of a single "ethnic Chinese economy" which extends across the whole of Southeast Asia, as if it formed one entire economic system, or a unified network of activities? Surely the answer must be: No. Or should we be thinking instead in terms of the main features of half a dozen or more quite distinct economic subsystems involving the local ethnic Chinese within the various national economies of the region (10 of them, if we look beyond the ASEAN countries), in all of which many of the 23 million Southeast Asian Chinese play very important roles? These subsystems have many common features but also some significantly divergent characteristics shaped by the local circumstances of each country, as we shall see. Hence I have modified the title to a less problematic one.[1]

We will do best to approach the subject by stressing the differences as much as the similarities, focusing on certain key features of the business institutions and practices which are common to all (or most) Southeast Asian Chinese business firms (see pp. 48–56) and the dynamics of change among them, which may differ from place to place and over time, instead of assuming that they all share some common essence embodied in race, culture, values or *guanxi*. I do not mean to deny or disparage the importance of China's great cultural heritage for the Southeast Asian Chinese, or of its most common manifestations in the region, which are still very significant (although perhaps diminishing in importance?) in the social, cultural, associational and economic life of most Southeast Asian Chinese communities. But the effects of Chinese culture on their business success should not be exaggerated by attributing the latter solely to Chinese value systems and their cultural roots, even though we certainly need to understand the influence of such factors much better than we yet do in order to know why they have been so successful. As an outsider, I will not presume to say much about that; instead I will be dealing more with the ways in which we try to explain these phenomena by reference to the interactions of structure and culture, rather than just with culture and values *per se*.

Unless it can be shown that the economic activities of the five main groups of Southeast Asian Chinese (let alone all 10 of them) can usefully be considered as one "economic system" in some meaningful sense – which I believe they cannot – we should use terms to describe their activities which will accurately reflect the reality that those groups have been growing apart over the last generation or two, gradually but inexorably, and have become quite distinctive communities with diverse economic and political interests, linguistic codes and capabilities, education systems and folkways. They will almost certainly continue to do so during the decades ahead, even though integrating forces may slowly knit some individuals together for particular business purposes, especially the wealthiest tycoons who control the largest business conglomerates of the region. But I am sceptical that the several national groups of ethnic Chinese are likely to grow together into anything like a single "Southeast Asian Chinese economic system" just for that reason, despite all the networks and linkages that may be established between them through the trade and investment flows across ASEAN's national boundaries. Insofar as any economic or political integration of Southeast Asia into a single politico-economic system is occurring through those trade and investment flows, it is still proceeding very slowly and hesitantly. And the role of the Southeast Asian Chinese in that process is merely instrumental – i.e. their firms may be the vehicles through which intra-ASEAN trade and investment is taking place, but they are not the driving force behind government policies on regional integration, which represent the crucial variable here. Nor are there many signs that the commercial, financial and personal linkages established between Southeast Asian Chinese businessmen throughout the region and the hub cities of Singapore and Hong Kong have yet done much to hasten the integration of the Indonesian, Malaysian, Thai or Philippine economies as a whole. Intra-ASEAN trade is still extremely small in comparison with the trade of each country with other parts of the world – and investment patterns likewise. Even the new AFTA scheme is proving only a very small and tentative step towards closer regional economic integration.

I want to urge that we should even try to avoid talking about "a Chinese economy" within any of these countries, as if it were something distinct from the national economy more broadly, despite the fact that there are sectors in which the Chinese are predominant in them and their institutions and methods of doing business do indeed stand out as distinctive. If we overstress the ethnic or cultural aspects of our story by doing this, particularly by stressing the similarities and linkages with the other economies of Southeast Asia and with Hong Kong-South China, we distract attention from the fact that the activities of "Chinese" enterprises in all countries of the region are becoming more intertwined with the activities of the indigenous sectors and increasingly indistinguishable from them. That process (which the Indonesians call *pembauran*, "mixing together", something that is essential if real assimilation or integration is to occur) still has a long way to go, even in the Philippines and Thailand where it has proceeded furthest; but there are many indications that such a process is gathering pace slowly throughout Southeast Asia, as economic growth expands the size of each nation's gross domestic product. Hence it is less misleading to talk about several Southeast Asian Chinese economies with increasingly different local characteristics rather than one single system, despite their many similarities and linkages. They have always been intimately intermeshed with the society and economy of the countries in which they live. The pattern of their economic activities in Indonesia has some very different features from that of Singapore or Thailand, or of the Philippine Chinese from Malaysia's. And we will learn more from closer investigation of the socio-economic chemistry behind those differences than we will by focusing on what the commonalities may tell us.

These points need to be stressed from the outset because there has recently been a spate of over-enthusiastic articles in the international financial press about the extent to which the overseas Chinese generally – and the Southeast Asian Chinese in particular – are becoming bound together into a vast cobweb of business transactions with "Greater China" (i.e. the fast-growing southern China zone covering Hong Kong, Guangdong, Fujian and Taiwan) as if their Chineseness alone is uniting them all into a "nation without borders" which transcends national boundaries and sovereignties.[2] These reports have been stimulated further by stories of big investments in "Greater China" by various tycoons from Southeast Asia, often embellished with highly misleading headlines to the effect that they are now "coming home" to their ancestral land almost as if in a "gold rush" fashion. Closer scrutiny of the pattern of investments occurring reveals that this interpretation is based on erroneous estimates of the number and size of the large investments that have yet taken place, which have mostly not been very large so far.[3] More seriously, those reports put an excessive emphasis on the common factor of race and kinship as an explanatory variable in all this. Yet they fail to indicate that there have been significant regional variations in the patterns of investment in China from various Southeast Asian countries which undermine the "coming home" interpretation.

It is in fact highly debatable whether or not a supra-national "powerful regional network" of overseas Chinese is emerging through their economic linkages, of the kind that Henny Sender has described in a much-quoted article written in 1992, seen very much from a Hong Kong angle. She has described them as constituting

> a powerful regional network [extending from Hong Kong throughout Southeast Asia] – informal though pervasive, with local variations, but essentially stateless, stitched together by capital flows, joint ventures, marriage, political expediency, and a common culture and business ethic …

What Sender has referred to as a single network would be more accurately described as a multiplicity of overlapping and interconnected local networks, many of which have long had loose personal and financial links with Singapore and Hong Kong. But it is very hard to assess the nature or durability of the connections between them. Even if such a single, tightly enmeshed network could be shown to exist, moreover, it could not be categorized as an "economic system" identical with the entire Southeast Asian Chinese population. The "network" metaphor – and it should be stressed that it is only a metaphor – implies a kind of octopus-like system of control by the great Chinese capitalists of the region, headed by Li Ka-shing in Hong Kong, Robert Kuok, Liem Sioe Liong and the Sophonpanich family in Malaysia, Indonesia and Thailand respectively, and various of the several hundred lesser tycoons who own nearly all the largest conglomerates throughout Southeast Asia. But the links that exist between these men appear to be very loose, personalistic and ad hoc; they are not tightly structured or institutionalized. Certainly these great tycoons are an important element in our picture of the newly emerging economies of Southeast Asia in the 1980s–90s, but they are not a controlling one, either individually or collectively, politically or economically. They represent only one small part of the totality of Southeast Asian Chinese economic activity in the region, a very significant part, admittedly, and perhaps the leading edge of it, which could become highly influential in the future. But for the present I think it would be better for us to focus on what is happening at the level of the less exalted yet more characteristic forms of Chinese business enterprise throughout the region, small and medium enterprises mostly, along with the socio-economic dynamics behind them.

There are two other reasons, theoretical and political, why it is important to stress the differences (sometimes merely incipient ones, admittedly) as much as the similarities among the Southeast Asian Chinese. One is that as time passes and the older China-born towkays and their children pass from the scene, the differences between them are likely to appear more striking and the similarities more evanescent than they have been so far, for they are steadily becoming more and more "Southeast Asian" in identity and characteristics (as Sino-Thai, Singaporean, Sino-Indonesian etc.) rather than simply "Chinese". Most have been gradually losing some parts of their "Chineseness" over the past half-century and will probably continue to do so, although they will almost certainly retain dual or multiple identities in some degree and there may be many swings of the pendulum from one side to the other in this respect. Another reason is that by putting too much emphasis on their common racial origins, as if that were the sole clue to their economic success, we implicitly give support to the notion that they should preserve their common Chineseness against any tendencies towards becoming Southeast Asian. If any trend towards a resinification of the Southeast Asian Chinese were to develop in the 1990s, or any real fear amongst indigenous Southeast Asians that they are again looking towards "Greater China" as their homeland or preferred field of economic activity, the danger of a backlash of hostility to them throughout the region could prove very serious, in some countries possibly undermining the very conditions which have made their remarkable prosperity possible.

Ethnicity, Multiple Identities and Business Success

What part, then, does the ethnicity of the Southeast Asian Chinese, or their racial origins or Chinese cultural heritage, play in all this? There is no doubt that some sort of link between ethnicity and economic roles is thought to exist both by the overseas Chinese in general who are proud of their success and by their indigenous rivals who resent it, although the connections are seen in many different ways. "Chinese ethnicity owes much to the fact that almost all Chinese are merchants ... The merchant niche and Chinese immigrant culture are interacting in several ways," observed Omohondro (1981: 83, 187) in his classic study of a Philippine Chinese commercial community in Iloilo. That community may not be entirely typical of most

Chinese communities in the Philippines, admittedly, or of others in Southeast Asia. But the links between ethnicity, economic roles, occupation, class and identity are very complex, too much so to be reduced to any simple set of generalizations.[4]

On the other hand, a lot of recent writings about "the overseas Chinese", defined so as to include not only those who have settled in Southeast Asia, but also those who live in Hong Kong and Taiwan, as well as others in North America, Australia and Europe, have been inclined to treat them all as if they are essentially the same people, all basically "Chinese", with similar business practices, institutions, values, culture and ideals, a "nation without borders", in the now fashionable phrase. Yet in those accounts the only common factor brought to the fore is their racial affinity, or else a few distinctively Chinese cultural characteristics, often subsumed under the broad rubric of "Neo-Confucianism".[5] Many of the writings which glorify their business achievements, moreover, implicitly stress either racial or cultural elements as the common explanatory factors behind the business successes of overseas Chinese all around the world, putting greater emphasis on their shared Neo-Confucian heritage as the key determinant than on the many differences in their cultural patterns.

That kind of approach tends to imply that the decisive factor in their success is embedded somehow "in their blood", or their genes, or else in their value systems, cultural heritage and family structures, all of which are thought to make them basically different in some way from the peoples among whom they live, as well as from other racial groups like the Japanese, Europeans, Indians or Australians. Such racially-oriented arguments can be dangerously misleading, for they suggest that we should be searching for some kind of hidden essence within the Chinese character, or in Chinese business organization or practice, or Chinese culture more generally, which will account for the superior success of so many ethnic Chinese businessmen over others.[6] To say that does not mean that cultural factors are irrelevant: merely that we should not rest more explanatory significance upon them than they will bear.

The reality is in fact very different on the socio-cultural and political level. Far from remaining uniformly Chinese, the Southeast Asian Chinese have been gradually becoming more and more "Southeast Asian", as mentioned above, hence less "Chinese" in outlook, not only in respect of their nationality, but also of their sense of identity (or identities), cultural characteristics and ideas about who they are or want to be.[7] Not many now want to be Chinese nationals and citizens of the Communist PRC, it seems, or of Taiwan. There is no reason, of course, why they cannot retain a strong "Chinese" cultural or "historical" identity while also adopting a local Southeast Asian political and national identity, along with the national loyalties that implies (Wang Gungwu 1988). But with a few exceptions they do not seem to have much cultural baggage in common these days, apart from a diffuse sense of Chineseness and an associated pride of race, some knowledge of Mandarin or a regional dialect (increasingly rare among the younger generation?), some appreciation of Chinese art and literature and a strong but vague belief in the superiority of "Neo-Confucian values", such as hard work and thrift as a basis for entrepreneurial success in East Asia.[8] To regard all the overseas Chinese, or even just the Southeast Asian Chinese, as bound together by some common bond of race or culture makes no more sense than it would to label the Canadians, Australians, New Zealanders and Americans as "the overseas British" (those of them of British ethnic origins, at least), and then proceed to explain their past successes in business or empire-building by reference to that feature alone, without noticing that most of them no longer think of themselves as British at all. It does not serve much purpose to use the term "Southeast Asian Chinese" as if they were a collective group any longer, except as a convenient shorthand term to bundle them together to highlight the point that over the past century many of them did indeed share similar experiences of emigration, adaptation to colonial rule, then adjustment to the tumultuous events of the 1940s and 1950s throughout Southeast Asia, when they were gradually coming to terms with the newly independent states of the region. But their circumstances have been changing steadily since then, in accordance with developments in the countries they reside in and the various economc roles they have taken on there.

Diverse Economic Roles

Many Southeast Asian Chinese are very wealthy and most are comfortably "middle class" in status and income, although many others are quite poor (those in rural areas in particular) or disadvantaged in various ways. They are not a homogeneous group in their economic roles or social status at all. The myth that nearly all of them are rich is associated in part with the frequently heard view that the Indonesian Chinese, for example, own about 70% of the commercial wealth of that country, or that in Thailand the Sino-Thai control more than 90% of the modern sector of the economy. The accuracy of such estimates is almost impossible to verify and they cannot be regarded as much more than approximate ball park figures.[9] For Malaysia we have official estimates of the extent of Chinese ownership of corporate property at the end of the NEP in 1990 (nearly 50%), which are by far the most reliable of such figures, but still suspiciously "rubbery" when closely examined at source. For lack of anything better, however, we simply have to be content with rough figures like these as the nearest we can get to the truth. Yet it is always important to notice just what they are said to represent and then to set them in context. In the case of Chinese commercial wealth in Indonesia, for example, we should notice that agricultural land is rarely included in such calculations; yet land is one of the most important forms of capital in the country (albeit undervalued in most calculations of aggregate capital), and one which is neither owned nor controlled by Indonesian Chinese to any significant extent. And there are several other sources of income (e.g. oil production and refining, plantation crops, even timber, until the 1980s) in which they have played very minor roles. I will elaborate on these matters more fully below, for some of the details are more interesting and more illuminating than broad generalizations on the subject.

It is undeniable that in all the ASEAN nations (except perhaps Brunei), Southeast Asian Chinese have been playing the leading entrepreneurial roles over recent decades and making major contributions to the economic development of the countries in which they resided. I will try to indicate below how important a part was played by other elements on the socio-economic scene, notably the state enterprises, the indigenous businessmen and foreign investors, and farmers. The contributions to development and growth made by the peasants, in particular, should not be overlooked although they are too often disregarded in discussions of this topic.[10] We should not attribute all the credit for the development that has occurred in those countries since the 1960s solely or primarily to the local Chinese, few of whom are now engaged in agriculture. Their contributions must be seen in proportion. They have indeed played prominent parts in the growth of the commercial, financial and manufacturing sectors of all these economies, which happen to have been the most rapidly growing sectors in most cases; so those of them who were engaged in such activities have in many cases become wealthy and very well-known. But little is heard about the many thousands of poorer Chinese throughout the region whose contributions to development have also been cumulatively important.

Thailand

Thailand is unique in that there are virtually no "indigenous Thai" private businessmen of substance – and relatively few even at the lower levels – in comparison with the Sino-Thai; hence nearly all the corporate wealth of the country is commonly said to be owned by Sino-Thai enterprises.[7] (It must be stressed, however, that the racial distinction between "Thai" and Sino-Thai is less significant in social or political terms and more blurred than anywhere else in Southeast Asia; assimilation has gone further there than elsewhere, although not at all social levels.) Foreign capital has not been a very intrusive factor, except as joint venture partners in the 1950s–70s, when the Sino-Thai were pioneering the economic development of postwar Thailand and establishing their strong economic dominance there; foreign investment has become more important in the 1980s, however. State-owned enterprises (SOEs) have been quite minor players on the economic scene, apart from the Crown Property Bureau (CPB) and the large Siam Cement Corporation, which is mainly controlled by CPB. The Sino-Thai have been active in virtually all spheres of activity, including many forms of cash crop cultivation (rubber, sugar, maize, kenaf, vegetables – although not much in rice cultivation; rice milling and rice trading, on the other hand, were dominated by them), as well as retail and wholesale trading, manufacturing industry, banking and finance, construction and real estate. A few Sino-Thai are even involved in the bureaucracy and politics, to a greater degree than in Indonesia or the Philippines.

Nearly 30 large corporate conglomerates under Sino-Thai control were listed in 1979 by Krirkiat and Yoshihara (1983) in a study of ownership patterns. The number has increased considerably since then, with many newcomers and some dropouts; but the basic pattern has not changed greatly. The "Big Four" banks (Bangkok Bank by far the largest; the Thai Farmers Bank as the second largest, Bank of Ayudha and Bangkok Commercial Bank, now tending to fall well behind the leaders) have dominated the financial sector since the 1960s, becoming large family-owned conglomerates that also control a lot of commercial, manufacturing and property investments also. About 20 to 30 large industrial conglomerates and several agro-industry enterprises (the foremost among them the fast-growing Charoen Pokphand conglomerate, now expanding fast into China and diversifying into telecommunications and other industrial fields) are catching up rapidly, some of them in joint venture relationships with Japanese, Taiwan or South Korean capital. But when we look below the level of such large-scale enterprises we see an enormous array of Sino-Thai SMEs (small and medium enterprises), from the traditional shop-house upwards, nearly all family firms employing a lot of family labour, whose mode of operation has changed relatively little over recent decades, just as we see in all other parts of Southeast Asia. The most dramatic changes are occurring at the higher levels.[11]

Malaysia

Malaysia reveals a far more complex pattern, mainly because of the ethnic cleavage between Malays and Chinese and because the part played by British capital was so dominant until the 1970s. But as British capital has been gradually reduced since then, Chinese capital has become increasingly prominent on most of the higher slopes of the economy's commanding heights, despite the constraints imposed by the government under the NEP between 1971 and 1990. The Malaysian Chinese are less dominant overall than their counterparts in Thailand, however, although their per capita incomes are still generally much higher. But they will almost certainly find the politico-economic environment increasingly unfavourable to them in the years ahead, particularly at the lower levels of society. While they have long been active in tin mining and plantation enterprise (rubber and palm oil, mainly), the future outlook for tin is bleak, while competition from SOEs and other countries is growing in rubber and palm oil. The Chinese play little or no part in oil production or other mining activities and they tend to be subordinate to MNCs in the major manufacturing industries such as electronics. The main fields of investment for the new and fast-rising Chinese tycoons of the 1980s have been property development, hotels and urban leisure activities for yuppies (including gambling), as well as construction, financial services and insurance and commercial services more generally. Robert Kuok has been exceptional in having had big investments in shipbuilding, steel manufacturing and machinery, but few others have followed in his wake (unlike in Thailand). Many of the new Chinese millionaires emerging in Malaysia in the 1980s, such as Vincent Tan, Khoo Kay Peng, Lim Than Kiat and Loy Hean Heong, relied heavily on "money politics" and their personal connections with leading Malay politicians to get established.[12] To that extent they conform to Yoshihara's picture of the "ersatz capitalist", although some of them could now claim to be a good deal more than that.

Structurally, there are few major differences between the forms of Chinese economic enterprise in Malaysia and Thailand. Small family firms have constituted the vast bulk of them since the late colonial era, some of them growing in size over time to become medium and large-scale enterprises, as in Thailand, and a few becoming large corporate conglomerates. The latter are less dominant than those in Thailand, however – and less numerous in relative terms, it seems – for SOEs and foreign investment have played a far bigger part in Malaysia in both the banking and manufacturing sectors. Partly because of such constraints, but also because of the discrimination against them and the sense of uncertainty created by racial animosities, many

Malaysian Chinese firms of all sizes have dispersed some of their capital outside Malaysia, mainly to Singapore and Hong Kong, but also to North America, Australia and Europe (not many to Indonesia, however, or Thailand), largely in real estate, apparently to a greater degree than any of the other Southeast Asian Chinese have done. This has been due partly to the wish to create a financial nest-egg beyond the border as reinsurance against any repetition of the 1969 racial troubles, partly to the effects of the mid-1980s downturn in the Malaysian economy, when the level of capital outflow became quite alarming for several years. One consequence of this – and of the long-established foreign-trade orientation of so many Chinese firms in Malaysia – has been that international networks of business and social contacts with other Chinese in Singapore, Hong Kong and further afield appear to have been relatively more numerous and diverse than those in Thailand or Indonesia.

The other noteworthy structural feature of the Malaysian Chinese economic activities has been the relatively developed state of its stock market, which has been the most active in the region, along with Singapore's, for over 30 years. Hence ownership rights to a sizable proportion of Chinese business are dispersed among many shareholders there, far more than elsewhere in the region (apart from Singapore), although control by a family group is still almost universal. Some interlinking of directorships and shareholdings has occurred, but still to a quite rudimentary degree so far. That feature will probably change considerably in due course, as corporatization proceeds further.

Singapore

Singapore, being essentially a Chinese city-state with a population about 77% ethnically Chinese, is unquestionably the major commercial and financial hub to which most of the overseas Chinese networks in the southern part of the region are linked (although not those in Thailand or the Philippines to any great extent) and a thriving metropolis. Yet it presents a number of anomalous features as regards the economic and social roles of its own Chinese private businessmen, who are not such eminent community leaders as elsewhere. They have not been politically influential there since the 1950s, nor outstandingly entrepreneurial or wealthy in comparison with others in the region. In some respects, in fact, they are becoming rather cautious and conservative in their business dealings, unlike their colonial-era forebears. Lee Kuan Yew's PAP government has relied far more on SOEs and foreign

MNCs than on local private capital to bring about the industrial and commercial development which Singapore needed urgently after its former status as an entrepot for Malaysia and Indonesia crumbled in the 1960s. He deliberately chose not to let his government become unduly beholden to Singapore's capitalists, but to make it their master, not their servant. So their role in Singapore's development has not been as great as that of the Sino-Thai or even the Malaysian and Indonesian Chinese. But it would be absurd to suggest there are no wealthy Chinese corporations in Singapore, or that none of the businessmen have any political influence (the most striking exception has been Wee Cho Yaw of the fast-growing UOB group, who has had good access to the PAP leaders for a long time). What is most striking, however, is that in general the island's big businessmen have played a less prominent part in charting its future economic strategy than in any other ASEAN country (except Brunei). None has played anything like the part that Liem Sioe Liong has played in Indonesia or the Bangkok Bank group in Thailand, or achieved their preeminence over others. They have been eclipsed in influence over policy by the civil servants, famously uncorruptible and capable, on whom Lee Kuan Yew has relied heavily since he came to office at the head of an avowedly Socialist government in 1959.[13] Nowhere else in the region are the leading Chinese towkays less beholden to the government for perks and contracts, or compelled to compete so vigorously on a level playing-field. Nowhere else is there so little corruption.

Singapore shows dramatically that it is the socio-economic context within which Chinese businessmen operate that mainly influences the character of their business operations and relations with the political authorities, not just their ingrained cultural predispositions. And yet the stifling of entrepreneurial drive in both the private business class and the SOEs by the all-pervasive control exercised by the government, albeit within the framework of a market-oriented economy, was noted by a government enquiry in 1985–86 as a major inhibition to vigorous development in the future, despite the island's overabundance of savings and investable capital (Krause et al. 1987; Lee and Low 1990). Singapore's traditional entrepot activities, shipping, inter-regional trade across most of Southeast Asia (formerly accumulating commodities like rubber, pepper, spices etc.; latterly directed more towards the supply and distribution of consumer goods) and to a lesser extent banking and finance which have long been the mainstays of the Singapore economy, have inevitably made Singapore the most international city of the region, with innumerable links to most cities in the southern part of the ASEAN region, and also with Hong Kong, Japan and other major capitals. Two of the biggest Singapore business groups with the widest international networks are the OCBC-Lee Rubber group and Robert Kuok's sugar-based empire (which is legally based in Malaysia, but originally in Singapore also and still with some interests there). Another is the Hong Leong group of enterprises, more diversified and property-oriented, and the UOB group. But they are merely the foremost among many others of lesser wealth and eminence, with diverse international connections.

Indonesia

Indonesia presents an utterly different picture in that the Sino-Indonesian minority is small (about 4% of the total population, probably) and in a much more vulnerable position socially and politically than its Thai and Malaysian counterparts.[14] Sino-Indonesians are able to exert almost no political influence at all, except through informal channels, less than any other Southeast Asian Chinese in the entire region. Yet they exercise a great degree of control over many of the modern, commercial sectors of economic life, although not to the same extent as in the other ASEAN countries, for the SOEs took over the big Dutch enterprises that were nationalized in 1957–58; hence Sino-Indonesians play only a small part in plantation enterprise or banking, and virtually none at all in oil or other mining activities (apart from tin on Bangka and Billiton in earlier times). Their main spheres of activity have always been retail and wholesale trade, local transportation services, food processing and some other manufacturing activities (the *kretek* cigarette industry and textiles in particular), plus various non-bank financial services in recent years and real estate, property development and construction, as elsewhere in ASEAN. Land ownership for agricultural purposes has virtually been closed to them since the colonial era and is still hedged around for them almost universally, even though almost all Sino-Indonesians are now Indonesian nationals and in principle have the same legal status as others.

The distinctiveness of the economic roles of the Sino-Indonesians can be attributed primarily to their restricted status in the colonial era and the early decades of independence, from which they are only slowly finding their way clear. The opportunities open to them have always been more limited than elsewhere. Because the dominance of Dutch capital posed far greater constraints upon them than did the much smaller amounts of British, American or French capital on the Chinese elsewhere in the region (and because of the less mercantilist trade regimes applying in the British colonies), they were barely able to get a foothold in plantation agriculture as their Malayan counterparts did.[15] During the decades of acute economic disruption between

1931 and 1968, the Depression, the Japanese Occupation, the armed struggle for independence and the late Sukarno era, some Chinese businessmen were able to make limited gains, although the low rates of economic growth and shortage of materials, capital equipment and finance imposed severe constraints on them all. But under Suharto's New Order they have been able to make dramatic advances as the economy has recovered to achieve unprecedented rates of growth and consumer demand. Sino-Indonesian businessmen have been able to benefit from those circumstances far more than the small indigenous business class (with a few favoured exceptions), because of their prior experience in commerce, their networks of market information, credit and trusted customers and suppliers, and in the most outstanding cases their political contacts.

Yet they have had to cope with two major obstacles, to a greater degree than any other group of Southeast Asian Chinese. One has been the legacy of overt discriminatory measures against alien Chinese in the 1950s–60s, officially much softened since then, now that nearly all of them are Indonesian citizens and closely connected to the ruling elite, but still widely prevalent in practice at the lower levels against virtually all Sino-Indonesians, in a variety of illegal but accepted forms. These exactions are not crippling to their economic activities although they are irritating and sometimes onerous, constant reminders of their vulnerable status as second-class citizens. Second, the Indonesian political system is still a highly patrimonialist, top-down power structure, in which access to crucial government contracts, subsidized credits, licences and monopolies depends largely on personal contacts with political leaders at the highest national and local levels. Almost all the big Sino-Indonesian capitalists of the Suharto era have relied heavily on such political connections. At lower levels of society close personal (and financial) relations with local officials are also necessary, although frequently more diffused and variegated.

The Philippines

The Philippine Chinese have been a very small minority throughout the 20th century, although a large proportion of the country's population has long had some degree of Chinese ancestry after several centuries of Chinese immigration, particularly the descendants of the 19th-century Sino-*mestizo* elite. Estimates of the numbers of "aliens", or self-identifying Chinese, used to range widely between 100,000 and a million prior to 1974, when admission to citizenship was at last opened up to them by President Marcos (one of his few highly commendable actions) and very generally taken up. The number of "aliens" has sharply diminished since then, but it is too early to conclude that the issue of ethnicity has yet receded into the background. Half a dozen or more outstandingly wealthy "Chinese" entrepreneurs have emerged since the Marcos period at the head of large conglomerates, similar to those in other Southeast Asian countries, which has aroused widespread resentment against the Chinese in the business world and retarded other tendencies towards rapid integration or assimilation of this tiny minority. It might be expected that the Philippines, with its long history of intermarriage and assimilation, will in due course follow along the same path as Thailand towards a point where ethnic differences become so blurred as to be irrelevant, but there is still a long way to go in that respect.[16]

As elsewhere in Southeast Asia, the Chinese grip on key economic roles in the Philippines is quite disproportionate to their numbers. But the most striking feature of the Philippines situation is that a very wealthy indigenous propertied class and a substantial group of ethnic Filipino entrepreneurs also exist alongside the self-identifying "Chinese" minority; hence there is not such a sharp polarization of economic roles as we see elsewhere in the region. But there are few other noteworthy features that demand our closer attention here, except that their links with nearby Taiwan and Fujian tend to be much closer than those of other Southeast Asian Chinese communities, most of them being of Hokkien ancestry.

At the lower levels, the poorer Chinese are concentrated mainly in the traditional Chinatown areas and occupations of Binondo (in Manila), Iloilo, Cebu and Davao, where their conditions of life and economic roles have long been very similar to those in the other major towns of Southeast Asia (Omohondro 1981). They tend to be widely and thinly dispersed in commercial occupations throughout the rural areas where many used to deal in rice and corn in the rural areas, or ran *sari-sari* stores until discriminatory measures in the 1950s drove them into other occupations. Some of the wealthier ones, along with many members of the Filipino elite, became manufacturing entrepreneurs in the 1950s to the 1960s, years of effective tariff and exchange rate protection. A few alien Chinese became wealthy during the Marcos era as cronies and financial intermediaries, although some of the older Chinese community leaders suffered from the depredations of the cronies like many other members of the elite. But the very low rates of growth in the Philippines since 1980 have been a major limitation on their expansion. A few of them are reported to be making substantial investments in Fujian, as well as Taiwan and Hong Kong, but apparently on a more modest scale than the other leading Southeast Asian Chinese investors in China.

Southeast Asian Chinese Economic Organization: Key Features

Three economic institutions are of central importance in any analysis of Southeast Asian Chinese economic organization: family firms (FF hereafter), which are the basic building blocks from which the entire edifice has been constructed; the various forms of commercial and financial networks that have been built up amongst many of the leading Chinese towkays, both international and local; and the huge conglomerates that have emerged over the last quarter-century or so in all the ASEAN countries (except Brunei).

The main point to be stressed here is that each of these institutions has had its own distinctive dynamics and characteristics, which need to be analysed separately, even though they are intermeshed and overlapping in various ways. The big conglomerates had their origins as FFs and are in virtually every case still controlled by holding companies that are family-owned (in some sense, with minor variations). They are subject to many of the same weaknesses (and strengths) as the small Chinese FFs that are found in hundreds of thousands throughout Southeast Asia. Few are yet joint stock companies in any real sense, even though some may embrace several such companies which are predominantly owned and controlled by the core family. Neither the larger joint stock companies nor the conglomerates are comparable in this respect to the Japanese *keiretsu*, or other MNCs, which are far more tightly integrated by interlocking directorships and shareholdings. They are all essentially personalistic in structure, like most Chinese economic institutions. Likewise, the far-flung networks for which the Southeast Asian Chinese are famous consist mostly of loosely-structured personal connections between the bosses of these conglomerates, or of smaller enterprises. They need to be analysed essentially in terms of the historical and institutional reasons why those personal links have been so important to the latter, not as if they all have some mysterious Chinese binding agent that holds them together on the basis of *xinyong*, or some other quality.

But we also observe that each of these three types of institution is undergoing significant long-term changes, not in entirely the same directions, as they become larger, more modern and more institutionalized.[17] The traditional Chinese family firms in Southeast Asia are likely to decline in numbers, or change in character, over the decades ahead as the structure of Chinese families changes along with the socio-economic environment within which they have flourished throughout the 20th century are modified under the impact of rapid growth. Chinese business networks will probably persist in some form, as they do elsewhere, although they are likely to change greatly in character, as they have in the past. The large conglomerates will almost certainly persist, although they too will change in structure as they become modernized and corporatized, hence more like large-scale organizations in other parts of the world, but will retain various Chinese characteristics (much like their Japanese and South Korean counterparts have done). No one could yet predict, however, what form that will take, nor the time-scale of the changes to be expected.

Family Firms

Virtually all accounts of the economic behaviour of the overseas Chinese emphasize the versatility, adaptability and entrepreneurial qualities of their family firms, as well as the particular characteristics of Chinese family structure, as the primary source of socialization and of the transmission of values conducive to business success. Other forms of socialization such as schools, clans and trade associations may also play a part in that transmission process, but the primary role of the family and the family firm seems indisputable. Little has been written about Chinese family firms as such in Southeast Asia, however, apart from Omohondro (1981) and some sections of the older ethnographic accounts of the Chinese (Willmott 1960; Tan Giok Lan 1963). But some clues can be found in the growing literature on the subject in Northeast Asia, especially the illuminating works of S.L. Wong (1980, 1988a, 1988b), from which we can look for parallels or deviations elsewhere. One would expect to find similar patterns in the Southeast Asian Chinese communities, although they may be less marked amongst those which are experiencing substantial modification of their older Chinese values. Where significant acculturation towards local customs and values has occurred, the family and the family firm could be expected to differ significantly from those of mainland China, Taiwan or Hong Kong. But until more empirical research is done on the subject, we can only make guesses in this area.

"The essence of Chinese economic organization is familism", observes Wong (1980: 58) in the earliest and still the best treatment of Chinese family firms. By familism he means any one of three things, or all of them: nepotism, or preferential recruitment, employment or promotion of kin; a paternalistic ideal of how superiors and subordinates should interact; and an emphasis on maintaining family ownership and control of business assets rather than subdividing them among siblings. These characteristics are not inherently related to each other, he notes, although they often go together. But, more significantly, he also notes, citing Freedman (1961–62): "What is relevant is not the dichotomy between kin and non-kin, but between 'personal and impersonal'" – for most Chinese have a strong antipathy to impersonal contacts as a basis for business dealings. Curiously, however, partnerships have been notably unstable among Chinese, he remarks. Relations between brothers are apt to be brittle and precarious, as many writers on Chinese families have noted, for younger brothers are often unwilling to defer to older brothers (as Indonesian siblings, for example, do much more easily), for reasons which stem from childhood socialization patterns. Hence they are inclined to press for the creation of new and autonomous ventures within the family firm in which they can themselves be bosses and not be subject to close control by the head of the firm, who will often but not always be the eldest brother.

Wong has devised a four-stage model of growth and disintegration of family firms (emergent, centralized, segmented, disintegrating), a more sophisticated version of the old Chinese saying about the three-generation cycle from rags to riches to ruin. He contrasts this life cycle of the Chinese family firm with Japanese and Philippine patterns to highlight its distinctiveness. Chinese enterprise tends to be "strong in entrepreneurialism (sic) but weak in management" (Wong 1988a: 197). Yoshihara has commented that no Chinese family firm can trace its origins back beyond the late 19th century, as several Japanese family enterprises can, Mitsui the most notable of them. He has also noted that they have not shown the same capacity as Japanese firms to bring in capable managers from outside the family and incorporate them into senior positions in the structure of the organization. There are some signs that this is changing in some of the larger firms, but there is still a long way to go in most cases.

Family enterprises still play an important part in business structures in most other parts of the world, of course, including USA, Europe and Japan. They are not a uniquely Chinese phenomenon, nor dependent solely on the value systems or tight family structures of the Chinese. The literature on the strengths and weaknesses of the large family firms to be found in other countries is extensive, for they are still numerous in France and Britain (Okuchi and Yasuoka 1984). What is most noteworthy in the case of the Southeast Asian Chinese FFs is the great multitude of small and medium enterprises of this kind found in nearly all parts of the region, as well as the uniquely important developmental roles they have played in the opening up of the commercial frontiers there earlier in the century. These have far exceeded the contributions of Mom-and-Pop corner shops in the suburbs of other countries. Many have grown to become much larger enterprises with little change of formal structure. But there have been few alternative forms of enterprise available in Southeast Asia since the 19th century *kongsi* until very recently; joint stock companies were virtually impracticable for them to create until stock exchanges came into being in the 1960s to the 1970s. Partnerships seem to have been rare among the Southeast Asian Chinese. Their intense desire to manage their own businesses has been a major factor in the small and fissiparous character of most family firms.

Networks

Networks of personal connections based on mutual trust (*xinyong*) have long been common in most commercial communities, not just in Chinese ones, although they have tended to change in character and become institutionalized in various ways for many types of transactions, particularly in order to ensure the reliability of contracts and repayment of debts. Networks have played an unusually prominent part among the Southeast Asian Chinese for two major reasons: one, that they have been so heavily involved in commercial operations across wide distances, and second, that their inherited preferences for personal contacts and *xinyong* as the basis for business dealings has been strongly grounded in their culture and value systems. Indeed, it has become elevated almost to the status of a national icon in many cases. "The most important organizational feature of Asian capitalist economies is that they are organized through networks of firms," observes Gary Hamilton (1991) in a study of business networks in this region.

The remarkable success of overseas Chinese business firms is often attributed in large part to the use they make of networks of various kinds, both local and international, giving them access to a wide range of personal contacts, credit, market information and sources of supply, as well as means of checking credit-worthiness of associates and imposing sanctions on defaulters on contracts. "Kinship and collegiality play roles analogous to those played by law and individuality in the West ... but with very different trajectories and outcomes" (Hamilton 1992: 48). Gordon Redding (1990) sees the "strength of network ties" as one of the fundamental sources of strategic effectiveness of overseas Chinese firms, which tend to be "weak organizations, but [with] strong linkages". Among indigenous Southeast Asians there has long been a widely held belief that Chinese businessmen hold an insuperable advantage over them in being able to tap these networks for almost limitless credit whenever they are in difficulties, thus enabling them to ride out business fluctuations more easily. There was a good deal of truth in that belief. It was also commonly said that the Chinese always stood by each other in crises. The combination of their ethnic solidarity and their wide-ranging networks stemming back to Singapore, Hong Kong and the two southeastern provinces of China seemed *prima facie* to provide a convincing explanation of their success.

Business networks of various kinds have played an important part in the economic life of Southeast Asian Chinese communities over a long period. They are likely to continue to do so well into the future. They have been an integrating factor of considerable importance within the ASEAN region, as well as between Southeast Asia and Greater China, and will probably continue to be so in the future also. Many of the wealthiest tycoons in the ASEAN countries have had close personal and business relationships with their counterparts in the other countries of the region (mainly in Singapore, or in Hong Kong, sometimes also Taiwan, although more rarely). But having said that, some caveats need to be entered against any tendency to exaggerate their influence in this respect.

It is usually only a few very wealthy Chinese who are in a position to develop such international networks of contact and mutual support. The vast majority of Southeast Asian Chinese are not, even many of the moderately well-to-do ones with salaried jobs or medium-sized firms. Many of them are plugged into local or kinship networks of various kinds, some of which may have loose personal ties with the bigger ones. The numbers in either category would be almost impossible to estimate, and it is hardly worth putting much effort into trying to do so. But it must be stressed that whereas large numbers of the Chinese in Southeast Asia may be members of some kind of rudimentary local network, which in the past have had important roles in the early stages of economic development there, most of them are not directly involved in today's more wide-ranging international networks.[18]

Next, the very concept of networks and networking is extremely loose. The term has been commonly used to refer to at least five distinctly different types of relationships in Southeast Asia. The first, in their most rudimentary form, were the early Chinese trading networks built up between the 15th and the 19th century; the second were the Chinese remittance system networks operating between about 1900 and 1941 which had their own distinctive institutional features. Trust played a crucial part in both types, although they were very different from later variants.[19] Third, the archipelagic network of shipping-commercial-financial contacts built up from the Singapore hub in the "Joseph Conrad era" of small steamers between the 1870s and 1940 were highly personalized and wide-ranging, making an important contribution to the gradual integration of local markets at that time through the intertwining of commerce, credit, market information and regular transport routes. But

Singapore's entrepot role as the hub of that trade was already crumbling before the Second World War and recovered only temporarily in the 1940s–50s. Fourth, new and quite special forms of network developed out of the smuggling trade and other forms of illegal shipping across the Straits of Malacca during and after the Japanese Occupation; but such activities were extremely risky in most cases, the networks highly ephemeral and they rarely survived long after conditions improved later (Twang 1988). Fifth, the postwar commercial and financial networks which have come into being in recent years, mainly on a basis of personal knowledge and trust, represent a more solid and enduring variant of the species, but do not rest on any special institutional foundations that distinguish them from the earlier varieties.

In short, in circumstances where market information and access to credit were key advantages in the early stages of economic growth, those older forms of network seemed to be the key to the success of overseas Chinese family firms, with their intensely personalistic character and reliance on *xinyong* and a need for reliable knowledge of the people they were dealing with. But as the larger of them become more corporatized, depersonalized and "modern" in character, the significance of these earlier forms of network is likely to diminish gradually, or change to become more like those of other commercialized economies.

Conglomerate Enterprises

One particularly noteworthy feature of the several hundred big conglomerates owned by Southeast Asian Chinese that have emerged throughout the region since the 1960s is that very few of them are vertically integrated industrial structures, or concentrated in one sphere of activity only. Most have a strikingly diverse array of interests, usually including real estate and property sections, financial services and banking or insurance (the boom sectors in those decades) as well as various forms of commercial services. Liem Sioe Liong's heterogeneous array of more than 240 companies (a 1988 estimate, probably larger by now) in his $3–$4 billion empire is merely an extreme example of that.[20] A few of the smaller conglomerates are developing more focused and efficient business strategies which benefit more from synergies and complementarities, but such groups are still the exceptions in all countries of Southeast Asia. The reasons for that state of affairs are to be sought more in the character of those national economies themselves than in any special features of Chinese business enterprise as such. Diversification makes better sense in such poorly integrated, risk-prone economies than putting too many eggs into one basket does.

To understand the economic rationale behind the emergence of large-scale conglomerates in Southeast Asia over the last 20 years or so, as opposed to the political aspects so frequently mentioned, there is no better starting point than the works of Nathaniel Leff (1976, 1978) on economic "groups", as he discerned them in Latin America. They contributed significantly to economic development, he argued, by helping to "relax the entrepreneurial constraint" on the pace of economic development in LDCs (1978: 670). The groups in those countries had their origins in the prior existence of market imperfections. They performed several of the functions formerly attributed to entrepreneurship: they generated growth and reduced transaction costs by internalizing them within the group, thereby integrating imperfect markets, generating economies of scale, gaining easy access to credit and thereby performing the capital accumulation function (which used to be regarded as the major bottleneck to growth in poor LDCs). The group, he says,

> can be conceptualized as an organizational structure for appropriating quasi rents which accrue from access to scarce and imperfectly marketed inputs. Some of these inputs, such as capital, might be marketed more efficiently, but in the conditions of LDCs they are not. Some ... are inherently difficult to market efficiently; for example, honesty and trustworthy competence on the part of high-level managers ... The absence of markets for risk and uncertainty also helps explain another feature of the groups' pattern of expansion – their entry in diversified product lines ... diversification has an obvious appeal in economies subject to the risks and uncertainties of instability and rapid structural change (1978: 667).

He suggests also that the group pattern of industrial organization conforms well to Leibenstein's (1968) theory of entrepreneurship and development. In Leff's words (1978: 667–668), Leibenstein has suggested that

> entrepreneurship in LDCs involves the opening of channels for input supply and for marketing of output in situations where a routinized market mechanism does not exist. In the absence of such "intermarket operators" some input and/or output quantities, qualities, and costs would be so beclouded by risk and uncertainty that investment and production in these activities would not take place ... The groups create a channel both for mobilizing and for allocating such inputs and outputs. In fact, the group can perhaps

> best be understood as an institutional innovation for internalizing the returns which accrue from interactivity operations in the imperfect market conditions of the LDCs. What has happened in effect is that the groups have appropriated as gains the *quasi* rents which Leibenstein envisaged would otherwise be foregone due to imperfect factor markets and insufficient entrepreneurship.

This approach to the phenomenon of conglomerate organization is very relevant to Southeast Asia, partly because it underlines the point that entrepreneurial dynamism is not just a quality to be sought in the motivations of individuals with the drive, foresight or frugality of the emigrant Chinese, but is something that may often be found also in large-scale impersonal, corporate enterprises also, regardless of the personal qualities of the chief executive. Hence our earlier searches for rags-to-riches entrepreneurs as the potential pioneers of capitalism in the 1950s (e.g. Geertz's elusive "shop-keeper revolution" to be led by petty traders in subsistence markets who would create the conditions for large-scale capitalism in Indonesia) were wrongly directed. It could even be argued that the Indonesian state oil company, Pertamina, under General Ibnu Sutowo, was just as important in the growth of Indonesian capitalism in the 1970s as was Liem Sioe Liong. State investment was then hardly less significant overall than that of the leading Chinese businessmen.

One limitation of Leff's approach, however, is that it does not in itself tell us much about how or why large groups have emerged, merely about their significance as agents of development in terms that fit comfortably within neo-classical economic theory. We still need to know whether they emerged because of some particular entrepreneurial qualities in their founders (or the men/women who pulled various firms together to reach critical-mass size), and if so what those qualities were. This leads us into other questions about the dynamics of efficiency in large-scale enterprise and how it arose.

Leff hints at political connections and the relationships of groups with governments and state policies as key factors behind their growth. There is little doubt that these have been unusually important in all the Southeast Asian countries, again for reasons which are to be found in the character of their political systems as much as the "pariah" status of the early Chinese immigrants. But the theoretical implications of this have not yet been investigated with Leff's contributions in mind, nor the relevant empirical data. Neither the Marxist literature on Southeast Asian conglomerates, nor works on the South Korean *chaebol* or the recent group of influential post-*dependencia* writings on the NICs have yet taken up the implications of Leff's suggestion that the conglomerates reduce their transaction costs by internalizing them, thereby generating abnormally high profits. It may be valid, or may not.

Contrary to the Leff hypothesis, in fact, Ramon Myers (1989: 288) has argued that in mainland China prior to 1949 and in Taiwan and Hong Kong

> Chinese firms have traditionally handled their transaction costs in the marketplace rather than trying to internalize those costs within the firm, an action requiring more impersonal interactions and a more complex assignment of tasks. This avoidance of impersonal ties and strong preference for personal ties to handle transaction costs is not only a salient feature of Chinese firm behaviour but flows well from specific Confucian values and behaviour.

Is Myers's approach valid for Southeast Asia also? If so, it too represents a major step towards a more satisfactory explanation of the links between values, structural factors and the economic behaviour of Chinese firms, both at home and abroad. But we can treat it as no more than a provisional working hypothesis in the Southeast Asian context at this stage, requiring corroboration; it is not yet an established explanation. For there is also evidence that in the overseas context, traditional values and behaviour patterns have been eroding longer and further than in the China-Hong Kong-Taiwan area. The traditional Chinese preference for personal relationships rather than reliance on impersonal market mechanisms may be weakening faster there than elsewhere.

"Pariah Capitalists", Rent-seekers, or "Real" Entrepreneurs?

The notion that Southeast Asian Chinese businessmen were mere "pariah capitalists" was popularized by the writings of Fred Riggs (1966) in the 1960s on the idea of "the bureaucratic polity" in Southeast Asia, based upon his observations of their dependence on the political support of government officials, either military or civil, in Thailand and the Philippines. More recently, Yoshihara (1988) has advanced the alternative idea that they were "ersatz capitalists", not real ones. Riggs' term seemed appropriate at the time he wrote, since the utter lack of political power of the Chinese in those countries in the 1950s made it hard to imagine how they could ever hope to bring about any effective changes in the socio-political systems prevailing there, which Riggs described as pre-capitalist "prismatic societies", caught stranded mid-way across the transition between traditional (or "fused") societies and modern (functionally differentiated, or "diffracted") societies as a consequence of colonial rule, with no interest groups strong enough to generate further change towards modernity and a conventionally capitalist economic and political system. His analysis had considerable *prima facie* plausibility at the time, for the term "pariah capitalists" seemed to apply also to Indonesian Chinese businessmen, although less so to the Chinese in Singapore or Malaysia, where the economic system was much more fully "capitalist" in character and Chinese businessmen more independent of political office-holders.

Thirty years later, however, we can see that capitalism has developed considerably throughout Southeast Asia, although to varying degrees in each country, and that the local Chinese businessmen can no longer be described as mere "pariahs" to the same extent as previously, even in Malaysia or Indonesia. It was not necessary for a strong and independent capitalist class to come into existence first and then gain political power before the institutions of capitalism could be created, as both the Marxist and Riggsian approaches to the problem had earlier inclined us to expect. The transition came about as a result of a variety of pressures from external economic forces as well as internal political changes. Not the least important of these, as Ruth McVey (1992) has well described, was the shift in attitudes among the former predatory officials whom Riggs had seen as preying upon the vulnerable Chinese businessmen for funds. They had gradually learnt that it was more profitable to collaborate with the businessmen as partners in the further creation of wealth than to behave simply as parasitical bloodsuckers. The gradual loosening up of the political system in Thailand was also a major factor in undermining the "bureaucratic polity" there and in enabling the wealthy Chinese to spread their political risks by building up contacts with a number of patrons, instead of having to rely heavily on one. Similar processes have been occurring also in other parts of Southeast Asia, although more slowly and with rather different socio-political dynamics from country to country.

Yoshihara's assertion that Southeast Asian Chinese businessmen are essentially "rent-seekers", or "ersatz capitalists", not genuine entrepreneurs, because they owe their success so largely to political connections, monopolies, subsidies, favours, contracts and cheap credits, has achieved wide acceptance throughout the region among people who are eager to believe that there must be something spurious about the "economic miracle" that has occurred throughout Southeast Asia in the 1980s. There is a lot of empirical evidence in favour of his view and he has provided us with much valuable information about those businessmen, which alone makes his work valuable. But his underlying theoretical approach is flawed, in my view, by his overstatement of the case, and his characterization of all five economic systems as "ersatz" is based too much on the adverse judgements he makes about them as individual capitalists, without applying a macro-level analysis of how and why the ASEAN economies more generally have proved so successful. Some of the businessmen (and governments) of the region must be doing something right. It cannot be denied that nearly all Chinese businessmen in the region have to rely on political connections in some degree to advance their interests, the foremost of them very heavily; hence many have benefitted greatly from subsidies or other favours in various forms. But the conclusion that they are not "real" capitalists for that reason does not follow, for the same could be said of numerous capitalists in all parts of the world, who are generally very happy to take advantage of any opportunities for rent-seeking behaviour that arise. Yoshihara defines "capitalists" too narrowly to be practicable in Southeast Asian circumstances.[21]

Further, if we say that these Southeast Asian businessmen are lacking in "genuine" entrepreneurial spirit or capacities, it becomes hard to explain how the various ASEAN countries have achieved such impressive rates of economic growth and the profound social transformations resulting from it over the last 20 or 30 years. Who else has carried out the investments that have brought about such great changes? State enterprises cannot be given the credit for much of that, nor the MNCs. The innumerable Southeast Asian Chinese enterprises throughout the region who now constitute the core of the private sector, small firms as well as large, "rent-seekers" and others, have been making major contributions to development and rapid growth through risk-taking investments, integrating markets, creating new productive resources and opportunities, eliminating inefficiencies and structural obstacles to trade, providing commercial and financial services and establishing many of the new manufacturing industries which are rapidly becoming export-oriented and competitive on world markets. Without those enterprises, whether they are "ersatz" or not, the Southeast Asian "economic miracle" of recent years would simply not have happened.

Even though there are many rent-seekers among the Southeast Asian Chinese, they cannot all be categorized as nothing more than that, although many perhaps can. We need to subdivide them more carefully than the bald general categorization of them as "ersatz" implies. Without going further into this matter, I will simply conclude with the observation that Yoshihara's argument would have been far more persuasive if he had not overstated it in the form of such a cast-iron theory. If he had simply said that many opportunities for rent-seeking have arisen and have been seized avidly by the local Chinese capitalists (and others), hence that some or many of them have little claim to be regarded as real entrepreneurs, the validity of his argument could hardly be denied. Yet many of them clearly have shown entrepreneurial talents of various kinds, such that it cannot be seriously maintained that they are not "real" capitalists except on a very idiosyncratic definition. By the demanding criteria set by Yoshihara, many countries conventionally regarded as "capitalist" would also have to be dismissed as merely "ersatz". Not only has he made his definition too stringent to be useful in this context, he has also lumped all the Southeast Asian Chinese together as if they were basically all the same, instead of recognizing that they are developing strikingly different local characteristics.

Conclusion: The Future?

Finally, we must touch briefly on a question that often arises about the future of the Southeast Asian Chinese and their family firms, their networks and conglomerates in the face of all the tendencies towards modernization and corporatization now impinging upon them. I think we must expect that all three types of institution will gradually change in character, but none of them will disappear entirely. Large conglomerates are a feature of most modern, institutionalized capitalist systems, so we will almost certainly see many more of them emerging in the decades ahead. In Southeast Asia they will retain some of their original Chinese characteristics (a preference for family control and personalistic rather than institutionalized linkages, almost certainly), despite tendencies towards convergence with some features of modern western or Japanese types of enterprise, such as joint stock companies, or greater reliance on professional management, separated increasingly from family ownership. They will probably not grow to resemble Japan's tightly interlocked *keiretsu*, nor the multi-owner western-style MNCs, for a long time. Their networks of personal and commercial relationships are also sure to persist, as they do in all capitalist societies, although they may well change in character as the context changes. (What effect will the communications and information revolution have upon them, the fax or e-mail technology?) The family firm in its classic Chinese form is more likely to change quite substantially, I believe, albeit gradually, as it adapts to the circumstances of a more modern, structured economic system, especially if the strongly collective bonds within the Chinese family become frayed in the 1990s by the corrosive influences of greed, consumerism and individual ambitions. But since family firms are still found throughout world, they are unlikely to disappear among the Southeast Asian Chinese for a long time.

To foresee the future in any of these respects, however, our first step should be to look back to the past, in order to see what these institutions have been changing from, as well as what into, and then ask how and why. A well-informed historical perspective will enable us to peer into the mists of the future more effectively than any teleological or essentialist theory about inexorable trends, intrinsic characteristics or "stages" of socio-economic change will let us do. The amazing transformations that have occurred in the Southeast Asian countries since the 1960s, and within the Chinese communities themselves, provide copious evidence of how unpredictable the course of history can be, even from one decade to another.

Endnotes

1 The words "Chinese" and "Southeast Asian Chinese" are used here in a loose sense to refer to all persons of Chinese ethnic origin and identification; where a particular nationality is relevant, it will be indicated. The estimate of numbers is taken from *The Economist*, 18 July 1992, p. 21 (but may be slightly inaccurate). Brunei will be left out of account in my discussion of the ASEAN countries, since the Chinese there play a subordinate part alongside the vast wealth of the Sultanate. Burma and the countries of Indochina will also have to be ignored, for lack of up-to-date information about the state of their Chinese minorities, although a new study of the Chinese in Vietnam by Tran Kanh (1993) contains valuable information on their economic roles.

2 For example, see "Homeward Bound", *Asia Inc.*, August 1993; "Chinese on the Rebound", *Australian Business Monthly*, March 1993, pp. 123–124; "There's No Place Like Home", *Manager* (Bangkok), Nov. 1992; Henny Sender, "Inside the Overseas Chinese Network", *The Institutional Investor*, August 1992, pp. 29–42; James Kao, "The Worldwide Web of Chinese Business", *Harvard Business Review*, March–April 1993. Kao says Chinese entrepreneurs are "becoming part of what I call a Chinese Commonwealth", not based on any one country, but "primarily a network of entrepreneurial relationships" reaching across national boundaries. The empirical data on which that observation is based may be essentially accurate, but the significance Kao attaches to them is highly dubious, for race is the only common element binding that "worldwide web" together. The problematic notion of "Greater China" has been given various interpretations, ranging from an essentially racial (and politically quite indefensible) concept of a "commonwealth" made up of all ethnic Chinese throughout the world to the narrower geographic notion of the south China-Hong Kong-Taiwan economic zone; see Wang Gungwu (1993), Harding (1993) and Wanandi (1993).

3 My conclusion here is based on the relatively small number of really large

investments from Southeast Asia in mainland China, as reported in the press so far. Total Southeast Asian investment in China was commonly estimated at about US$8–9 billion in late 1993, although any such figure must be treated with reserve. Nearly half of that was apparently from Singapore, much of it apparently in many relatively small sums of a few million dollars. Three big Southeast Asian Chinese tycoons, Dhanin Chearavanand (Chearavanont) (Charoen Pokphand group, Thailand), Robert Kuok (Malaysia-Hong Kong) and Liem Sioe Liong (Indonesia) seem to account for nearly half of the total Southeast Asian amount, but have all been involved in investments in China for over a decade; they all have sums in the order of half to one million dollars (or more) invested there. A handful of others, notably Mochtar Riady (Indonesia) and Oei Hong Liong (Singapore-Hong Kong) are engaged currently in large-scale, highly speculative projects of similar dimensions, recently started; but few others of that magnitude have been reported. Nor have many been mentioned in the intermediate range between about $10–500 million, puzzlingly, although it may be that some or many such investments have been made through Hong Kong channels, or simply not publicized. Yet there does appear to be a puzzling gap between the relatively few large investments and the far more numerous small investments which are merely testing the water in China. How much Southeast Asian money is flowing into China by way of Hong Kong is unknowable. It appears, however, that most of the big Southeast Asian Chinese conglomerates have so far invested only small amounts in China directly.

4 See J.A.C. Mackie (1988), "Economic Roles and Ethnic Identities of the Southeast Asian Chinese: A Comparison of Thailand and Indonesia" in Cushman and Wang eds. (1988). The perils of generalizing about the overseas Chinese or Southeast Asian Chinese as if they were homogeneous can be seen in the treatment of them in Joel Kotkin's *Tribes. How Race, Religion and Identity Determine Success in the New Global Era* (1993). Because his picture of them is based almost entirely on individual Chinese from Northeast Asia (especially Taiwan) or USA, it is strikingly misleading if applied to the Southeast Asian Chinese in several respects, although he seems unaware of this.

5 Hofheinz and Calder (1982) advance the most explicit argument that Neo-Confucian culture and values have been crucially important factors behind the rapid growth of "Eastasia" (virtually, the countries of Sinitic culture, including Japan and the two Koreas), although they denied that they were resorting to cultural determinism as such.

6 In the "inheritance versus environment" controversy over issues like this, it is better to incline towards the latter camp, even if the former is interpreted broadly to cover cultural heritage as well as purely genetic factors, since we get more clues from it towards an explanation of the success of so many Chinese through a close analysis of the environment within which they have been operating, the context and circumstances in which they have so often been oustandingly successful (although sometimes not), than from any invocation of their intrinsic Chineseness.

7 On multiple identities, see the illuminating discussion by Wang Gungwu, "The Study of Chinese Identities in Southeast Asia", in Cushman and Wang eds. (1988).

8 The exceptions are certain traditional Chinese business practices and institutions, discussed below, and what one might call a "Hong Kong-based cosmopolitan superculture", marked by blatant consumerism and a preoccupation with money or what it can buy, to which many of the younger-generation overseas Chinese yuppies are now aspiring in many parts of the world.
9 The elaborate calculations by Wu and Wu (1980) of how much of the commercial capital of various Southeast Asian countries was Chinese were commendably ambitious in aim, but based on such sweeping and unrealistic assumptions (often unconsciously quite racist in their assumptions) that the conclusions simply do not stand up to close scrutiny.
10 Java's rice farmers, for example, have achieved increases of productivity per hectare of 2–300% in rice cultivation since the introduction of the new Green Revolution technology in the late 1960s, a major contribution to the growth of the national economy since then. Thai farmers brought about both an extension and diversification of crop production in the early years of rapid growth in the 1960s (although not such spectacular rice productivity increases).
11 For fuller information on the foremost Sino-Thai capitalists, see Suehiro (1989) and Hewison (1990).
12 On the Malaysian Chinese and their stake in the economy, the most informative studies, some now slightly outdated, are Tan Tat Wah (1984), Lim Mah Hui (1981), Jesudason (1989), Heng Pek Koon (1992) and Sieh Lee Mei Ling (1992). I am much indebted to Peter Searle, who has recently completed a Ph.D. dissertation on this subject in the Department of Political and Social Change, ANU, for information on this aspect of the situation in Malaysia.
13 Lee was initially extremely suspicious of Singapore's wealthiest businessmen of all races because of their hostility to the PAP and its Marxist ideology, although he has gradually become less so since he has become less Marxist.
14 No reliable figures on the number of ethnic Chinese in Indonesia have been collected since the 1930 census; all later estimates (as for 1980 in Suryadinata 1989: 1 or *The Economist*, 18 July 1992: 1), appear to be based on calculations that they still represent either 3 or 4% of the total population, although even that can be only an informed guess.
15 Only the remarkable Oei Tiong Ham Concern managed to break into the sugar sector in a big way, with four sugar mills and a range of ancillary services; but no others could compare with him in that (Yoshihara 1989).
16 For the most up-to-date treatment of the issue of integration processes among the Philippines Chinese, see the papers by Theresita Ang See and Theresa Carino in this volume.
17 That is not to say that there will be an inevitable trend towards convergence with Western business structures in all respects, although there probably will be in some. One has only to think how very different Japanese firms are from American, or British firms from both, to realize how strongly national traditions and characteristics persist.
18 I have discussed these issues more fully in Mackie (1992a and 1992 b).
19 The actual workings of the cobweb-like networks of structures and mechanisms involved in the transmission of remittances from early Chinese emigrants to

Southeast Asia back to southern China are best documented in George Hicks (1992).

20 Estimates of Liem's fortune are taken from various issues of *Forbes* and *Fortune*. For fuller information on his career and business strategies, see Soetiyono (1989), Siregar and Widya (1989) and Sato (1993).

21 Yoshihara does not even regard Singapore's capitalists as of the "genuine" variety, because they rely so heavily on foreign technology, since Singapore does not yet produce its own. Nor do many other advanced capitalist countries, however, in large part.

References

Cushman, Jennifer and Wang Gangwu (eds.), *Changing Ethnic Identities of the Southeast Asian Chinese since World War II*, Hong Kong: University of Hong Kong Press, 1988.

Freedman, Maurice, "The Family in China: Past and Present", *Pacific Affairs*, Vol. 24, No. 4, 1961–62, pp. 323–326.

Hamilton, Gary (ed.), *Business Networks and Economic Development in East and Southeast Asia*, Hong Kong: Centre of Asian Studies, University of Hong Kong, 1991.

Harding, H., "The Concept of Greater China: Themes, Variations & Reservations", *China Quarterly*, Dec 1993, No. 136, pp. 660–684.

Heng Pek Koon, "The Chinese Business Elite in Malaysia", in McVey (ed.), 1992.

Hewison, K., *Bankers and Bureaucrats: Capital and the Role of the State in Thailand*, New Haven: Yale University Southeast Asia Studies Monograph No. 34, 1990.

Hicks, G., *Chinese Remittances in Southeast Asia, 1910–1940*, Singapore: Select Books, 1993.

Hofheinz, Jr. R. and Calder, K., *The Eastasia Edge*, New York: Basic Books, 1982.

Jesudason, J.V., *Ethnicity and the Economy: The State, Chinese and Multinationals in Malaysia*, Singapore: Oxford University Press, 1989.

Krause, L.B., Koh Ai Tee and Lee Tsao Yuan, *The Singapore Economy Reconsidered*, Singapore: ISEAS, 1987.

Krirkkiat Phipatheritham and Yoshihara Kunio, *Business Groups in Thailand*, Singapore: ISEAS, 1983.

Lee Tsao Yuan and Linda Low, *Local Entrepreneurship in Singapore: Private and State*, Singapore: Times Academic Press, 1990.

Leff, Nathaniel H., "Capital Markets in the Developing Countries: The Group Principle" in Ronald I. McKinnon (ed.) *Money and Finance in Economic Growth and Development*, 1976.

Leff, Nathaniel H., "Industrial Organization and Entrepreneurship in the Developing Countries: the Economic Groups", EDCC, 1978, Vol. 26, p. iv.

Leibenstein, H., "Allocative Efficiency v. 'x–efficiency'", *American Economic Review*, 1966, Vol. 56, pp. 392–415.

Lim, Linda Y.C. and Gosling, L.A. Peter, (eds.), *The Chinese in Southeast Asia*, 2 vols, Singapore and Ann Arbor: Maruzen and University of Michigan, Center for South and Southeast Asian Studies, 1983.

Lim Mah Hui, *Ownership and Control of the One Hundred Largest Corporations in Malaysia*, Kuala Lumpur: Oxford University Press, 1981.

Mackie, J.A.C., (ed.), *The Chinese in Indonesia: Five Essays*, Melbourne: Thomas Nelson, for AIIA, 1976.

Mackie, J.A.C., "Changing Economic Roles and Ethnic Identities of the Southeast Asian Chinese: A Comparison of Indonesia and Thailand", in Cushman and Wang (eds.), 1988.

Mackie, J.A.C., "Changing Patterns of Chinese Big Business in Southeast Asia" in *Southeast Asian Capitalists*, Ruth McVey (ed.), 1992a.

Mackie, J.A.C., "Overseas Chinese Entrepreneurship", *Asia-Pacific Economic Literature*, 1992b, Vol. 6, No. 1, pp. 41–64.

McVey, Ruth, *Southeast Asian Capitalists*, Ithaca: Cornell Southeast Asian Program Publications Program, 1992.

Myers, Ramon, "Confucianism and Economic Development: Mainland China, Hong Kong and Taiwan", *Chung-hua Institution for Economic Research*, Taipei, Conference Series, 1989, Vol. 13, pp. 281–302.

Okuchi, A. and Yasuoka, S. (eds.), *Family Business in the Era of Industrial Growth*, Tokyo: University of Tokyo Press, 1984.

Omohondro, John T., *Chinese Merchant Families in Iloilo: Commerce and Kin in a Central Philippine City*, Athens, Ohio: Ohio University Press, 1981.

Redding, S. G., *The Spirit of Chinese Capitalism*, Berlin and New York: de Gruyter, 1990.

Riggs, F.W., *Thailand: The Modernization of a Bureaucratic Polity*, Honolulu: The East-West Center Press, 1966.

Sato, Yuri, "The Salim Group in Indonesia: The Development and Behaviour of the Largest Conglomerate in Southeast Asia", *The Developing Economies*, 1993, Vol. XXXI, No. 4, pp. 408–441.

Sender, Henny, "Inside the Overseas Chinese Network", *The Institutional Investor*, Aug 1991, pp. 29–43.

Sieh Lee Mei Ling, "The Transformation of Malaysian Business Groups", in McVey, (ed.), 1992.

Siregar, S.E. and Widya, K.T., *Liem Sioe Liong: Dari Futching ke Mancanegara*, Jakarta: Panca Merdeka, 1989.

Soetiyono, Eddy, *Kisah Sukses Liem Sioe Liong*, Jakarta: Indomedia, 1989.

Suehiro, A., *Capital Accumulation in Thailand, 1885–1985*, Tokyo: The Center for East Asian Cultural Studies, 1989.

Suryadinata, L., *Pribumi Indonesians, the Chinese Minority and China*, Singapore: ISEAS, 1978.

Suryadinata, L., "Chinese Economic Elites in Indonesia: A Preliminary Study" in Cushman and Wang, (eds.), 1988, pp. 261–288.

Suryadinata, L., *The Ethnic Chinese in the ASEAN States*, Singapore: ISEAS, 1989.

Tan Giok-lan, *The Chinese of Sukabumi: A Study in Social and Cultural Accomodation*, Ithaca: Cornell Modern Indonesia Project, Monograph Series, 1963.

Tran Kanh, *The Ethnic Chinese and Economic Development in Vietnam*, Singapore: ISEAS, 1993.

Twang Peck-yang, *The Transformation of the Trading Minorities in Indonesia, 1940–50*, Ph.D. thesis, Research School of Pacific Studies, ANU, 1988.

Wanandi, Yusuf, "China's Asia Card", *Far Eastern Economic Review*, Vol. 25, November 1993, p. 32.
Wang Gungwu, "Greater China and the Chinese Overseas", *China Quarterly*, No. 136, December 1993.
Willmott, David, *The Chinese of Semarang*, Ithaca: Cornell University Press, 1960.
Wong Siu-lun., "The Chinese Family Firm: a Model", *British Journal of Sociology*, 1980, Vol. 36, No. 1, pp. 58–72.
Wong Siu Lan, *Emigrant Entrepreneurs; Shanghai Industrialists in Hong Kong*. Hong Kong: OUP, 1988a.
Wang Siu Lan, "The Applicability of Asian Family Values to Other Socio-cultural Settings", in Berger and Hsiao, 1988b.
Wu Yuan-li and Wu Chun-hsi, *Economic Development in Southeast Asia*, Stanford: Hoover Institute, 1980.
Yoshihara Kunio, *The Rise of Ersatz Capitalism in South-east Asia*, Singapore: Oxford University Press, 1988.
Yoshihara Kunio (ed.), *Oei Tiong Ham Concern: The First Business Empire in South-east Asia*, Kyoto: Centre for South-east Asia Studies, 1989.

4

The Ethnic Chinese and Ersatz Capitalism in Southeast Asia

Yoshihara Kunio

Introduction

A strange logic is sometimes used for explanation. For example, some Japanese leftists who are concerned with the Philippines argue that the country is poor because Japan is located nearby to exploit it. The Philippines' $700 per capita GNP is about one-fortieth Japan's, which is the second highest in the world today (after Switzerland). The Philippines' poverty and Japan's affluence may be unrelated events, but for those who subscribe to a "world system" approach, the two are interrelated. But if the Philippines' poverty is due to Japan's exploitation, one wonders why Taiwan, which is nearer to Japan, is doing better than the Philippines, with a per capita GNP of over $10,000. It seems more logically sound to argue that the Philippines is poor largely because of its own problems.

In Southeast Asia, ethnic Chinese capitalists seem to suffer from a similarly strange logic. Although it is difficult to show statistically, it seems safe to say that they dominate the capitalist sector of Southeast Asia.[1] This fact is often taken as the cause of the poor economic performance of some countries in the ASEAN region (e.g. Indonesia). Critics of the ethnic Chinese argue that those countries have not been doing as well as they should, because the ethnic Chinese are conscienceless capitalists, exploiting the weak, seeking monopoly profits, speculating on land and stocks, bribing government officials, and serving as a conduit for capital flight. But the real reasons for their poor economic performance may lie elsewhere. One can easily hypothesize that one basic reason is that their culture lacks a strong work ethic. If this is true, the dominance of the ethnic Chinese in the capitalist sector of the economy (or the private sector as a whole) can be a result of it, instead of its cause.

Thailand and Malaysia have been doing better than the Philippines and Indonesia. While the per capita GNP of the latter two is hovering around \$700, Thailand's is about \$1,700 and Malaysia's \$2,500. Thailand in particular has been enjoying high growth in the past several years, and has doubled its income between 1987 and 1991. But one cannot extrapolate to the future from the record of the past several years. The economic record of the recent past has been good because they depended heavily on foreign capital, and in view of increasing competition from other countries, especially China which took half of foreign investment in the region in 1992, it is unlikely that the strategy will continue to work in the future. When economic growth slows down or the economy declines, people will blame Chinese capitalists for this, although they are not the real reason. In Malaysia, where the ethnic Chinese remain a distinct minority, they can easily become scapegoats.

Singapore and Brunei will continue to enjoy a high standard of living in the foreseeable future because the former has built a strong institutional framework which encourages private initiative and has a strong work ethic largely because of its history as a country of immigrants (especially Chinese), while the latter enjoys favourable resource endowments. But in other ASEAN countries, because of a weak work ethic, economic growth will not be sustained over time, and it will be difficult for them to follow the path of industrial countries. As a result, people's economic expectations will be frustrated, and capitalists will become the target of their frustration, whether they are Chinese or not. But in the countries where the Chinese are a distinct minority, they earn an additional enmity because of their ethnicity.

Culture, Institutions, and Economic Growth

From the neoclassical economists' point of view, economic development is sustained economic growth. Their main concern is how the dependent variable of GNP or per capita GNP is related to other economic variables, such as investment, saving, export, etc. Institutional economists, on the other hand, while accepting the relations pointed out by neoclassical economists, are interested in examining how the structure of institutions and their interdependence affect the parameters defining those economic relations.

What has come out from neoclassical economists' investigation is that there is a high correlation between export performance and economic growth in the fast growing countries of East Asia. One can explain this in terms of Keynesian economics by viewing exports as a demand, but it would be more correct to view the relation as follows. Economic growth requires import increase since, if the economy grows, it requires additional raw materials and manufactured goods (intermediate and capital goods) as inputs, many of which must be imported because they are not available in the country, more expensive, or poorer in quality. Import increase can be financed only by export increase, which can be sustained only if the country is able to change the export composition from primary to manufactured goods and within the latter, from labour intensive goods to more value added goods such as machinery.

Institutional economists would ask what type of institutional arrangement is supportive of, for example, export increase. A market economy would be a better institutional arrangement for this than a planned economy. But not all market economies perform equally well. For a market economy to perform well, it depends on the government for supply of public goods, so one crucial question becomes how well the government is fulfilling this task. Another question may be how extensively and how well the government is intervening in the market economy. As government intervention increases, the economy approaches a planned economy, which is, of course, an undesirable state. But from this, one cannot argue that the less intervention, the better, since Japan, Korea, and Taiwan were subject to more government intervention than such countries as Thailand, yet did better. Here, the quality of government intervention becomes an important issue. In addition, there are numerous other institutional questions affecting efficiency, especially in connection with export increase.

An institutional approach can throw new light on the problems a country is facing in economic growth. For example, the Philippines, which used to enjoy twice as high income as Thailand in the early 1950s, now produces per capita income only half as much as Thailand ($735 vs. $1,605 in 1991). The poor economic performance of the Philippines *vis-a-vis* Thailand is related to the decline of the government's ability to provide public goods and increased intervention in the market economy. As for Thailand, the government did not intervene much since it was aware that its bureaucratic capability was limited, and the ability to provide public goods, although it is still limited compared with such a country as Singapore, improved over time possibly because being authoritarian, the government was under more pressure to "perform". If this is true, one might ask, why didn't Marcos' martial law perform as well as Thailand's authoritarian government. The answer in this case seems to be that the Philippines did not have an indigenous authoritarian tradition in the recent past, whereas Thailand had been an authoritarian country (first under the absolute monarch and then under the military) and improved it to meet the needs of modernization.

But if one turns from comparison of the Philippines and Thailand to that of Korea and Thailand, culture emerges as an important factor. As pointed out above, export increase can be sustained only if export composition changes over time. The most difficult part in this is to change from labour intensive goods to more value added goods such as machinery. In the 1980s, Thailand increased the exports of textiles and other labour intensive goods virtually on their own. True, Japanese and other foreign capital was involved in the production of labour intensive goods for export, but Thai capital was more important in this. But the next stage was more difficult. Thus, in increasing electronic and other machinery exports, Thailand had to depend greatly on foreign, especially Japanese, capital. But since its in-flow to Thailand was limited, it became a constraint on the export increase of more value added goods.

In the 1950s and the first several years of the 1960s, Korea was poorer than Thailand. In 1968, Korea caught up with Thailand in per capita GNP for the first time. After this, Korea continued to grow faster, and outdistanced Thailand. Now, it is enjoying about three times as high income as Thailand. The reason for this is the faster increase of exports in Korea, especially of machinery exports. From the mid-1970s, Korea began increasing machinery exports rapidly, and surpassed the $1 billion mark in the second half of the 1970s, the $10 billion mark in the mid-1980s, and reached $30 billion in 1991. In contrast, in Thailand, machinery exports became important only in the second half of the 1980s, and amounted to $6.9 billion in 1991. In addition, unlike Thailand, since Korean machinery exports were undertaken mostly by national capital, their contribution to national income was so much greater.

In machinery exports, Thailand did not do as well as Korea primarily because it lacked technological capability. Technology is a crucial factor for the emergence of new exports as old exports become less competitive with the rise of wages. Without the ability to create new exports, export increase cannot be sustained; if it cannot be sustained, economic growth cannot be sustained. One can argue that one main reason why Korea could grow faster than Thailand is that it built the technological base more effectively. In the following section, I want to take Thailand as the representative case of Southeast Asia, and contrast it with Korea's technological progress.

Technologyless Industrialization in Thailand: A Contrast with Korea

I once argued that industrialization in Southeast Asia is 'technologyless'.[2] This is because I could not see a rise of firms with technological capability in the region. If this is true, one might ask, how did certain Thai entrepreneurs set up sophisticated industries? For example, Tawon Pornprapha is engaged in motor vehicle and parts production. His activities appear quite technologically sophisticated, and he is sometimes hailed as an industrial pioneer of the country. But the fact is that he is a Japanese comprador (to be more precise, Nissan's comprador). Important components are supplied by the Japanese company, and those which are produced locally are made under the technical supervision of the Japanese company. He is essentially the distributor of Nissan cars, with the difference that he has assembling and parts producing plants. Technologically, however, he is almost 100% dependent on the Japanese licensor. So, under the present set-up, it would be impossible for him to become technologically independent and start exporting his products. His technological dependency is not temporary but, being structural, permanent.

One might say that Thailand has produced a number of industrial entrepreneurs who are not compradors. For example, pharmaceutical producers (such as Svasti Osathanugraph of Osothsapha) produce drugs under licence from foreign countries, but they are far more independent than the automobile producer. If they use foreign patents, they do not depend on one company; and often they tie up with more than just a few companies. Sometimes they pirate foreign patents and produce generic products. So, they have a great degree of freedom. But there is little technology involved in much of what they do. A large part of their operation is to mix imported chemicals (according to the formulas supplied by their foreign licensors) and bottle the products.

Those in textiles, steel, cement, and petrochemicals (especially downstream products) have no foreign licensors and accordingly enjoy a greater degree of freedom in the procurement of raw materials and the marketing of their products. At the same time, their operation is fairly capital-intensive and appears technologically quite sophisticated – a sign of industrial progress. However, it is machines which make their operation appear sophisticated. Raw materials are fed into the machines at one end, and the final products come out at the other end. If there is any technological sophistication in such plants, it is in machines. But the machines are imported, so there is nothing sophisticated in what these industrial entrepreneurs are doing.

One might say that this was also true in Korea not so long ago. But Korea was not so totally dependent on foreign companies as Thailand is today. If Korea could not produce the machines it needed, it had to import them, and in fact, imported a great deal; but that is all it did. Unlike Thai entrepreneurs, Korean entrepreneurs did not, in general, depend on foreign companies for the layout of their factories or installation of machines. There was already little of "plant exports" in the 1970s. But a typical Thai entrepreneur essentially bought a plant from a foreign company as a turn-key project. If his staff did not know how to operate it, he could enlist a foreign engineering company to give the necessary training before the plant was completed. If this was not enough, he could hire its technicians to stay at the plant. Even if this was unnecessary, he may have later depended on the engineering company or the supplier of the machines when something went wrong, for his technical staff tended to lack the technical ability to make complicated repairs.

Although technical capability differed from one plant to another, the situation described above was not exceptional. Industrial entrepreneurs were able to run manufacturing plants that required technical competence far beyond what they could muster within their own country because foreign companies could fill the gap – of course, for a fee. They were willing to undertake this because it was profitable. And it was profitable because the government, in its eagerness to promote industrialization, provided protection and subsidies (though the Thai government did not do this as much as other governments in the region). In Korea, the government also offered protection and subsidies to industrial entrepreneurs, but their industrialization was more commensurate with their own technological progress.

Because the overall level of technical competence was low in Thailand, the entrepreneurs who aspired to be industrialists had to depend on foreign technology even though it was terribly expensive. There was no effective local substitute for the technology needed for the advanced industrial activities the government was promoting. The situation was different in Korea: technology had to be imported, but this was minimized by substituting local technology whenever possible. It could do this because there were a number of better trained engineers and skilled workers. And it paid to train them further because it was more likely to lead to technological independence, product innovation, and cost reduction.

Today's large technological gap frustrates in many ways Thai efforts to catch up with the technology of developed countries. This problem should not be overemphasized, however, for against similar odds, Korea has been catching up rapidly. Until recent years, Thailand cared little about science and technology. In the late 1970s, in order to demonstrate to the people that the country needed to make a faster progress in technology, the government created the Ministry of Science, Technology, and Energy. However, it amounted to no more than a gesture. With little budget, the ministry came to be referred to as the 'cemetery ministry', and in July 1985, its minister, Damrong Lathaphipat, committed suicide. He may have had other reasons for killing himself, but his act was also taken as a protest against the Sixth National Economic and Social Development Plan which gave science and technology the cold shoulder.[3] This incident was interpreted by some people as showing that if one became serious about science and technology in Thailand, one would end up killing oneself as Damrong did.

There are a number of indicators of the technological backwardness of Thailand. For example, there are no privately owned shipyards in the country which can build ships greater than a few thousand tons, despite the importance of ocean transport. Shipbuilding is not like a turn-key project, in which imported machines play a central role; it is more like building a house.[4] Each ship has a different design and requires various kinds of skilled workers at different stages of production. And unless jobs are done properly, it can sink. But even though building a large ship is technologically more complicated than, say, melting scrap iron and making steel products or producing cement from limestone and clay, by today's standards it does not require much scientific and technological sophistication. Even so, there are no Thai companies which can build a large ship even for the domestic market. In Korea, however, as early as 1974, a 260,000 ton tanker was exported. Several years later, Korea began challenging Japan in shipbuilding, and is now becoming the largest shipbuilder in the world.[5]

If Thailand becomes an NIC, this can only be through foreign capital since the country does not have dynamic industrial entrepreneurs of its own. As a new development on the Thai industrialization scene that augurs Thailand's entry into NIC status, some might point to the plan of some Thai companies to export cars and automobile parts (such as engines), but these are all foreign (Japanese) joint ventures. Damrong's suicide is symbolic of Thailand's technological backwardness as well as its unwillingness to push for technological progress. The only things Thai industrialists can export are processed primary products, garments, textiles, and other labour-intensive products.

In contrast, such Korean conglomerates as Hyundai and Samsung compete in the world market. Hyundai has the largest shipyard in the world, and is also challenging Japanese producers in car manufacturing. Samsung is a major chip maker in the world, and competes with Japanese and American firms in this market (especially DRAM chips). The rise of such Korean firms was made possible by the country's technological progress. For this, Korea emphasized science and technical education, and has now 46.5 scientists and technicians per 1,000 population, compared with 1.2 in Thailand.[6]

Technology and Culture

Technology, income, and institutions are interrelated. For example, R & D is dependent on how much money can be spent, so that to promote technological progress, Korea, with a higher level of income, is in a better position than Thailand. The effect of institutions on income was discussed when the economic performance of Thailand and the Philippines was compared. But the causation is not always one way; income can influence institutions. For example, as income rises, people become better educated, and more people come to live in cities; these are favourable factors for the rise of democracy (or authoritarian government becomes more difficult to maintain).[7] And institutions can influence technology, and vice versa. For example, the market economy is believed to be more conducive to technological progress than the planned economy because its competitive environment induces business enterprises to seek a technological advantage over others. In turn, technology can influence institutions. For example, centralized government (such as Communist government) over a large territory has become possible only with the progress of transportation and communications technology.

Although technology, institutions, and income are three important interrelated variables, culture has to be introduced as another variable to complete the picture. If it is defined as a value system, culture is related to institutions, but here, by postulating that technology depends on income, institutions, and culture, we want to single out the effect of culture on technology. Of course, culture is a dependent variable as well (for example, it changes as income rises), but for the sake of argument, it is taken as an independent variable. This can be justified since culture, as the result of the past historical evolution, does not change rapidly.

Some people argue that culture doesn't have anything to do with the present technological gap between Thailand and Korea. They explain the gap in terms of government leaders' recognition of the importance of technology and willingness to promote it. Sarit and his successors in Thailand paid little attention to technology until the 1980s, while Park Chung-hee in Korea began promoting it soon after he came to power in the early 1960s. But it is one thing for government leaders to recognize the importance of technology, while it is quite another for people to respond to it. One can easily argue that Thai leaders were realistic enough to foresee a poor response by people to the government's plan to promote technology and that they decided to rely on Japanese and other foreign companies for most of industrial technology. On the other hand, Park Chung-hee believed that Koreans could absorb technology, and in fact, they did under the government's direction and incentives. One can easily argue that Thailand's success in economic development (*vis-a-vis* other developing countries) was made possible by the realistic assessment of the people's response, for it enabled the country to avoid the costly mistakes other countries made with extensive government intervention.

The first scholar who has called our attention to culture as a determinant of development is Max Weber, who argued that the Protestant ethic explains the rise of capitalism in the West.[8] In recent years, his theory was discredited by the rise of capitalism in Catholic countries as well as East Asia, but Weber's contribution can be appreciated more if one does not regard his theory as a general theory but as a local theory applying only to Protestant countries in a specific period of time. The rise of capitalism in East Asia is now often attributed to the Confucian ethic (as the East Asian counterpart of the Protestant ethic in the West).

But one wonders why it is necessary to seek a development-promoting value system in religion (or moral teaching in the case of Confucianism). In the case of Max Weber, although it is not clear whether he is entirely right, if one is willing to give him the benefit of the doubt, the rise of Protestantism was important in the 18th and 19th centuries since people were religious then. In East Asia, however, Confucianism or other religions have been much less binding in the past century or so, and it seems that a development-promoting value system arose for different reasons.

What does such a value system consist of then? One value is to attach great importance to work in life. Work is the opposite of sleeping in the daytime, drinking, playing games, sports and musical instruments, gambling, gossiping, chatting, singing, dancing, watching or listening to an entertainment programme on TV or radio, and reading for fun or to kill time. Work is not fun and requires one to exert effort. Of course, life cannot be sustained without entertainment or fun, so there has to be some room for leisure and merry occasions, but work must be a dominant value.

Another central value in a development-promoting value system is that people should be spurred to improve themselves (materially, socially and intellectually, but not so much spiritually) over life time or over other people. Work (or study in the case of children in school) can be an end by itself to some extent, but it must be directed for improvement. When work and the desire for improvement are combined, one works hard to improve one's life and does so systematically. Society may be improvement-oriented, but it may lack emphasis on persistent efforts to attain it through work if work is not emphasized. For example, Philippine society attaches importance to improvement, but traditionally, it did not place great emphasis on hard work as its means. This is reflected in its folk hero, Juan Tamad (Juan the lazy), who attaches importance to success but glorifies an easy way of attaining it (for example, courting a rich man's daughter successfully).

Work- and improvement-emphasizing values affect productivity through two channels. One is to raise productivity directly with more working days, longer working hours, and higher intensity of work per hour. The other is indirectly through human capital formation. An important part of this is acquisition of technical know-how. Technical know-how, unlike knowledge on culture and society, is internationally standardized, and how well it is acquired or how advanced it is can be easily tested in the international market when goods produced with it are exported. In other words, there is no cultural relativity in technical know-how, and countries with stronger work- and improvement-emphasizing values can do better in technological competition. Science and technical subjects are not fun, and attract only those with strong work- and improvement-emphasizing values. They may attract others initially or keep them until the end of schooling, but their mastery tends to be poor. And after they enter companies, those with strong work- and improvement-emphasizing values continue to work on what they studied in school or continue to learn new skills or new knowledge. Only persistent efforts can bring about the technological progress which contributes to fast economic growth.

Koreans work hard. In 1986, Korean workers in the manufacturing sector worked 54.7 hours per week. There is no comparable data for Thai workers,[9] but if they worked as much as those in industrial countries (which was roughly 40 hours per week), Koreans must have worked a little over 30% more hours than Thais. It is said that Koreans are the hardest working people in the world. As to the desire of people to improve themselves, one indicator is the percentage of children in secondary schools. In Thailand, it is about 30%, but in Korea, it is close to 100%. True, income difference is a factor for the different percentages, but even when Korea had a lower income, it had a higher percentage. The percentage of high school graduates advancing to colleges or university in Korea is now the second highest in the world after the United States.[10] Koreans are said to be "a fiercely upward-moving people".[11]

Thais do not emphasize work and self-improvement as much as Koreans do. On the other hand, Thais attach greater importance to calmness (*choey*), fun (*sanuk*), and being comfortable (*saduak* and *sabay*). If they want to improve themselves, their efforts are sometimes directed to improvement in the next life, since, being Buddhists, many of them believe in transmigration of souls and want to accumulate merit in this world (*tham bun*) for a better next life.

True, Thai culture is changing, and many middle-class people are hard-working and success-oriented (in this world), but for the majority of Thai people, especially those in rural areas, leisure seems to be more important and work less important than for the Koreans.

Why the difference? A culture has been shaped by many factors in the past. One is how man interacted with nature. Two economies can be equally poor, but one may produce enough (food, etc.) without man working very hard, while the other require man's efforts to overcome the constraints set by nature, such as several months of cold winter and the scarcity of productive land (Korea has the second highest population density in the world).[12] For example, in Korea, people experienced famine a number of times because, since population tended to increase to the limit of what nature could support with the existing technology, weather changes (like an unusually early winter) could easily affect the crop of marginal lands. True, calamities were sometimes brought about by forces beyond man's control, but they could be often avoided by planning, diligence, and frugality. These values naturally became important in such a country as a matter of survival. In contrast, in Thailand, it seems that forces affecting man tended to be beyond his control, and values emphasizing the adjustment to nature seem to have become more important than those encouraging man to subdue it with hard work and planning. Besides, since nature was generally bountiful (as epitomized in King Ramkhamheang's words "In water there are fish, in the field there is rice"), there was no strong need to overcome nature.

Of course, man's interaction with nature is not the only factor. In the case of Korea, the destruction of class barriers during the Japanese period may have been important. During that period, the government and business elites were mostly Japanese, but since they left after the Pacific War, they were filled by Koreans after that. But before new elites were formed, the Korean War came. The war killed many people, did extensive damage to property, and dislocated numerous people. It had a great levelling effect on society. As a result, Korea in the mid-1950s was a classless society, in which people could move up with their own initiative. This seems to have been one factor for people's enthusiasm for education and business undertaking. In contrast, Thailand has not gone through such a traumatic period as Korea has, and there is greater continuity in society. As a result of this, the values emphasizing mental calmness and status quo seem to have remained more important.

How representative is Thailand of the four ASEAN countries (Thailand, Malaysia, Indonesia, and the Philippines; hereafter called the ASEAN Four)? True, all of them have different cultures. As for religion, while Thailand is a

Buddhist country, Malaysia and Indonesia are Islamic countries, and the Philippines is a Christian (predominantly Catholic) country. This religious difference alone gives rise to cultural diversity. But if there is any major difference among the ASEAN Four in the value system affecting technology (and productivity), the other three may be more achievement-oriented than Thailand.

As to the work ethic, however, there does not seem be a major difference. During the colonial period, a number of Western observers have pointed out a weak work ethic is a major problem for various countries in the region.[13] One might argue that their views were biased, but some ethnic Chinese have been pointing out the same thing. Although many of the ethnic Chinese who hold the view express it only privately, ethnic Chinese in Singapore, constituting a dominant majority in the island republic, have been more frank. For example, the Singapore Malay specialist, Tham Seong Chee, attributes Malay "backwardness" to their work ethic.[14] They tend to view indigenous Southeast Asians as 'soft' people and Chinese and Koreans as 'hard' people.[15]

Some Southeast Asians admit that a weak work ethic is a problem. The Filipino revolutionary leader of the late 19th century, Jose Rizal, wrote on "the indolence of the Filipinos".[16] More recent Southeast Asian writers have not put the problem as bluntly as Jose Rizal did, but they recognize it as a cause for underdevelopment (for example, Mochtar Lubis and Mahathir bin Mohamad).[17] Recently, when the production manager of the Indonesian integrated steel mill, Krakatau Steel, was asked whether its productivity could ever reach the levels of South Korea, he replied; "[Indonesian] culture is different. The Korean is very tough; we are a tropical people. You have to handle people differently [here]."[18]

A weak work ethic can be compensated by lower wages when labour intensive goods are produced for export, but if a country wants to move to production of more valued added goods (such as machinery) for export, lower wages cannot be of much advantage. For production of such goods, technology is not all embodied in machines, and an important part of it must be provided by workers, but if they are not up to international standards, they cannot produce the goods or if they can, the goods are not exportable. I once argued that Southeast Asian capitalism is ersatz because industrial capitalism, lacking necessary scientists, engineers, and skilled workers, cannot overcome the export barriers an economy faces as its income rises.[19] A poor quality of government intervention, discrimination of ethnic Chinese, and lack of emphasis on science and technology on the part of government, were offered as factors causing such a technological situation. But when a weak work ethic is introduced as an additional barrier, the problem of technology becomes a much fundamental problem confronting the ASEAN Four.

The Ethnic Chinese vs. Indigenes in the ASEAN Region

If culture is a determinant of the economic performance of a country or an ethnic group, as has been argued so far, it is tempting to use cultural difference, in particular difference in work orientation, to explain why ethnic Chinese do better in economic competition with indigenes. But a more popular explanation is the network theory. According to this theory, because the Chinese have long had well-structured, extensive business networks, they are in a much better position to compete with the indigenes.

The lack of a business network was, until recent years, a major obstacle even to an indigene with a strong work ethic. In starting a business, for example, he would have no one who could help him to get training, for his father and his relatives would probably be peasants. If he approached an established business organization and actually managed to get a job, it would be a lowly one, the experience of which would hardly be sufficient to embark on any significant business on his own.

Capital was also a major problem for the indigene, unlike for the Chinese, who had a network through which to find someone who could help him get started in business. In pre-war Malaya and Indonesia, for example, there was no bank for an indigene to go to. He could not approach a Chinese bank, since the Chinese did business among themselves. Even if he could find someone willing to lend him money, he had to pay higher interest rates. It was also difficult for the indigene to obtain supplies on credit, since it was the Chinese who monopolized the distribution network and they did not trust indigenous traders.

In some areas where the Chinese did not penetrate, either by choice (this was especially so in the Philippines where the Chinese had to concentrate on lucrative areas because their number was small due to restricted immigration) or because of exclusion by the colonial government, indigenous traders were born and developed their own networks, but these were weak compared with Chinese networks. For one thing, an indigenous network tended to be more location-specific, since the geographic spread of an indigenous ethnic group was more limited. But a Chinese network could much more easily link up with a national or even an international network. A Hokkien network in a town in East Java, for example, could be linked to another Hokkien network in a town in Sumatra, and if necessary, to the one in Singapore or any further place where there were Hokkiens.[20]

In understanding Chinese networks, it is important to bear in mind that, in the pre-war period, these excluded not only indigenes but also many other Chinese. The broadest group was a speech group (Hokkien, Teochiu, etc.). In addition, there were narrower groups based on other ties, such as native place. In the postwar period, these ties loosened and new ties formed in the new places of residence. Networks now have a broader base than the speech group, but this is not usually broad enough to cover non-Chinese.

In the pre-war period, not every one who spoke, for example, Hokkien, could belong to a Hokkien network. Of course, to be able to speak Hokkien and have a 'Hokkien personality' was a necessary condition for entry to that network, but a number of other conditions had to be met. The most crucial of these was what the Chinese call *shinyung* (trustworthiness).[21] This was important because business was often done with a verbal promise and because even if there was a contract, its enforcement was inefficient and costly when it was broken (at least, this is how the Chinese perceived the administrative justice in their countries of residence).[22] A Chinese with *shinyung* would not break a promise or contract, so only such people were kept in the network.

None had *shinyung* from the beginning. Those who wanted to enter business had to go through a training period, and only those who finished it successfully could enter a network with the endorsement of their masters. Then, in the course of their career, they could either lose *shinyung* and drop out of business, or win greater *shinyung* and establish themselves as traders. There was always a possibility that someone with a certain amount of *shinyung* could cheat the network or fail it unwillingly, but it was minimized by the fact that the Chinese formed a closed, minority community. Being a minority, business and social life were so interwined that severe social sanctions were imposed on those who were dishonest in business. But at the same time, gossip was exchanged in social gatherings and the meetings of trade and other business associations, and any worthwhile information (often negative) was fed back to the network so that it could adjust its evaluation of its members' *shinyung*.

As pointed out above, the organizational basis of networks changed over time, and what was true in the pre-war period no longer holds.[23] But Chinese business networks still exist, and they still operate on the basis of *shinyung*. The indigenes, who have never been given a chance to prove themselves, are excluded from these networks and cannot compete with the Chinese on an equal basis. In the postwar period, some Southeast Asian governments established banks, trading companies, and other institutions to break the Chinese monopoly on networks, but these efforts were not enough to counterbalance the disadvantages the indigenes face in competition with the Chinese.

In Thailand, institutional constraints constituted another reason for the failure of indigenous networks to develop. In the 19th century, the Thai government required Thai peasants to perform corvee labour, which meant that they could not leave their villages for the entire year. It can be argued that this corvee obligation handicapped the Thais who wished to enter business. In contrast, Chinese immigrants were given greater freedom in movement. At the same time, the Chinese were more lightly taxed than the indigenous Thais because the government wanted to induce Chinese immigration; and this tax discrimination may also be argued to have worked against the Thais.

These constraints may have discouraged Thais from entering business; but similar constraints were absent in the other Southeast Asian countries, where there were, in fact, more constraints on the Chinese than on the indigenous population. In these countries, restrictions were placed, for example, on Chinese travel and residence: the Chinese were required to live in designated areas and to obtain permits to travel to other areas. It is true that these were gradually removed, but in Java, they remained until as late as 1919 (and this freedom was extended to the Outer Provinces in 1926). There were also similar restrictions in the Philippines during the Spanish period, though they were removed earlier than in Java (in the mid-19th century).

Networks and institutional constraints may have been important, but they are not a complete explanation for the greater success of Chinese in business. One has to bring in cultural differences as another explanatory variable. The Chinese are not innately commercially oriented and hard-working. Certainly, the majority of the Chinese in China were not like that. But the Chinese in Southeast Asia may have had these qualities, at least more so on the average than the indigenes in the pre-war period, partly because the bulk of them were immigrants who were lured by better economic opportunities and wanted eventually to return to China. Of course, they did not start from scratch but were helped by existing networks and this makes it difficult to isolate how independent their value orientation was. It appears to have been an important factor, however. In the Philippines, for example, the Chinese *mestizos* (who were treated like the indigenes by the Spanish Administration) tended to dominate business whenever the number of Chinese shrank due to expulsion and restriction of immigration, and to be pushed out of the areas the Chinese re-entered when they were allowed to return. In Malaya, the Chinese took over tin mining from the Malays in the mid-19th century, which again seemed to have little to do with networks.

After a long period of stay, and also from the second generation onwards, the Chinese tended not to work hard for money (at least not as hard as the first generation). After all, such a life was not enjoyable, and a number of Chinese opted, at least partially, for an indigenous way of life.[24] In Thailand and the Philippines, this could be accomplished relatively easily by marrying and being absorbed into indigenous society (absorption did not often follow marriage for the first generation, but from the second generation, it was quite common, even if the father remained within the Chinese community). Nevertheless, in the pre-war period, a constant influx of new immigrants kept alive the work ethic and commercial orientation of the Chinese community. And in early postwar years, the inflow of Chinese stopped (which will be bound to have serious effects on the value system of the Chinese in the long run), but being the descendants of recent immigrants, they retained a stronger work ethic and commercial orientation than the indigenes, and in the countries where the Chinese were discriminated against, their lives and properties threatened, and their future uncertain, such values were kept alive as a way of survival.

The Ethnic Chinese in a Weak Economy

One might ask how the ASEAN Four can be a weak economy. Except for the Philippines, the other three have recorded healthy growth in the past several years, and are widely hailed as new 'little dragons'. But such a view is too optimistic. A couple of decades ago, it was Latin American countries (such as Brazil) which were thought to be on the way to development, but the 1980s was a decade of stagnation for them. They could not overcome the barriers a higher level of income created because, I believe, they did not have a strong work ethic. As argued earlier, it is a necessary condition for raising productivity over time. Malaysia and Thailand, the two ASEAN countries which have been doing better than the other two, will face similar problems as their incomes grow, and chances are that their growth will slow down then. Like Latin American countries, they do not have a strong work ethic which is required to overcome such barriers. If they do better than Latin American countries for some reason, they will slow down at a slightly higher level. They do not have the same growth potential as Korea.

After all, the Chinese were brought in to the region because the indigenes did not have a strong work ethic and could not perform the tasks that the Chinese could or were willing to do. On the other hand, they were not much needed in countries such as Korea where people had a strong work ethic, and if they went there, they played only a marginal role in their economic development. There, indigenous people performed the task the Chinese undertook in the ASEAN region. Contrast this situation with, for example, Thailand where Chinese were needed as coolies, merchants and artisans, since the Thais generally wanted to remain in rural areas. Traditional Thai society was not much work- and achievement-oriented.

In Thailand, the Chinese problem does not seem to exist. The ethnic Chinese may not disappear, but, since many of them are being absorbed into Thai society, they are a shrinking group (if you define ethnic Chinese as those who either speak Chinese or retain a great deal of Chinese values). Though the economy may not meet the people's expectations, the ethnic Chinese will not be singled out as the target of attack. If they are criticized, it will be because they are business leaders (or capitalists) who do not deliver economic liberation, which capitalism "promises". In the Philippines, the Chinese problem still exists, but compared with the early 1970s, the situation has greatly improved for the ethnic Chinese, and it appears that, although the Chinese problem remains an irritating one for the ethnic Chinese, it will decline in importance as a national problem.

The problem will be serious for Malaysia and Indonesia where Islam acts as a line of separation between the Muslim majority and the Chinese minority. The problem will become less serious if the economy continues to grow at a healthy rate and thus can meet the rising economic expectations of the Muslim majority, but as argued above, this cannot be expected. This is basically because the Muslim majority does not have a strong work ethic which overcomes the barriers created by a rising level of income, but they are reluctant to admit this. Instead, they will put the blame on Chinese capitalists and the ethnic Chinese businessmen in general.

In this age of anti-heroes, capitalists are often disparaged and equated with monopolists, speculators, and rent-seekers (seekers of political connections for unearned profits). But they need not be, and their reputation improves if capitalism performs. In Japan, for example, Honda Soichiro and Matsushita Konosuke are respected for their contribution to the Japanese economy. So, Chinese capitalists can be respected like Honda and Matsushita, but their chances are not good, because the economy in which they operate is not strong. The best they can hope for is that they earn the respect of people who work under them. In the case of Honda and Matsushita, they became respectable because they headed the manufacturing companies which became nationally as well as internationally respectable companies. But they could not bring this about themselves; they depended greatly on the people who worked for them as well as on the Japanese economic system which provided a favourable environment.

I am somewhat reluctant to use the term "ersatz capitalists". Not all capitalists who operate under ersatz capitalism are ersatz. Japanese companies' industrial compradors in the ASEAN region are not ersatz capitalists, for example. They have responded to the environment and became successful; although their companies cannot become Samsungs and Hyundais, that is not their fault. There are many other capitalists in the region as genuine as their counterparts in Korea. Many of those operating large hotels, banks, and department stores have become successful by responding to the market needs of people. If the term "ersatz capitalist" has any meaning, it should be applied to the capitalist who thrives on political connections. Most of Marcos' cronies in the early 1980s were such examples. It can be also applied to speculators and corporate raiders who do not bring real benefits to the economy. And it can be applied to capitalists who take money out of their countries where capital is needed for national development.

In Malaysia and Indonesia where the Chinese problem will remain, if the economy stagnates and this raises political temperatures, the ethnic Chinese will come under attack, and the business environment will deteriorate (with more government regulations and state enterprises). This will make it more tempting for Chinese capitalists to engage in unproductive or counterproductive economic activities, resulting in a rampant growth of ersatz capitalists. Since this worsens the economy, the ethnic Chinese will come under further attack, this time focusing on their ersatzness. As a remedy, the government will undertake further measures to restrict capitalist institutions, which will in turn weaken the economy further and make ersatz economic activities more widespread. This is a vicious circle which will destroy capitalism as well as the potential for economic development.

This may be unduly pessimistic, but whether this will be correct or not depends importantly on whether the business environment will deteriorate due to a fundamental Islamic movement. If it is regarded as a movement to create an Islamic state, whatever its supporters may say, it is anti-rational (as well as anti-scientific), anti-materialistic, and anti-capitalistic (more government-interventionist). If the term "anti" is objectionable, it should be understood to mean that it stands for something opposite, though it may not mean to go all the way in that direction (at least, there is no consensus among its supporters on how far they want to go).

A fundamental Islamic movement grows and declines for reasons which we cannot discuss here, but it is sufficient to note that Malaysia and Indonesia may come under its influence. One effective check against this is continuous economic growth, but because of a weak work ethic, this cannot be expected.

So, if the fundamental Islamic movement grows for non-economic reasons at the time when the economy is not doing well (or declines), this can unleash frontal attacks on capitalism and capitalists. To make the situation worse, since most capitalists are ethnic Chinese (most genuine capitalists are), Muslim prejudice will make rational checks extremely difficult.

The worst scenario may not materialize, but the two countries can move in that direction. What is difficult to estimate is the strength of fundamental Islam in the future. In a way, it is strange that in the age of rapid transportation and instant communications which are shrinking the world, such an "anachronistic" movement as fundamental Islam is merging on the horizon. But this can be understood better if we remember that modern institutions often fail to solve our problems. Such a movement can become strong in the countries where people are not well educated and face a bleak economic reality.

Endnotes

1 Some people offer statistical estimates, but these are on dubious grounds because data on corporate assets are not comprehensive in Southeast Asia and because the definition of ethnic Chinese is somewhat vague. One such estimate was given recently by David K.P. Li, chief executive of the Bank of East Asia in Hong Kong: "[In] Indonesia, Malaysia, Thailand and the Philippines ... up to 70% of each country's private sector is controlled by overseas Chinese." "Watch for a Prosperous China Soon", *International Herald Tribune*, 5 October 1993.

2 Yoshihara Kunio, *The Rise of Ersatz Capitalism in Southeast Asia*, Singapore: Oxford University Press, 1988, Chapter 5, and Krirkkiat Phipatseritham and Yoshihara Kunio, "Thailand: Industrialization without Development", *East Asian Cultural Studies*, March 1989.

3 *ASEAN Forecast*, September 1985, p. 132.

4 This analogy was suggested to me during my interview with Mr Kitajima Jun, the representative in Jakarta of Mitsui Engineering & Shipbuilding Co., June 1986.

5 Korea's share of the tonnage of ships built in the world surpassed Japan's for the first time in the first quarter of 1993 (Korea's 26% vs. Japan's 20%). *Asahi Shinbun*, 14 July 1993.

6 United Nations Development Programme, *Human Development Report*, New York: Oxford University Press, 1991, p. 128.

7 Ronald Inglehart, "The Renaissance of Political Culture", *American Political Science Review*, December 1988. See also Samuel Huntington, *The Third Wave: Democratization in the Late Twentieth Century*, Norman: University of Oklahoma Press, 1991.

8 Max Weber, *The Protestant Ethic and the Rise of Capitalism*, translated by Talcott Parsons, New York: Charles Scribner's Sons, 1958.

9 According to IL0's *Year Book of Labour Statistics*, 1976, in the period 1966-1972,

Koreans worked 55.6 hours per week in non-agricultural sectors, compared with the 47.2 hours of Thai (that is, Koreans worked 18% more). But some say the Thai figure is too high.

10 Bhung Nak Song, *The Rise of the Korean Economy*, Hong Kong: Oxford University Press, 1990, p. 62.

11 Jon Huer, *Marching Orders: The Role of the Military in South Korea's "Economic Miracle" 1961–1971*, New York: Greenwood Press, 1989, p. 190.

12 Countries with an area of less than two thousand square kilometres (such as Singapore and Hong Kong) are excluded. Bangladesh has the highest population density.

13 For the observations of Westerners during the colonial period, see, for example, John Crawfurd, *Journal of an Embassy to the Courts of Siam and Cochin China*, rpt, Kuala Lumpur: Oxford University Press, 1967, pp. 20, 343–344, and 555; Clive Day, *The Policy and Administration of the Dutch in Java*, rpt, Kuala Lumpur: Oxford University Press, 1966, pp. 345–348, 356–357, and 361; James Low, *The British Settlement of Penang*, rpt, Singapore: Oxford University Press, 1972, pp. 8–9; Ernest Young, *The Kingdom of the Yellow Robe*, rpt, Kuala Lumpur: Oxford University Press, 1982, pp. 9, 138, and 206; J.H. Boeke, *Indische Economie*, Vol. 1, Haarlem: H.D. Tjeenk Willink, 1940, p.19; F.A. Swettenham, *British Malaya*, London: Allen and Unwin, 1955, p. 136; and C.G. Warnford-Lock, *Mining in Malaya for Gold and Tin*, London: Crowther and Goodman, 1907, pp. 32–33.

14 Tham Seong Chee, *Malays and Modernization*, 2nd ed., Singapore: Singapore University Press, 1983, various pages.

15 One such a view is quoted in *The Economist*, 10 July 1993.

16 "The Indolence of the Filipinos" appears in E. Alzona, tr. and ed., *Selected Essays and Letters of Jose Rizal*, Manila: Rangle and Sons, 1964.

17 Mochtar Lubis, *The Indonesian Dilemma*, trans. F. Lamoureux, Singapore: Graham Brash, 1983, pp. 33–34; and Mahathir bin Mohamad, *The Malay Dilemma*, Kuala Lumpur: Federal Publications, 1970, pp. 20–28 and 85.

18 *Far Eastern Economic Review*, 29 July 1993, p. 58.

19 Yoshihara, Chapter 5.

20 In the pre-war period, the Minangkabaus probably had the best business network among the indigenous groups of Southeast Asia, but because they were not as widespread as the Chinese, even in Indonesia, their network was not very extensive. At that time, particularly in business, Indonesia's indigenous groups could not transcend their ethnicity.

21 On the importance of *shinyung*, (*xinyong*) see Clifton Barton, "Trust and Credit: Some Observations Regarding Business Strategies of Overseas Chinese Traders in South Vietnam", in Linda Y.C. Lim and Peter Gosling, (eds.), *The Chinese in Southeast Asia*, Vol. 1, Singapore: Maruzen Asia, 1983. This article is not on an ASEAN country, but there is no reason to think that the working of *shinyung* is different.

22 For an economic theory of *shinyung*, see Janet Landa, "The Political Economy of the Ethnically Homogeneous Chinese Middleman Group in Southeast Asia: Ethnicity and Entrepreneurship in a Plural Society", in Linda Y.C. Lim and Peter Gosling, (eds.).

23 On the changing character of Chinese organizations in Singapore (though not a

network in particular), see Cheng Lim Kean, *Social Change and the Chinese in Singapore*, Singapore: Singapore University Press, 1985.

24 On the assimilation of the Chinese to indigenous society, see, for example, Botan, *Letters from Thailand*, translated by Susan Fulop Morell, Bangkok: D.K. Book House, 1977.

5

The Economic Role of the Indonesian Chinese

Christianto Wibisono

This paper examines the economic position of the Chinese in Indonesian economy. It deals with the history which led to the birth of both state owned conglomerates and private sector conglomerates, the ethnic components of the private sector conglomerates, especially the ethnic Chinese component, their relative strength, their impact on the Indonesian political stability.

Much has been written about the so-called economic domination of the Chinese in Southeast Asian countries, including Indonesia. A recent issue of *Asiaweek* quoted from the Nomura Research Institute that Indonesian Chinese who account for 3.5% of Indonesian population, possess 73% share of listed equity.[1] The magazine argues that the figure represents Chinese holdings in listed companies not under state and foreign control. However, the figure does not accurately reflect the economic position of the Chinese in Indonesia.

If we scrutinize the real figure of BPS (Central Bureau Statistics) on elaboration of GDP according to economic sector, we would come to a more realistic figure of the ownership structure of the Indonesian economy. Agriculture still holds almost 20% of the nation's GDP and this sector is almost 100% indigenous. If the manufacturing sector which contributes 21.3% of GDP is largely owned by the Chinese as calculated the Nomura Research Institute of 73%, it means that the Chinese are controlling 15.5% of the GDP. In trading and retailing which account for 13.9% of the GDP, it may be said that the Chinese presence is overwhelmingly dominant. However, in comparable mining and quarrying sector, the Chinese private sector is smaller than the state owned as well as the foreign MNCs.

The Indonesian Economy

Up to 1957, the Indonesian economy was based on the Dutch structure. Three large Dutch banks: Nederlandsche Handels Maatschappij (NHM), Nationale Handels Bank (NHB), and Escompto, as well as Big Five Dutch trading houses remained active, along with BPM (Royal Dutch Shell), Stanvac and Caltex of the United States, plus Dutch and European companies involved in the plantation sector, as well as other multinational corporations (MNCs).

The ethnic Chinese segment of Indonesian society held the role of middlemen between the Dutch or MNCs and consumers. Some Chinese entrepreneurs like Oei Tiong Ham and Be Biauw Tjoan had expanded into industry and banking, but they were a minority. Among the indigenous populace several names such as Djohan Djohor, Rahman Tamin, Agus M. Dassad, H. Abdul Ghany Aziz, Achmad Bakrie and Nitisemito came to the fore successfully during the colonial period.

Once the sovereignty of the Indonesian republic was recognized, the new government immediately took steps to correct and reform the economic system left behind by the colonial power.

State Owned Conglomerates

The first state owned venture was Bank Negara Indonesia, set up on July 5, 1946. The next was Central State Plantation I in 1948 followed by the Central State Plantation II on 23 October 1950. As part of the Round Table Agreement on Indonesian independence, public services were transferred to the Indonesian government. Among these were railroad and telecommunication services, pawnshops and the forestry services. The electricity companies under Dutch concession in the colonial period were nationalized.

The Indonesian government continued to take steps to strengthen the national economy and Bank Negara Indonesia established the State Industrial Bank (Bank Industri Negara, BIN), which is now called Bapindo. BIN set up subsidiary firms like PELNI, Djakarta Lloyd and began to design the cement factory that eventually become PT Semen Gresik. The Government also set up the firm which would become Indonesia's Garuda Airlines. The nationalization through the purchase of all shares in the Javasche Bank in 1953 was the beginning of the central bank, Bank Indonesia. The three Dutch private banks, NHM, NHB and Escompto continued to hold the largest portion of the Indonesian banking business.[2]

The Benteng programme meant to strengthen the position of indigenous businessmen was introduced in the 1950s. This programme was meant to balance the strength of businessmen of Chinese descent and indigenous entrepreneurs. The government continued to establish state owned firms to compete with the powerful Dutch and multinational corporations. Among state firms set up in this period were Pantja Niaga and Indonesian Services Company.

The 1955 election failed to generate political stability. Four major parties which emerged after the elections struggled among themselves. Local and regional uprisings such as those in West Java, South Sulawesi and Aceh, as well as the Irian Jaya conflict made the political situation unfavourable. At the end of 1956, the labour sector, heavily influenced by the Indonesian Communist Party (PKI), began to clamour for nationalization of all Dutch property. The Army then took these companies over and the Republic of Indonesia suddenly owned hundreds of state firms.[3]

The three Dutch Banks (NHM, NHB and Escompto) were nationalized and renamed BEII, BBD and BDN. The Big Five trading houses, Borsumy, Geo Wehry, Internatio, Jacobson van den Berg and Lindeteves, were taken over and split up to became Budi Bhakti, Juda Bhakti, Sejati Bhakti, Fajar Bhakti, Tri Bhakti, Tulus Bhakti, among others.

Dutch contracting firms formed the basis for PT Adhi Karya, Amarta Karya, Hutama Karya, Waskita Karya and Wijaya Karya, while all the Dutch plantation interests became the State Plantation Company. Dutch manufacturing firms were also taken over with NV Braat becoming PN Barata, NV Bromo becoming PN Boma, NV Vulkan becoming PN Bisma and NV de Industrie becoming PN Indra, which eventually became PT Boma Bisma Indra.

In a rationalization programme which followed these takeovers the central government transferred authority over some enterprises to local and regional administrations. Among these were the Dutch brewery in Jakarta which became PT Delta Djakarta and in which the Jakarta Metropolitan Administration still owns a 30% share.

On the national level a socialistic pattern was followed and the state firms were classified according to sector or specialization and put under the authority of the relevant ministry. This eventually led to the eclipse of the influence of the trading houses as many of the state firms sold their products or services directly.

About this time the Chinese business sector began to shift from the role of go-between to a larger one: creatively channelling the allocations (quotas) of the state firms into the market. Even though they were playing an important role, the government issued regulation PP 10/1959 preventing alien businessmen from doing business or trading in the rural areas. Although some Chinese traders were actually Indonesian citizens and were entitled to continue doing business, local populations often misunderstood this and several racial incidents occurred.

On a macro level the policy of the Manipol political regime which was essentially anti-business however, appeared ambiguous. On one hand the government confiscated private sector enterprises like the Oei Tiong Ham Concern in 1963 and sentenced businessman Liem Koen Nio to death for economic subversion. On the other hand, it gave special licences to businessmen such as Bram Tambunan, Abdurachman Aslam and Markam.

Under this economic system of etatism and the paternalistic political system, the Indonesian economy rapidly worsened. The Irian Jaya conflict and the confrontation with Malaysia took their toll, with the aborted communist coup (G30S-PKI) representing the turning point. After a period of about six months of crisis the new Order Government took over in March of 1966.

In 1967 the Indonesian government promulgated Law No. 1 which was meant to open the door for foreign investment. The Dutch and European firms confiscated during the Irian Jaya and Malaysian conflicts were returned. And in 1968 Domestic Investment Law No. 6 was issued to stimulate the return of the capital.

The number of state firms was reduced radically. The remaining companies were reclassified as Perjan, Perum of Persero under Law No. 9, 1969. The private sector (domestic and foreign interests alike) were strengthened with the PMA Law and PMDN Law which came into effect with the launching of the First Five Year Development Plan (Pelita I) on 1 April 1969. Foreign assistance in the form of loans from the IGGI nations began to aid the economic reconstruction.

Within five years the economy had advanced radically. Its social and political impact was seen clearly in the public's discontent over certain quarters which had benefitted more than the indigenous populace. The Malari demonstrations of 1974, which occurred during the visit of PM Kakuei Tanaka of Japan to Jakarta, which involved the burning of the PT Toyota Astra Motor building and the Senen Market project, reflected the racial sentiments that had come to the fore again.

The issue of collusion and collaboration between the business sector and officials was widely discussed in the press in 1970, when the *Nusantara* daily exposed the chronology of the establishment of PT Bogasari Flour

Mills by Liem Sioe Liong. The *Indonesia Raya* daily under Mochtar Lubis revealed the collusion between Arief Husni (Ong Seng Keng) and the assistant to the president (Aspri) Lt. Gen. Soeryo in the Coopa scandal. These and other articles brought to the attention of the public the trend towards the development of huge business groups based on their relationship with officials. The Malari explosion exposed public discontent but was only one aspect of the social tension which also involved political conflict between Armed Forces Commander Gen. Sumitro and presidential assistants (Aspri) Ali Mutopo and Sujono Humardani who were exploiting the sensitive issues known as SARA (an acronym for tribal affiliations, race, religion and socio-economic class). Malari began a new era in the political development of the nation.

From the economic viewpoint, the energy crisis and the renewed importance of oil at the first half of the 1970s played a major role in the changing patterns of the Indonesian society. Although the people expressed discontent and bitter criticism over corruption in Bulog (Logistic Agency), Pertamina (oil) and the forestry sector, which motivated the formation of Commission IV, Pertamina continued to expand rapidly. With the *Nusantara* daily's exposure of the Bogasari and Taman Mini issues and criticism of other forms of business collusion printed in the domestic media, came government action against the press which eventually led to the closing down of *Indonesia Raya*, *Nusantara*, *Pedoman* and others.

Since then the political and economic pendulums have swung back towards etatism partially due to the government's huge profits from oil sales. In order to correct the situation that had developed over about eight years in which foreign investment and domestic capital, seen as being dominated by the Chinese, had played a major role, the government set up the credit programme known as Kredit Investasi Kecil in order to stimulate indigenous firms to develop and strengthen their position.

The expansion of state firms continued, however, even though Pertamina experienced a major crisis in 1976 when it could not pay its debts of US$10 billion. President Director Ibnu Sutowo was replaced and a special team was formed to save the firm.

In 1981 the Indonesian Business Data Center (PDBI) released its premier report on the internal composition of PMA & PMDN companies. The figures were startling: The state owned sector accounted for 58.75% of the PMDN equity with non-indigenous business interests holding 28.95%, leaving only 14.3% in the hands of indigenous Indonesians. In PMA, the state owned firms hold a portion of 9.24%, the non-indigenous business 9.7% and indigenous business 12.77%.[4]

The targets set for the First through Third Five Year Plan (Pelita I–III) were surpassed because of the heavy influx of oil funds, but the target for Pelita IV proved too optimistic, with the government counting on a base price of US$.25 per barrel for oil which did not materialize. The drastic drop in oil prices created a new situation. In March 1984 the Armed Forces Commander Gen. L.B. Moerdani announced that the use of the terms indigenous and non-indigenous in discussions of economics should be avoided.

Since Pelita V began in 1984 a new generation of state owned subsidiaries has sprung up which have been set up by foundations owned by officials. These include the Dharmais, Supersemar and Dakab (Dana Bhakti Kesejahteraan Keluarga Besar Golkar), which is chaired by President Soeharto himself in his private capacity.

These foundations own shares in all kinds of subsidiaries to state firms as well as companies in the private sector. For example, Pertamina owns 45% of the shares in PT Tugu Pratama Indonesia (TPI), while 35% is owned by PT Nusantara Ampera Bhakti which in turn is owned by Dharmais and Supersemar Foundations. PT TPI set up insurance companies for which they have a captive market through their relationship with the mother bank. Another example is PT PP Berdikari which was formed through the merger of the three firms owned by businessmen with links to the presidential palace during the Old Order. It has undergone a metamorphosis with one of its most successful subsidiaries, PT Bank Duta, being 90% owned by Dharmais, Supersemar and Dakab Foundations (each with 30%) with 10% held by employees. Ownership in state companies by their subsidiaries through pension funds, foundations, officials, or local governments has led to the phenomena PDBI calls quasi-BUMN or quasi state owned enterprises. Included in this category are subsidiaries of the state owned companies Pertamina, Krakatau Steel, Pusri, Garuda and state banks.

The History of Private Sector Conglomerates

The private sector is considered a driving force in continued development efforts. The strength of the private sector is hoped to originate in conglomerates while smaller firms also play a role.

The term conglomerate or business group is unpopular in Indonesia due to its historical background in which anti-capitalist, and anti-business sentiments have long existed.

This factor makes anti-trust legislation difficult to institute because we do not perceive the system as purely capitalistic. It is said that as a state based on Pancasila we do not need anti-monopoly legislation because we are not a capitalistic nation. This is indeed a paradox in light of the fact that huge business groups have been formed in Indonesia, among them being Salim, Astra, Bimantara and other conglomerates. It is ostrich politics to ignore this phenomenon and to lull the people of Indonesia into thinking that there is no problem with monopoly or oligopoly. In fact, there is the danger that the activities of the large business groups can no longer be controlled. All over the world nations have established anti-trust laws, although business interests have often been able to get around them. This makes the situation in Indonesia more critical as we seem to have taken a pro-monopoly stance with the excuse that the public's interests can best be protected through the state owned firms or the private firms given licenses for monopolies. In this context, the private sector business conglomerates in Indonesia deserve serious observations and considerations.

Compared to state owned firms, the development of the private sector conglomerates has not been that straightforward. The political climate of the 1950s and early 1960s which made it difficult for business to survive is one of the reasons. It is very difficult to find a group that has survived intact from before the Second World War.

If we want to trace the history of conglomerates in Indonesia, we have to go back to the formation of the Oei Tiong Ham Concern during the colonial period. This firm, however, no longer exists. The socialistic etatistic regime (Old Order under Soekarno) brought an end to the activities of the group and to those of others, such as that run by Liem Koe Nio of Surabaya who was sentenced to death. Then we have the three indigenous businessmen, Abdurachman Aslam, Bram Tambunan and Markam, who enjoyed the protection of the Sukarno regime and could not survive after the Old Order was replaced with the New Order. Very few glimpses of some influence left by firms set up before the Second World War are visible today. The small establishments of Warung Tinggi coffee (1878), Bango soy sauce and kecap (1928), and indigenous businessmen H.M. Sulchan and Hasyim Ning, are examples of businessmen who have survived the changing of regimes. (Hasyim Ning's interests in Fiat and Ford were strong up to 1974 when the Astra company of William Soeryadjaya who first set up business in 1957 began to take over in the automobile sector.)

Very few businesses founded before the revolution or in the Sukarno period still exist and most of the major firms today are newcomers with protective facilities provided by bureaucracy, as well as some which have grown on the strength of the market.

Based on the history put forth above the configuration of Indonesian conglomerates is divided into the following categories:

BUMN Conglomerates (State Owned)

This type of conglomerate is established by the state through formally set up state owned firms or their subsidiaries. This type of conglomerate in Indonesia involves 180 purely state owned companies and 635 subsidiaries which are partially owned by those 180 state firms. Latest official figures released by the government reveals that the total sales of those 180 BUMN reached Rp. 68,4 trillion with total assets of Rp. 232 trillion.

Bureaucratic Capitalist Conglomerates

The conglomerates included in this category are private sector firms set up by former officials and, or relatives of officials, including sons, daughters and wives. Of the 300 groups reached in this report as many as 14 groups or 4.6% fell into this category of businesses owned by former officials, while only 9 groups or 3% fell into the category of firms owned by the family of officials.

Crony Capitalist Conglomerates

This term is used in connection with business conglomerates formed on the basis of special licensing, or protection provided to friends of officials in an unfair or biased manner. Of the 300 groups studied, 14 or 4.67% fell into this category.

Genuine Private Sector Conglomerates

This type of conglomerates may have developed on its own or been inherited from businessmen who set up enterprises during the colonial or Sukarno periods. These firms in general have gained success through creativity and innovation. In general they are considered stronger than the crony capitalist or bureaucratic capitalist owned conglomerates. These market forces conglomerates account for 263 or 87.67% of the 300 conglomerates studied.

Combined Conglomerates

Combined conglomerates are joint or cooperative ventures between the four types of conglomerates listed above. It is quite difficult to identify whether any of the businesses listed in this category actually fall into any of the above categories because their formation is so confused (mixed up).

For example Eka Tjipta Widjaja (Oei Ek Tjiong) of the Sinar Mas group has gone into business with Ibnu Sutowo. With the Salim Group Sinar Mas has set up a joint venture Sinar Mas Inti Perkasa and Sadang Mas which was later shattered. Also Ometraco under the leadership of Ferry Teguh

Santosa and Bimantara with Eka Tjipta Widjaja founded Bimantara Eka Santosa which is building Plaza Indonesia next to Hotel Indonesia in Central Jakarta.

The Salim Group conglomerate, by far the largest, and based on special licensing has set up several joint ventures with other conglomerates. With Krakatau Steel, Salim set up the Indosteel group and with Atang Latief's group he set up the Indo Mobil Group. The second largest conglomerate in Indonesia, Astra, has also cooperated with other groups in order to consolidate its power. An example of this is the joint venture Astra was set up with Pakarti Yoga, PT Federal Motor which they have developed into a major automotive components business.

In summary it can be said that over the 20 years of the New Order government the middle level of business has grown into conglomerates which have been cooperating with each other through the setting up of joint ventures.

In the decades toward the end of the 20th century it is clear that the constellation of Indonesian conglomerates involves a complex mixture of interrelationships between state owned firms and crony capitalist and bureaucratic capitalist, as well as the genuine private sector business conglomerates. For this reason it is very difficult to assess the exact source of wealth of Indonesia's individual conglomerates.

In the case of the issuance of special licence or protection it is extremely difficult to determine whether these things are actually being done because the firms so benefitted are infant industries which must be protected. It is clear in terms of industries like the aeronautics firm IPTN. What is at issue is the schedule for the development of these industries and when they will be able to stand on their own. And in the case of the private owned firms that are given protection, the issue of whether the firm can be competitive in an open market is of vital importance. The public should clearly be concerned with how long they will be required to pay the price of supporting these fledgling, protected industries.

Management Pattern of Indonesian Conglomerates

Many of Indonesia's conglomerates, throughout its history, have been developed and managed by families, examples being Oei Tiong Ham Concern, Bakrie & Brothers, and the Salim and Astra conglomerates. Of the 300 groups studied, 221 or 73.67%, use family style managements, while 54 of the other groups are husband-wife ventures and 79 are non-family ventures.

Family management, however, has its weaknesses, educational levels and managerial skills being two of them. This is understood by the Indonesian conglomerates and in 1989 led to Bakrie & Brothers' payment of Rp. 1 billion for the services of Tanri Abeng, who has a Masters degree in business management. The training of second and third generations of the families with conglomerates is also being undertaken. It is clear, however, that if the conglomerates are to survive they must shift from the pattern of family oriented management to more professional systems.

Educational Levels of Indonesian Conglomerates

To start with two concrete examples of educational levels in firms here we need to mention Liem Sioe Liong, who lack adequate formal education, and Masagung who only went to elementary school. These two men, despite what may be seen as educational handicaps have succeeded greatly in business.

From the data studied by PDBI it was found that five of the key figures in conglomerates under family management had only studied in elementary schools and 18 had senior high school education. Only 61 has any tertiary education and 25 of these did not graduate.

On the other hand, the businessmen who will inherit these enterprises eventually have a better level of education than the founders of these family run conglomerates. There are 43 of these potential heirs who have had university educations. On the other hand, 52 of the founders of non-family conglomerates have university educations.

Regeneration of Indonesian Conglomerates

In this study PDBI observed businesses established before the Second World War and their regeneration processes. Of the 300 groups studied only 29 (9.67%) had been established before 1950. These include the Salim, Hasyim Ning, H.M. Sulchan, Jamu Nyonya Meneer, Jamu Jago and Djisamsoe conglomerates.[5]

The giant Astra conglomerate was not established until 1957 and is one of 55 groups (18.33%) established between 1951 and 1960. Between 1961 and 1970 there were 85 groups established, or 28.33%, while from 1970 to the present 108 groups (36.0%) have been formed.

The data indicates that most groups were established after the Second World War and that most are therefore still managed by the first and second generations. Of the 221 classified as family conglomerates, 107 groups are still run by the first generation, 110 involve the second generation in management and only 4 have gone to the third generations. Of the groups that have passed into the hands of the second generation only 29 are completely controlled by that generation without the presence of the first generation. Of the groups managed by the third generation, 3 are managed entirely by the generation.

Ranking of Indonesian Conglomerates

In 1988 the total sales of the 300 largest conglomerates is Rp. 68.6 trillion, while the BUMN had only Rp. 40 trillion or 58.4%.

In 1990 the BUMN managed to increase their sales to Rp. 60.9 trillion or 63.1% of the 300 conglomerates sales at Rp. 96.7 trillion. Afterwards the BUMN continued to decline with only 55.2% in 1991 at Rp. 62 trillion compared to Rp. 112 trillion of the top 300. In 1992 the top 300 reached Rp. 132 sales or 51.5% of GDP while the state owned only managed to make Rp. 68 trillion assets or only 51.8% of the top 300. In correspondence with those sales data, the tax returns of the state owned conglomerates drastically declined from its 65% portion in fiscal year 85/86 at Rp. 615.5 billion compared with Rp. 364 billion by private sector. In fiscal year 91/92 the ratio was turned upside down, with the private sector paying Rp. 3.4 trillion or 68.3% of total income tax returns while the BUMN only paid Rp. 1.6 trillion or 31.7%.

If we speak of business concentrations and oligopoly, then we see that the sales growth of Indonesian conglomerates indicate this trend. In 1988 the dozen conglomerates with sales exceeding one trillion rupiah each, held 33.8% of total sales compared to 26% in 1987. The 10 groups with sales between Rp. 0.5 – 1 trillion held 9.8% of total sales while those with less than 0.5 trillion are 278 groups which make the bulk of the groups having 56.4% of total sales. The Salim group topped the list of conglomerates worth several trillions, followed by Astra, Sinar Mas, Djarum, Gudang Garam, Lippo, Dharmala, Jan Darmadi, Mantrust, Moh. Hasan and Bimantara in 1988.

In 1992, 21 groups manage to enter the trillion rupiah sales club at Rp. 61.5 trillion or 46.6% of total sales and 41 groups had sales between Rp. 500 billion but below the one trillion figure. These 41 groups made Rp 26.8 trillion or 20.3% of the total. The remaining 238 had sales between Rp. 50 – Rp. 500 billion of a total of Rp. 43.7 trillion or 33.1% of total sales of the top 300 largest Indonesian conglomerates.

The growth of those conglomerates does not change the sales concentration pattern. In 1993, most of the sales over Rp. 1 trillion were controlled by 23 conglomerates whose sales amounted to Rp. 68.5 trillion, which is 47.8% of the total sales of Rp. 144.4 trillion. There were 45 conglomerates with sales between Rp. 0.5 trillion and 1 trillion. They captured 21.5% total sales (Rp. 31.03 trillion). The rest was controlled by conglomerates with Rp. 50 – Rp. 500 billion of sales. Conglomerates in this class control Rp. 44.4 trillion (30.8%) sales. In 1993 there was no conglomerate having sales below Rp. 50 billion. The lowest sales groups were Asaba and Propelat, each with Rp. 80 billion. There were 42 conglomerates whose sales were between Rp. 50 and 100 billion totalling Rp. 3.8 trillions (2.6%).

When we scrutinize the top 300 according to the ethnic origin of their major ownership, we will find that 197 or 65.7% are Chinese, with 18 groups considered as assimilation units where the Chinese and indigenous businessmen have joint ownership. The pure indigenous are represented by 85 groups. In terms of sales value, the 197 Chinese conglomerates control 77% of top 300 total sales at Rp. 101.7 trillion. The remaining 23% are made by those 85 indigenous and 18 assimilationist groups.[6]

Recently there is strong polemic regarding the Chinese conglomerates' domination of the Indonesian economy. The government had officially stated that there is no formal plan to adopt the ethnic-favouritism policy such as the former Malaysia's NEP.

However the government is under heavy pressure from some elements of the society to reconsider the fact that the Chinese are more capable in creating business opportunities in the favourable macro economic climate and they are lobbying for an ethnic differentiation policy.

The problem in Indonesia if compared with Malaysia is that the so called *pribumisasi* policy always failed to produce a substantial number of *pribumi* businessmen. Ever since the Benteng programme of the 1950s Prof Sumitro as Minister in charge of Economic Affairs had taken a policy of special treatment for the *pribumi* (at that time it was called *asli* businessmen).

While the Malaysian government had strongly implemented the NEP in actual operation with the result that *bumiputera* in Malaysia have succeeded in raising their corporate ownership from merely 2% to around 20% within 20 years of the NEP period, in Indonesia the State-owned Enterprises or the BUMN which are considered as the new *pribumi* economic fortress, are in their declining position continuously.

The ethnic dichotomy of profession was maintained tightly with no opportunities given to the Chinese in the non-business sector of the society. For the Indonesian Chinese, the widest avenue to reach top career is business, while in other professions like the civil service, army and others, there is a strict quota system which deter the interest of the Chinese.

Conclusion

There is no doubt that there are two types of private sector conglomerates in Indonesia, namely ethnic Chinese and indigenous conglomerates. The strength of Chinese conglomerates is far greater compared to the indigenous ones. Although these Chinese are already Indonesian citizens, and Indonesians are not defined in ethnic or racial terms, primordial sentiments in Indonesia are still very strong. There is still a strong prejudice against the ethnic Chinese in Indonesia. Anger is often targeted at the ethnic Chinese conglomerates rather than indigenous groups. The April 1994 riot in Medan which originated in a workers' demonstration, had turned into mob terrorism, killing one Chinese businessman, burning cars, damaging shops, houses and factories at Medan Industrial Estate and its vicinity.

One scholar asserted that the government is still reluctant to solve the Chinese problem, "because those who are in power need the Chinese as a scapegoat and a 'hostage' for their political manoeuvring".[7] If this is true, the elite should not play with fire because this would lead to disaster.

However, I am still optimistic that rationality and a modern approach will eventually prevail upon the irrational and primodial behaviour of the present Indonesian elite because this is the only way for the Indonesian nation to progress.

Endnotes

1 *Asiaweek*, 20 October 1993.

2 For a concise history of Indonesian state owned enterprises, see *Profile and Anatomy of BUMN* (State Owned Enterprise), Jakarta: Indonesian Business Data Center, 1987, 1st edition.

3 A very useful reference source which covers this period is the dissertation by John O. Sutter, "Indonesianisasi: A Historical Survey on the Role of Politics in the Institution of A Changing Economy from the Second World War to the Eve of the General Election 1940–1955", Ithaca: Cornell University, Ph.D thesis submitted to Political Science Department, 1959.

4 For further details, see *Survey Report on Foreign and Domestic Investment*, Jakarta: PDBI, 1980.

5 Most of the data in this part are derived from *Conglomeration Indonesia*, Jakarta: Indonesian Business Data Center, 1980, 1st edition.

6 The data will be included in the second edition of *Conglomeration Indonesia*, forthcoming.

7 "Wawancara Dengan Arief Budiman", *Matra*, No. 93, April 1994.

6

The Entrepreneurial Propensity of Singaporean Graduates*

Chew Soon Beng and Azlan bin Ghazali

Introduction

The recent interest in entrepreneurship comes about as a result of the emerging trend of focusing on market forces as instruments of growth in a number of countries. Leading this group of countries are the former planned economies of China, Vietnam and East European countries. Free enterprise economies such as Singapore, Malaysia and Thailand also encourage the private sector to play an even greater role in their respective economies and in the region as well. The entrepreneur is the agent of growth at least in the private sector, if not in the national economy. Thus, it is pertinent to analyse the behaviour of the entrepreneur.

Many researchers in the area of entrepreneurship focus on the profiles of Chinese entrepreneurs in the Southeast Asian region. Others, such as Chan and Chiang (1994) for example, analyse the behaviour of the immigrant-entrepreneur, based on interviews of Singapore's Chinese business pioneers conducted by the Oral History Department. Their analysis leads them to describe an entrepreneur as one who has to learn early in life to acquire the basic capabilities of conforming to and transforming social norms which would enable him to achieve, under hostile economic constraints, objectives which are more often for the interests of the extended family/clan than for his own self. At that time, to the Chinese entrepreneurs, migration to Southeast Asia was the inevitable option given the deficit economy prevailing in the early decades of this century in many Chinese villages. Chan and Chiang conclude that:

> Our entrepreneur was a village boy, an immigrant, a sinkheh, a sojourner then becoming a settler, a boss as well as a "family-izing"

man. It is within the various contexts of having to cope with these multi-faceted dimensions and roles that a person was socialized to join that special group called entrepreneurs.[1]

It can be safely said that these business pioneers were able to overcome various difficulties to achieve their objectives. The difficulties that entrepreneurs face today are very different from those in the past. Moreover, the goals of the would-be entrepreneurs are also very different, often being more self-focused than that of past entrepreneurs. Nevertheless, the basic attributes which are necessary for an entrepreneur to be successful are still the same: that is, a successful entrepreneur must have the qualities of perseverance, resourcefulness and sound business acumen.

The entrepreneur is the agent of foreign investment. The entrepreneur brings in capital, management and production know-how to generate value-added in the production process. China, since its economic reform in 1978, has been able to attract a significant inflow of foreign investment. A substantial portion of foreign investment in China originates in the private sectors of Taiwan, Hong Kong and the ASEAN countries.

Singapore is both a capital recipient and an exporter.[2] Singapore wants to build its external economy which will enable the republic to tap the growth of the booming economies in the region. In order to build the external economy, we need to have entrepreneurs who are ready to invest abroad.The types of investment that Singapore needs are those in the areas of manufacturing, recreation, retail, real estate and banking. Thus, the Singapore government has been encouraging entrepreneurship in these areas.

There are various types of entrepreneurs. A food hawker may be regarded as an entrepreneur, so also is a contractor in the renovation business, or a trader, a taxi driver, an industrialist, a hotelier, or a banker, etc. But in the move abroad, only those entrepreneurs with substantial capital are able to contribute to the building of our external economy. This implies that the kind of Singapore entrepreneurs who are greatly in demand by China are the capital-rich who are ready to invest in the areas of manufacturing, recreation, retail, real estate, banking and finance, etc.

The road to entrepreneurship today is different from that which existed in the postwar era. We are now an independent nation which has seen three decades of rapid economic development. The workforce is highly educated. The premise of this paper is that the future entrepreneur of Singapore in the areas of manufacturing, recreation, retail, real estate and banking is likely to be an educated person in that he would be a person who holds a tertiary degree.

Thus, this paper focuses on the determinants of self-employment among the graduates of tertiary institutions. We believe that a good understanding of the decision of our graduates regarding self-employment will help in the formulation of policies which would encourage or at least not hinder the development of entrepreneurship.

The Theoretical Framework

Singapore graduates are in a way more fortunate that their counterparts elsewhere because the Singapore government is very concerned about graduate unemployment.[3] Consequently, the graduate population has not been excessively high. (However, this policy of stringent control on tertiary enrolment will change in the 1990s.) Consequently, during the 1970s and 1980s, Singapore graduates generally were able to command a good career either in the public sector or in MNCs in the private sector. Nevertheless, many graduates have opted for self-employment.

The aim of this paper is to find out the reason(s) why these graduates opted for self-employment; why graduates forgo a comfortable life and opt for a risky business venture. It is the premise of this paper that self-employment is a risky business venture. It is risky because it involves giving up a career and facing the possibility of losing all the investment and of being in debt for the rest of one's life. With self-employment, the stream of income becomes unstable. We believe that a graduate will go through a cost-benefit analysis before opting for self-employment. It may be argued that those business pioneers mentioned by Chan and Chiang did not go through such a cost-benefit analysis. It is possible that some of them are born risk takers. Nevertheless, many of them did not have any option. Those entrepreneurs had the foresight and courage to venture abroad. On the other hand, most of today's would-be entrepreneurs, we believe, take a calculated risk in deciding whether to opt for self-employment.

The paper postulates the following hypotheses concerning the decision-making process of an employed graduate in Singapore:

Hypothesis 1: The household decision-making process

This applies only to married graduates. We postulate that a typical household would want to maximize household income and simultaneously minimize variation in total household income. The objective here is much narrower, unlike that of business pioneers of yesteryear who invested for the benefit of the entire extended family or village or clan. Thus, given that a couple are employed, they can maximize their household income if one of them were to opt for self-employment. As stated earlier, self-employment is risky, but it also opens up the possibility of a substantial increase in household income. Thus, while one of them opts for self-employment, the other member continues to enjoy a steady income through salaried employment. In this case, the stable stream of income provides for the basic needs while self-employment provides the possibility of increasing household income by leaps and bounds.

This argument is presented in Figure 6.1. AB represents the earnings of a salaried employee in Singapore, who ensures for himself a steady stream of income throughout his working lifetime. When a graduate salaried employee decides to become self-employed, he moves from Q in Figure 6.1 to X where he uses his savings to start his business. If he is very successful, his income profile can be represented by income profile XGY. If his business is a failure,

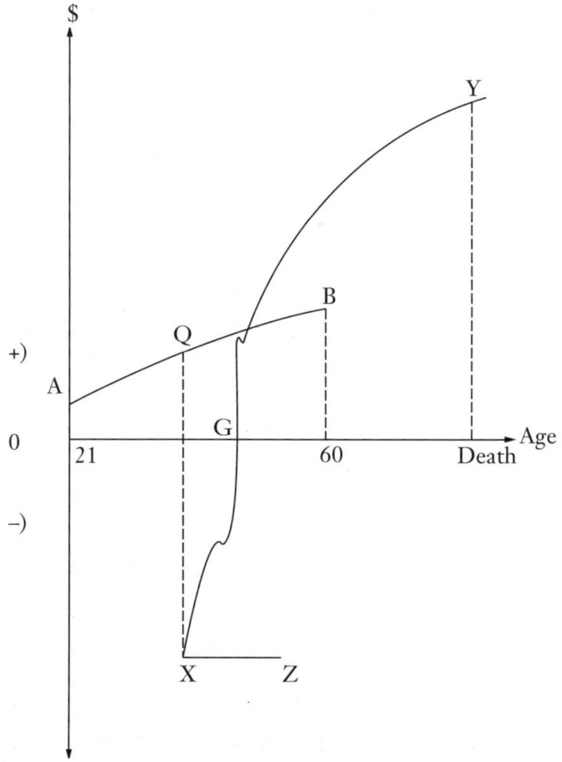

Figure 6.1: Income Streams of Salaried and Self-employed

then his income profile can be represented by XZ. He will then rejoin the labour market as a salaried employee although he might not be able to get a job which pays a wage as high as his previous wage rate Q. He may attempt self-employment again at a later stage. Of course, if he is marginally successful, his income stream will be somewhere below GY. It goes without saying that the income stream of the self-employed is cyclical.

There is evidence in support of the household decision-making process hypothesis. In China, many couples take advantage of the new economic reform making use of exactly this strategy: while one partner continues to remain in salaried employment with the state, the other joins the private sector either as a salaried worker or as a self-employed person. In this way, the family enjoys a steady income and at the same time opens up the possibility for the family to become rich if self-employment proves to be very successful.

We believe that our married graduates adopt the same strategy. That is, while one spouse opts for self-employment, the other spouse anchors the family with a stable career. Once the self-employed is successful, the other spouse may join the business or quit the labour market all together.

Prediction: A graduate is more likely to opt for self-employment if his spouse has a steady income.

Hypothesis 2: The graduate acquires the skills necessary to an entrepreneur at a minimum cost

As self-employment is costly and risky, a would-be entrepreneur must master the art of doing business if he is to avoid failure. He must have complete knowledge of the product or service that he supplies. He must know his competitors. He must also have a good knowledge of management in the areas of human resource, accounting, legal matters, marketing, inventory, production, technology transfer, business-client relations, employer-employee relationship, business-government relationship and union-management relationship.

Most of these skills cannot be obtained from textbooks. If one were to start a business and learn all these skills at the same time, the cost is very high and business failure is common as illustrated in Figure 6.1.

The best way to acquire all these skills is through salaried employment. When a person is employed as a marketing manager, for example, he learns the art of marketing. He gets to know the market very well. Moreover, he learns while he is being paid, and generally he learns without having to pay dearly for his mistakes. Through his work, he also gets to learn about human resource management, production, inventory, business-client relationship, etc., depending on the variety of jobs he has been exposed to.

The best time to undertake self-employment is when the graduate senses that his probability of success is the greatest. Besides learning, he also needs savings for his investment in self-employment. As shown in Figure 6.1, the salaried employed quits at Q to be self-employed.

Prediction: The graduate is more likely to opt for self-employment as his working experience increases.

Hypothesis 3: The probability of self-employment falls as age increases

Self-employment is risky but the return is very high. The drain on the energy of the self-employed is very high. When a graduate becomes older, his desire to take risks is reduced. Consequently, the drive to excel as a self-employed person is lessened. Also, the gain as a self-employed person appears to be smaller as one gets older. In other words, if X is nearer to 60 years of age, the area under GY is smaller.

Prediction: The probability of being self-employed falls as age increases.

Hypothesis 4: The mind-set of an entrepreneur is influenced by close relatives and friends

A graduate would probably be contented with salaried employment until he meets his relatives or friends who are entrepreneurs. Through contact with them, his mind-set changes. He discovers that there is an alternative way of making a living or making a contribution to the household.

Prediction: The probability of being self-employed is greater if relatives and close friends are entrepreneurs.

If we put all these hypotheses together, we can examine the various factors which influence entrepreneurship. If one spouse is a salaried employee, the probability of being self-employed increases. If relatives or close friends are entrepreneurs, the probability of being self-employed also is greater. These two conclusions may appear contradictory; but they are not, as explained earlier. Also, the probability of being self-employed is lower when a graduate is older, but is greater when he has more working experience. These two conflicting factors imply that the graduate-entrepreneur will begin at an age around 40.

The above-mentioned hypotheses will be tested making use of data on Singapore graduates. We also want to determine whether these hypotheses vary with ethnicity.

Analysis of Survey Data

The sample which this study is based is derived from a survey of university graduates in Singapore. Table 6.1 shows the composition of the sample. The first source of the sample was the alumni associations. The rest were obtained from directories. A total of 7300 questionnaires were sent out. The number of usable questionnaires obtained was 2462. This gives a response rate of 33.7%. Among the respondents, 208 (8.5%) are self-employed graduates and 2254 (91.6%) are employed graduates.

Table 6.1: Sample of Study

Source	Number	Percentage
Alumni Associations		
National University of Singapore	5000	68.5
Nanyang Technological University	1307	17.9
Canadian Alumni	318	4.4
New Zealand Alumni	219	3.0
Directories		
Marketing Institute of Singapore	227	3.1
Massachusetts Institute of Technology Club	54	0.7
Others	175	2.4
Total	7300	100.0

Race

Table 6.2 shows the breakdown of the respondents by race. Among the respondents, 2293 are Chinese. Of this number, 186 (8.1%) are self-employed and 2107 (91.9%) are salaried employees. The non-Chinese graduates, which comprise of Malays, Indians and Others, number 169. Of these, 22 (13.0%) are self-employed and 147 (87.0%) are salaried employees.

Table 6.2: Employment Status by Race

Race	Self-Employed (%)	Employed (%)	Total (%)
Chinese	186 (7.6)	2107 (85.6)	2293 (93.2)
Non-Chinese	22 (0.9)	147 (6.0)	169 (6.9)
Total	208 (8.5)	2254 (91.6)	2462 (100.0)

Notes: Percentages in parentheses
Percentages do not sum up to 100.0 due to rounding errors

Sex

Among the 2293 Chinese graduates, 1326 (57.8%) are males and 967 (42.1%) are females. Among the Chinese self-employed graduates, 146 (79%) are males and 40 (22%) are females (see Table 6.3).

Among the non-Chinese graduates, the males number 94 (55.6%) and the females number 75 (44.4%). Among the non-Chinese self-employed, the males number 16 (73%) while the females number 6 (27%).

Table 6.3: Singapore Graduates by Sex

	Male Number (%)	Female Number (%)	Total Number (%)
Chinese			
Self-Employed	146 (78.5)	40 (21.5)	186 (100.0)
Employed	1180 (56.0)	927 (44.0)	2107 (100.0)
Total	1326 (57.8)	967 (42.2)	2293 (100.0)
Non-Chinese			
Self-Employed	16 (72.7)	6 (27.3)	22 (100.0)
Employed	78 (53.1)	69 (46.9)	147 (100.0)
Total	94 (55.6)	75 (44.4)	169 (100.0)

Notes: Number of Chinese = 2293
Number of Non-Chinese = 169
Rounding-off error may occur

Age

Table 6.4 shows the number of Chinese and non-Chinese self-employed graduates in different age groups. Among the 186 Chinese self-employed graduates, 38% are in the 30–39 year age group and 30% in the 40–49 year age group. This is quite consistent with our theoretical prediction that the self-employed is likely to opt for self-employment around the age of 40, but we need econometric evidence for support.

Among the non-Chinese self-employed graduates, 41% are in the 30–39 year age group and 23% are in the 20–29 year age group. Thus, the non-Chinese graduates opt for self-employment at an earlier age than their Chinese counterparts.

Table 6.4: Singapore Graduates by Age

	20–29 Number (%)	30–39 Number (%)	40–49 Number (%)	50 & above Number (%)	Total Number (%)
Chinese					
Self-Employed	38	71	55	22	186
	(20.4)	(38.2)	(29.6)	(11.8)	(100.0)
Employed	1117	743	215	32	2107
	(53.0)	(35.3)	(10.2)	(1.5)	(100.0)
Total	1155	814	270	54	2293
	(50.4)	(35.5)	(11.8)	(2.4)	(100.0)
Non-Chinese					
Self-Employed	5	9	3	5	22
	(22.7)	(40.9)	(13.6)	(22.7)	(100.0)
Employed	80	48	16	3	147
	(54.4)	(32.7)	(10.9)	(2.0)	(100.0)
Total	85	57	19	8	169
	(50.3)	(33.7)	(11.2)	(4.7)	(100.0)

Notes: Number of Chinese = 2293
Number of Non-Chinese = 169
Rounding-off error may occur

Marital Status

The marital status of the Chinese and non-Chinese graduates are given in Table 6.5. Of the Chinese graduates, 50% are singles and 49% are married.

However, among the Chinese self-employed graduates, 70% are married. This is not inconsistent with Hypothesis 1 concerning the household decision-making process of an entrepreneur. We have the same findings for non-Chinese self-employed graduates.

Table 6.5: Marital Status of Singapore Graduates

	Single Number (%)	Married Number (%)	Divorced/ Widowed Number (%)	Others Number (%)	Total Number (%)
Chinese					
Self-Employed	48 (25.8)	131 (70.4)	7 (3.8)	0 (0.0)	186 (100.0)
Employed	1095 (52.0)	994 (47.2)	15 (0.7)	3 (0.1)	2107 (100.0)
Total	1143 (49.8)	1125 (49.1)	22 (1.0)	3 (0.1)	2293 (100.0)
Non-Chinese					
Self-Employed	3 (13.6)	18 (81.8)	1 (4.5)	0 (0.0)	22 (100.0)
Employed	79 (53.7)	66 (44.9)	2 (1.4)	0 (0.0)	147 (100.0)
Total	82 (48.5)	84 (49.7)	3 (1.8)	0 (0.0)	169 (100.0)

Notes: Number of Chinese = 2293
Number of Non-Chinese = 169
Rounding-off error may occur

Sibling Order

The sibling order of the graduates is categorized into the eldest, somewhere in between, and the youngest in the family. Table 6.6 shows the percentage distribution for sibling order of the Chinese and the non-Chinese graduates.

Of the Chinese graduates, 44% belong to the category of somewhere in between, 33% to the category "eldest" and 19% to the category "youngest". This distribution is also true of the Chinese self-employed, the non-Chinese graduates and the non-Chinese self-employed.

Thus, sibling order does not seem to be important here in deciding whether a graduate would opt for self-employment.

Table 6.6: Sibling Order of Singapore Graduates

	Eldest Number (%)	Somewhere in Between Number (%)	Youngest Number (%)	Total Number (%)
Chinese				
Self-Employed	67 (36.0)	83 (44.6)	36 (19.4)	186 (100.0)
Employed	696 (33.0)	924 (43.8)	487 (23.1)	2107 (100.0)
Total	763 (33.3)	1007 (43.9)	523 (22.8)	2293 (100.0)
Non-Chinese				
Self-Employed	10 (45.5)	10 (45.5)	2 (9.1)	22 (100.0)
Employed	51 (34.7)	68 (46.3)	28 (19.0)	147 (100.0)
Total	61 (36.1)	78 (46.1)	30 (17.8)	169 (100.0)

Notes: Number of Chinese = 2293
Number of Non-Chinese = 169
Rounding-off error may occur

Presence of Self-Employed Spouse

Table 6.7 shows whether the married graduates have a self-employed spouse. Among the 131 Chinese self-employed graduates, only two have a self-employed spouse. At the same time, among the 994 Chinese graduate salaried employees, 38 (26%) have a self-employed spouse. The data therefore supports Hypothesis 1.

Presence of Self-Employed Parents

It is known that parents often influence their children's occupation. In this case, the presence of self-employed parents is important in determining whether one should opt for self-employment for the following reasons: Firstly, the mind-set of an entrepreneur is constantly impressed upon the children. Secondly, the skills of learning to do business can be easily acquired. Thirdly, some of the children are likely to take over the business.

Table 6.7: Presence of Self-Employed Spouse among Married Graduates

	Absent Number (%)	Present Number (%)	Total Number (%)
Married Chinese			
Self-Employed	129	2	131
	(98.5)	(1.5)	(100.0)
Employed	956	38	994
	(96.2)	(3.8)	(100.0)
Total	1085	40	1125
	(96.4)	(3.6)	(100.0)
Married Non-Chinese			
Self-Employed	17	1	18
	(94.4)	(5.6)	(100.0)
Employed	61	5	66
	(92.4)	(7.6)	(100.0)
Total	78	6	84
	(92.9)	(7.1)	(100.0)

Notes: Number of Chinese = 2293
Number of Non-Chinese = 169
Rounding-off error may occur

Table 6.8: Presence of Self-Employed Parents among Singapore Graduates

	Absent Number (%)	Present Number (%)	Total Number (%)
Chinese			
Self-Employed	148	38	186
	(79.6)	(20.4)	(100.0)
Employed	1602	505	2107
	(76.4)	(24.0)	(100.0)
Total	1750	543	2293
	(76.4)	(23.7)	(100.0)
Non-Chinese			
Self-Employed	18	4	22
	(81.8)	(18.2)	(100.0)
Employed	121	26	147
	(82.3)	(17.7)	(100.0)
Total	139	30	169
	(82.2)	(17.8)	(100.0)

Notes: Number of Chinese = 2293
Number of Non-Chinese = 169
Rounding-off error may occur

Table 6.8 shows that, among the 186 Chinese self-employed graduates, 38 (20%) indicated that their parents are self-employed. This finding lends support to Hypothesis 4.

It should be noted that among the 2107 Chinese graduate salaried employees, 505 (24%) indicated that their parents are self-employed. It is possible that some of these graduates would opt for self-employment later in life.

Presence of Self-Employed Siblings

Table 6.9 shows, among the 186 Chinese graduate self-employed, 52 (28%) have siblings who are self-employed. And among the 2107 Chinese graduate salaried employees, only 16% have siblings who are self-employed. This finding also supports Hypothesis 4.

Table 6.9: Presence of Self-Employed Siblings among Singapore Graduates

	Absent Number (%)	Present Number (%)	Total Number (%)
Chinese			
Self-Employed	134	52	186
	(72.0)	(28.0)	(100.0)
Employed	1763	344	2107
	(83.7)	(16.3)	(100.0)
Total	1897	396	2293
	(82.7)	(17.3)	(100.0)
Non-Chinese			
Self-Employed	20	2	22
	(90.9)	(9.1)	(100.0)
Employed	122	25	147
	(83.0)	(17.0)	(100.0)
Total	142	27	169
	(84.0)	(16.0)	(100.0)

Notes: Number of Chinese = 2293
Number of Non-Chinese = 169
Rounding-off error may occur

Presence of Self-Employed Close Friends or Relatives

According to Table 6.10, among the 186 Chinese graduate self-employed, 92 (50%) indicated that they have self-employed close friends and relatives. Thus, Hypothesis 4 is supported. It should also be noted that almost 49% of the Chinese graduate salaried employees also have self-employed close friends and relatives. It is possible that some of them might opt for self-employment later in life.

Table 6.10: Presence of Self-Employed Close Friends or Relatives among Singapore Graduates

	Absent Number (%)	Present Number (%)	Total Number (%)
Chinese			
Self-Employed	94 (50.5)	92 (49.5)	186 (100.0)
Employed	1091 (51.8)	1016 (48.2)	2107 (100.0)
Total	1185 (51.7)	1108 (48.3)	2293 (100.0)
Non-Chinese			
Self-Employed	12 (54.5)	10 (45.5)	22 (100.0)
Employed	67 (45.6)	80 (54.4)	147 (100.0)
Total	79 (46.7)	90 (53.2)	169 (100.0)

Notes: Number of Chinese = 2293
Number of Non-Chinese = 169
Rounding-off error may occur

Degree Level of Graduates

Graduates are categorized into five levels of degree-holders: Bachelor, Honours, Post-graduate Diploma, Masters and Ph.D. Table 6.11 shows the breakdown of the Chinese and non-Chinese graduates by degree level.

An American researcher, Wolpin (1977), finds that self-employed persons have fewer years of schooling compared to salaried employees. Our study here differs from that of Wolpin's as we only focus on graduates. Nevertheless, among the Chinese graduates, there are proportionately fewer graduate self-employed with an Honours degree or with a Ph.D compared to graduate salaried employees.

Table 6.11: Degree Level of Singapore Graduates

	Bachelor	Honours	Post-Grad Diploma	Masters	Ph.D	Total
	Number (%)	Number (%)	Number (%)	Number (%)	Number (%)	Number (%)
Chinese						
Self-Employed	112	27	19	25	3	186
	(60.2)	(14.5)	(10.2)	(13.4)	(1.6)	(100.0)
Employed	1197	525	136	233	16	2107
	(56.8)	(24.9)	(6.5)	(11.1)	(0.8)	(100.0)
Total	1309	552	155	258	19	2293
	(57.1)	(24.1)	(6.7)	(11.3)	(0.8)	(100.0)
Non-Chinese						
Self-Employed	10	6	0	6	0	22
	(45.5)	(27.3)	(0.0)	(27.3)	(0.0)	(100.0)
Employed	80	30	16	18	3	147
	(54.4)	(24.5)	(10.9)	(12.2)	(2.0)	(100.0)
Total	90	36	16	24	3	169
	(53.2)	(21.4)	(9.5)	(14.3)	(1.8)	(100.0)

Notes: Number of Chinese = 2293
Number of Non-Chinese = 169
Rounding-off error may occur

Professional and Non-Professional Degrees

A law graduate has two choices. As a salaried worker, he can work as a lawyer or an non-law employee. As a self-employed, he can start a law firm or a non-law firm. Unfortunately, our data do not distinguish among these alternatives.

Generally speaking, the behaviour of graduates with a professional degree differs from those with a non-professional degree. It all depends on the prospects of salaried employment. In other words, if a law graduate has a good career, he is less likely to start a law firm, much less a non-law firm. Thus, it is important to distinguish between professional and non-professional degrees.[4]

The following types of degrees are categorized as professional degrees: Engineering, Architecture (including Building and Estate Management), Medicine (including Dentistry), Pharmacy, Accountancy and Law. Graduates

Table 6.12: Professional Degree Holders by Faculty

Faculty	Self-Employed (%)	Employed (%)	Total (%)
Engineering	30 (5.0)	565 (95.0)	595 (100.0)
Architecture	9 (11.0)	73 (89.0)	82 (100.0)
Medicine	34 (29.8)	80 (70.2)	114 (100.0)
Pharmacy	3 (11.5)	23 (88.5)	26 (100.0)
Accountancy	13 (4.1)	307 (95.9)	320 (100.0)
Law	10 (13.0)	67 (87.0)	77 (100.0)
Total	99 (8.2)	1115 (91.8)	1214 (100.0)

Notes: Architecture includes Building and Estate Management
Medicine includes Dentistry
Percentages in parentheses

Table 6.13: Non-Professional Degree Holders by Faculty

Faculty	Self-Employed (%)	Employed (%)	Total (%)
Science	32 (7.2)	411 (92.8)	443 (100.0)
Arts & Social Sciences	39 (8.3)	429 (91.7)	468 (100.0)
Business Administration	38 (11.3)	299 (88.7)	337 (100.0)
Total	109 (8.7)	1139 (91.3)	1248 (100.0)

Notes: Science includes Computer Science
Percentages in parentheses

in Science (including Computer Science), Arts and Social Sciences, and Business Administration are categorized as non-professional degree holders.

Tables 6.12 and 6.13 show the breakdown of the respondents by type of degree. Generally, graduates with a professional degree except engineering and accountancy graduates have a higher propensity to be self-employed.

Table 6.14 shows the distribution of the Chinese and non-Chinese graduates by degree type. For the Chinese graduate self-employed, 52% came from non-professional streams, compared to 50% for the Chinese graduate salaried employees. In the case of the non-Chinese graduates, the percentage was 54% and 59%, respectively.

Table 6.14: Degree Type of Singapore Graduates

	Professional Number (%)	Non-Professional Number (%)	Total Number (%)
Chinese			
Self-Employed	89	97	186
	(47.8)	(52.2)	(100.0)
Employed	1054	1053	2107
	(50.0)	(50.0)	(100.0)
Total	1143	1150	2293
	(49.9)	(50.2)	(100.0)
Non-Chinese			
Self-Employed	10	12	22
	(45.5)	(54.5)	(100.0)
Employed	61	86	147
	(41.5)	(58.5)	(100.0)
Total	71	98	169
	(42.0)	(58.0)	(100.0)

Notes: Number of Chinese = 2293
Number of Non-Chinese = 169
Rounding-off error may occur

Table 6.15: Local and Overseas Graduates

	Local Number (%)	Overseas Number (%)	Total Number (%)
Chinese			
Self-Employed	148	38	186
	(79.6)	(20.4)	(100.0)
Employed	1905	202	2107
	(90.4)	(9.6)	(100.0)
Total	2053	240	2293
	(89.5)	(10.5)	(100.0)
Non-Chinese			
Self-Employed	15	7	22
	(68.2)	(31.8)	(100.0)
Employed	121	26	147
	(82.3)	(17.7)	(100.0)
Total	136	33	169
	(80.5)	(19.5)	(100.0)

Notes: Number of Chinese = 2293
Number of Non-Chinese = 169
Rounding-off error may occur

Table 6.16: Years of Working Experience of Singapore Graduates

	5 & below Number (%)	6–10 Number (%)	11–15 Number (%)	16–20 Number (%)	21–25 Number (%)	26–30 Number (%)	30 & above Number (%)	Total Number (%)
Chinese								
Self-Employed	46	50	26	26	17	10	11	186
	(24.7)	(26.9)	(14.0)	(14.0)	(9.1)	(5.4)	(5.9)	(100.0)
Employed	1165	513	220	127	57	13	12	2107
	(55.3)	(24.3)	(10.4)	(6.0)	(2.7)	(0.6)	(0.6)	(100.0)
Total	1211	563	246	153	74	23	23	2293
	(52.8)	(24.6)	(10.7)	(6.6)	(3.2)	(1.0)	(1.0)	(100.0)
Non-Chinese								
Self-Employed	6	4	3	2	3	1	3	22
	(27.3)	(18.2)	(13.6)	(9.1)	(13.6)	(4.5)	(13.6)	(100.0)
Employed	88	27	17	10	3	0	2	147
	(59.9)	(18.4)	(11.6)	(6.8)	(2.0)	(0.0)	(1.4)	(100.0)
Total	94	31	20	12	6	1	5	169
	(55.7)	(18.4)	(11.9)	(7.1)	(3.6)	(0.6)	(3.0)	(100.0)

Notes: Number of Chinese = 2293
Number of Non-Chinese = 169
Rounding-off error may occur

Local and Overseas Graduates

Table 6.15 provides an indication as to whether the place of training makes a difference to the option to be self-employed. According to this table, among the Chinese graduate self-employed, 20% are trained overseas, compared to 10% for the Chinese graduate salaried employees. However, we are unable to determine whether overseas graduates have developed better business acumen or whether they are less successful in the search for salaried employment.

Number of Years of Working Experience

Hypothesis 2 states that working experience is indispensable if one wants to opt for self-employment. It goes without saying that one cannot be learning forever. The graduate must decide on the optimal time to go for self-employment.

Table 6.16 shows the number of years of working experience of graduates. Among the Chinese graduate self-employed, 25% have five years or less of working experience and 27% have 6–10 years of working experience. Thus, slightly more than 50% have adequate working experience. But there are 6% of the self-employed with more than 30 years of working experience.

We have examined the various features of Singapore graduates. However, in order to determine conclusively the various factors affecting the employment choice of Singapore graduates, we employ the regression analysis, to which we shall now proceed.

Estimation and Testing of Hypotheses

In this section, binary probit analyses are carried out on different sections of the sample to estimate the significance of the variables on the employment decision of the different groups of graduates. The employment choice of each graduate is modelled as a binary choice between self-employment and salaried-employment. The probit estimates of the graduate's employment decision between self-employment and salaried-employment can be represented by the equation:

$$Yj = B_1MALE + B_2AGE + B_3MARRIED + B_4POSN + B_5NDEPEN + B_6SPOUSE + B_7PARENTS + B_8SIBLINGS + B_9CFREN + B_{10}EDUC + B_{11}LOCAL + B_{12}PROFQ + B_{13}YWORK + e$$

The binary probit model is obtained by assuming that the random error term, e, is normally distributed. The rationale for this assumption is that the random term or disturbances includes a number of unobserved but independent components. By the central limit theorem, the random term approximates a normal distribution function. The binary employment choice of the graduate, j, between self-employment and employment is defined as:

Yj = 1 if self-employed,
   = 0 if employed.

The operational definitions of the variables in the binary probit equation are as follows:

MALE:	dummy variable taking the value 1 if the graduate is a male and 0 otherwise
AGE:	age of the graduate in years
MARRIED:	dummy variable taking the value 1 if the graduate is married and 0 otherwise
POSN:	dummy variable taking the value 1 if the graduate is the eldest child and 0 otherwise
NDEPEN:	number of dependents
SPOUSE:	dummy variable taking the value 1 if spouse is self-employed and 0 otherwise
PARENTS:	dummy variable taking the value 1 if self-employed parents are present and 0 otherwise
SIBLINGS:	dummy variable taking the value 1 if self-employed siblings are present and 0 otherwise
CFREN:	dummy variable taking the value 1 if self-employed close friends or relatives are present and 0 otherwise
EDUC:	ordinal variable for degree level – 1 for Bachelor degree, 2 for Honours degree, 3 for Post-Graduate Diploma, 4 for Masters and 5 for Ph.D
LOCAL:	dummy variable taking the value 1 if local graduate and 0 otherwise
PROFQ:	dummy variable taking the value 1 if graduate has obtained a professional qualification awarded by a professional body and 0 otherwise
YWORK:	number of years of working experience since graduation

Probit Analysis for All Graduates

Table 6.17 shows the probit estimates of employment for the entire sample. The total number of graduates is 2462, of whom 2254 (91.55%) are salaried employees and 208 are self-employed. For each variable to be significant at the 95% level, the t-ratio must be greater than 1.960.

The first significant variable is MALE. The t-ratio for this variable is 3.783 which is greater than 1.960. The variable has a positive coefficient, which means that male graduates are more likely to be self-employed compared to female graduates.

The next significant variable among all graduates is AGE. The maximum likelihood probit estimate for this variable is a negative coefficient. Therefore, the probability of being self-employed decreases with age.

CFREN has a negative significant estimate. This means that graduates with self-employed close friends or relatives are less likely to be self-employed themselves.

The variable, EDUC, also has a negative estimate. Therefore, the higher the degree level of the graduate, the lower the probability of him being self-employed.

Table 6.17: Probit Estimates of Employment Decision for All Graduates

Variables	Maximum Likelihood Estimates	Standard Errors	T-ratio
MALE*	0.3375	0.0892	3.783
AGE*	–0.0478	0.0063	–7.582
MARRIED	0.1446	0.0949	1.524
POSN	0.1116	0.0830	1.345
NDEPEN	0.0114	0.0273	0.417
SPOUSE	–0.3445	0.3178	–1.084
PARENTS	–0.0071	0.0958	–0.074
SIBLINGS	0.1556	0.0980	1.588
CFREN*	–0.1660	0.0787	–2.108
EDUC*	–0.2011	0.0392	–5.128
LOCAL*	–0.7193	0.1022	–7.040
PROFQ*	0.3245	0.0826	3.929
YWORK*	0.0884	0.0090	9.872

Notes: * denotes statistical significance at 95% level
No. of Observations: 2462 (SE: 208, E: 2254)
$t_{(0.95;2462)} = 1.960$

The relationship between the variable, LOCAL, and self-employment is also negative. This is shown by the negative coefficient. Local graduates therefore are less likely to be self-employed than foreign graduates.

PROFQ has a positive coefficient. Thus, graduates with professional qualifications are more likely to be self-employed.

The last significant coefficient for all graduates is the variable, YWORK. The probability of being self-employed increases with the number of years of working experience.

Probit Analysis for Chinese Graduates

The results of the binary probit analysis on Chinese graduates are given in Table 6.18. The total number of Chinese graduates is 2293, of whom 2107 (91.89%) are salaried employees and 186 (8.11%) are self-employed. The critical value of the t-ratio is again 1.960. Variables with t-ratios greater than 1.960 are significant at the 95% level.

The first significant variable is MALE. It has a positive coefficient. Therefore, male Chinese graduates are more likely to be self-employed than female Chinese graduates.

Table 6.18: Probit Estimates of Employment Decision for Chinese Graduates

Variables	Maximum Likelihood Estimates	Standard Errors	T-ratio
MALE*	0.3536	0.0937	3.775
AGE*	–0.0457	0.0066	–6.887
MARRIED	0.1110	0.0993	1.117
POSN	0.1059	0.0876	1.209
NDEPEN	0.0108	0.0288	0.374
SPOUSE	–0.5065	0.3829	–1.323
PARENTS	–0.0033	0.1000	–0.033
SIBLINGS*	0.2054	0.1013	2.027
CFREN	–0.1511	0.0824	–1.834
EDUC*	–0.2158	0.0417	–5.172
LOCAL*	–0.7589	0.1082	–7.011
PROFQ*	0.3205	0.0868	3.691
YWORK*	0.0853	0.0094	9.046

Notes: * denotes statistical significance at 95% level
No. of Observations: 2293 (SE: 186, E: 2107)
$t_{(0.95;2293)} = 1.960$

AGE is also significant but with a negative coefficient. This means that among Chinese graduates, the likelihood of being self-employed decreases with age.

SIBLINGS has a positive significant coefficient. This implies that Chinese graduates with self-employed brothers or sisters are more likely to be self-employed too.

Chinese graduates with higher degree levels are less likely to be self-employed. This is shown by the negative coefficient for the variable, EDUC.

Also, local Chinese graduates are less likely to be self-employed than foreign Chinese graduates. This because the probit coefficient for the variable, LOCAL, is negative.

PROFQ has a positive coefficient, which implies that Chinese graduates with professional qualifications are more likely to be self-employed.

The last significant variable for this group of graduates is YWORK. The likelihood of the Chinese graduate being self-employed increases with the number of years of working experience, as YWORK has a positive coefficient.

Probit Analysis for Non-Chinese Graduates

The total number of non-Chinese graduates is 169, of whom 147 (86.98%) are self-employed and 22 (13.02%) are salaried employees.

There are two significant variables for this group of graduates, as shown in Table 6.19. The first is the variable, AGE. The t-ratio for this variable is 3.217, which is greater than the critical value of 1.960. Therefore, this variable is significant at the 95% level. The coefficient of the variable being negative, it indicates that the likelihood of being self-employed decreases with age for the non-Chinese graduate.

The other significant variable is YWORK. This variable, however, has a positive coefficient. Therefore, the likelihood of being self-employed increases with the number of years of working experience among non-Chinese graduates.

Probit Analysis for Chinese Professional Degree Graduates

There are a total of 1143 Chinese graduates with professional degrees, of whom 1054 (92.21%) are salaried employees and 89 (7.79%) are self-employed. Table 6.20 shows the probit estimates for this group of graduates.

Table 6.19: Probit Estimates of Employment Decision for Non-Chinese Graduates

Variables	Maximum Likelihood Estimates	Standard Errors	T-ratio
MALE	0.2235	0.3326	0.672
AGE*	–0.0724	0.0225	–3.217
MARRIED	0.5381	0.3573	1.506
POSN	0.0793	0.2898	0.274
NDEPEN	0.0160	0.0953	0.168
SPOUSE	–0.1402	0.7566	–0.185
PARENTS	0.0373	0.3570	0.105
SIBLINGS	–0.6474	0.4512	–1.435
CFREN	–0.1760	0.2915	–0.604
EDUC	–0.1005	0.1310	–0.767
LOCAL	–0.2690	0.3396	–0.792
PROFQ	0.3280	0.2988	1.098
YWORK*	0.1273	0.0322	3.956

Notes: * denotes statistical significance at 95% level
No. of Observations: 169 (SE: 22, E: 147)
$t_{(0.95;169)} = 1.960$

Table 6.20: Probit Estimates of Employment Decision for Chinese Professional Degree Graduates

Variables	Maximum Likelihood Estimates	Standard Errors	T-ratio
MALE	0.2206	0.1460	1.511
AGE*	–0.0612	0.0108	–5.639
MARRIED	0.1267	0.1449	0.875
POSN	0.0288	0.1311	0.220
NDEPEN	–0.0074	0.0419	–0.177
SPOUSE	–0.2484	0.4326	–0.574
PARENTS	0.1595	0.1432	1.114
SIBLINGS	0.2468	0.1483	1.664
CFREN	–0.1929	0.1224	–1.577
EDUC*	–0.2020	0.0583	–3.463
LOCAL*	–0.4822	0.1775	–2.717
PROFQ*	0.5000	0.1282	3.902
YWORK*	0.1149	0.0146	7.883

Notes: * denotes statistical significance at 95% level
No. of Observations: 1143 (SE: 89, E: 1054)
$t_{(0.95;1143)} = 1.960$

The first significant variable for this group is AGE. Its negative coefficient indicates that self-employment is less likely as age increases for Chinese with professional degrees.

The variable, EDUC, has a negative coefficient also. Therefore, the higher is the degree level of the Chinese professional degree holder, the lower is the probability of his being self-employed.

The next significant variable is LOCAL, which has a negative coefficient. This implies that Chinese professional degree graduates from local universities are less likely to be self-employed compared to those from foreign universities.

PROFQ has a positive significant coefficient. Therefore, Chinese professional degree holders with professional qualifications awarded by professional bodies are more likely to be self-employed.

Finally, YWORK, which has a positive coefficient, is also statistically significant. We can therefore conclude that the probability of being self-employed increases with the number of years of working experience for Chinese professional degree graduates.

Probit Analysis for Non-Chinese Professional Degree Graduates

The number of non-Chinese graduates with professional degrees is 71, of whom 61 (85.92%) are salaried employees and 10 (14.08%) are self-employed.

Table 6.21 shows the results of the probit analysis. The first significant variable is AGE. As with the regressions for the other groups of graduates, this variable has a negative coefficient. Thus, the probability of being self-employed decreases as age increases for non-Chinese graduates with professional degrees.

PROFQ is also a significant variable. Its positive coefficient leads us to conclude that the possession of professional qualifications from professional bodies increases the likelihood of non-Chinese professional degree graduates to be self-employed.

Finally, YWORK is also a statistically significant variable. Its positive coefficient indicates that the likelihood of self-employment increases with the number of years of working experience.

Probit Analysis for Chinese Non-Professional Degree Graduates

There are a total of 1150 Chinese graduates with non-professional degrees, of whom 1053 (91.57%) are salaried employees and 97 (8.43%) are self-employed.

Table 6.21: Probit Estimates of Employment Decision for Non-Chinese Professional Degree Graduates

Variables	Maximum Likelihood Estimates	Standard Errors	T-ratio
MALE	–0.8047	0.7059	–1.140
AGE*	–0.1117	0.0547	–2.042
MARRIED	0.9210	0.8864	1.039
POSN	–0.7470	0.5994	–1.246
NDEPEN	–0.0927	0.1761	–0.526
SPOUSE	3.3790	296.207	0.011
PARENTS	1.4487	0.8239	1.758
SIBLINGS	–1.0154	1.1539	–0.880
CFREN	–1.1633	0.8579	–1.356
EDUC	–0.0424	0.2271	–0.187
LOCAL	–0.4079	1.0118	–0.403
PROFQ*	2.1411	0.9281	2.307
YWORK*	0.2607	0.1112	2.344

Notes: * denotes statistical significance at 95% level
No. of Observations: 71 (SE: 10, E: 61)
$t_{(0.95;71)} = 1.960$

Table 6.22: Probit Estimates of Employment Decision for Chinese Non-Professional Degree Graduates

Variables	Maximum Likelihood Estimates	Standard Errors	T-ratio
MALE*	0.4931	0.1275	3.867
AGE*	–0.0372	0.0087	–4.282
MARRIED	0.1532	0.1415	1.083
POSN	0.1353	0.1220	1.109
NDEPEN	0.0256	0.0409	0.627
SPOUSE	–4.3917	337.285	–0.013
PARENTS	–0.1723	0.1442	–1.195
SIBLINGS	0.2273	0.1431	1.589
CFREN	–0.1297	0.1154	–1.124
EDUC*	–0.2189	0.0612	–3.579
LOCAL*	–0.8874	0.1445	–6.140
PROFQ	0.1422	0.1270	1.120
YWORK*	0.0606	0.0129	4.687

Notes: * denotes statistical significance at 95% level
No. of Observations: 1150 (SE: 97, E: 1053)
$t_{(0.95;1150)} = 1.960$

MALE is the first significant variable for this group of graduates (see Table 6.22). It has a positive coefficient, which leads us to conclude that male Chinese non-professional degree graduates are more likely to be self-employed compared to the female Chinese non-professional degree graduates.

AGE has a negative coefficient. This means that the probability of self-employment decreases with age for Chinese graduates with non-professional degrees.

The negative coefficient of the statistically significant variable EDUC indicates that as the degree level increases, the less likely it is that graduates of this group would be self-employed.

Chinese graduates with non-professional degrees from local universities are less likely to be self-employed since the variable LOCAL has a negative coefficient.

Finally, the coefficient of the statistically significant YWORK is positive. Therefore, the probability of being self-employed again increases with the number of years of working experience for these graduates.

Probit Analysis for Non-Chinese Non-Professional Degree Graduates

Table 6.23 shows the results of the probit analysis for non-Chinese graduates with non-professional degrees. The total number of graduates in this category is 98, of whom 86 (87.76%) are salaried employees and 12 (12.24%) are self-employed.

The only significant variable for this group of graduates is YWORK. It has a positive coefficient. Therefore, the likelihood of non-Chinese graduates with non-professional degrees being self-employed increases with the number of years of working experience. All the other variables are not significant at the 95% level.

Conclusion

As Table 6.24 (which classifies the sample of graduates by ethnic group and professional or non-professional degree) shows, two factors are found to be consistently important in the decision-making process of graduates for each sub-group of graduates. These two factors are age and years of working experience of the graduate. Figure 6.2 shows that these two factors have a conflicting influence on the decision-making process of being self-employed. Thus, the time that the graduate is likely to embark on self-employment is when the two curves meet.

Table 6.23: Probit Estimates of Employment Decision for Non-Chinese Non-Professional Degree Graduates

Variables	Maximum Likelihood Estimates	Standard Errors	T-ratio
MALE	0.2242	0.5329	0.421
AGE	–0.0614	0.0441	–1.392
MARRIED	0.9042	0.6163	1.467
POSN	0.5869	0.4200	1.398
NDEPEN	–0.0241	0.2319	–0.104
SPOUSE	–4.1390	376.384	–0.011
PARENTS	–0.5484	0.5902	0.929
SIBLINGS	–0.4732	0.6647	–0.712
CFREN	–0.3865	0.4710	–0.821
EDUC	–0.4803	0.3041	–1.579
LOCAL	–0.0072	0.6583	–0.011
PROFQ	–0.3011	0.5674	–0.531
YWORK*	0.1173	0.0551	2.130

Notes: * denotes statistical significance at 95% level
No. of Observations: 98 (SE: 12, E: 86)
$t_{(0.95;98)} = 1.960$

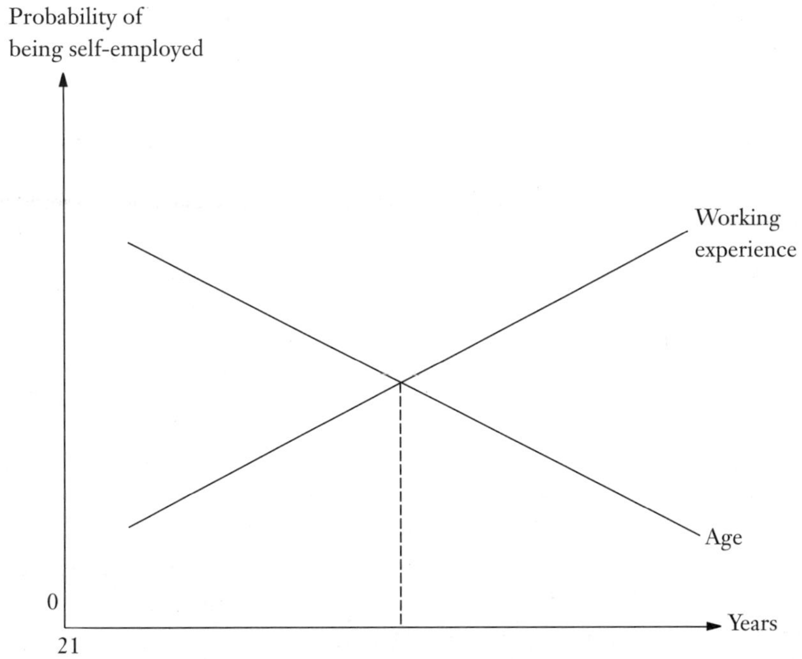

Figure 6.2: Self-Employment Decision

Table 6.24: The Significant Variables among the Different Groups of Graduates

	MALE	AGE	CFREN	SIB-LINGS	EDUC	LOCAL	PROFQ	YWORK
All Graduates	+	–	–		–	–	+	+
Chinese Graduates	+	–		+	–	–	+	+
Chinese Prof Graduates		–			–	–	+	+
Chinese Non-Prof Graduates	+	–			–	–		+
Non-Chinese Prof Graduates		–					+	+
Non-Chinese Non-Prof Graduates								+

Notes: + represents a positive relationship between the variable and the likelihood of being self-employed
– represents a negative relationship between the variable and the likelihood of being self-employed

MALE	:	dummy variable taking the value 1 if the graduate is a male and 0 otherwise
AGE	:	age of graduate in years
CFREN	:	dummy variable taking the value 1 if self-employed close friends or relatives are present and 0 otherwise
SIBLINGS	:	dummy variable taking the value 1 if self-employed siblings are present and 0 otherwise
EDUC	:	ordinal variable for degree level, 1 for Bachelor degree, 2 for Honours degree, 3 for Post-Graduate Diploma, 4 for Masters and 5 for Ph.D
LOCAL	:	dummy variable taking the value 1 if local graduate and 0 otherwise
PROFQ	:	dummy variable taking the value 1 if graduate has obtained a professional qualification awarded by a professional body and 0 otherwise
YWORK	:	number of years of working experience since graduation

Working experience alone will not make a graduate more inclined to be self-employed. The self-employed mind-set has to be injected by relatives or friends who are entrepreneurs. Indeed, we find evidence that the presence of siblings who are entrepreneurs is a relevant factor which makes the Chinese graduate more likely to be self-employed. However, this variable is not found to be important for non-Chinese graduates.

If we want to encourage graduates to be self-employed, we should not over-emphasize entrepreneurship. Rather, graduates should be encouraged to undergo a period of salaried employment in order to prepare themselves for self-employment. They must make use of salaried employment to learn the art of doing business. Whereas the business pioneers of yesteryear had learnt early in life to acquire the basic capabilities of an entrepreneur under hostile conditions, as observed by Chan and Chiang (1994), our graduates today are fortunate in that they can learn the skills of business in costless comfort while building up their savings. Unfortunately, sometimes many graduates become afraid to take risks because they have become too accustomed to a comfortable life. However, when the labour market for graduates shrinks increasingly due to the increased supply of graduates, many graduates will naturally seek self-employment eventually.

Some researchers recently argue that we should remove our safety nets such as the Central Provident Fund (CPF) scheme in order to encourage our graduates to be self-employed. It should be noted that the CPF scheme has a social role to play and has contributed to the full employment situation in Singapore. One cannot remove the CPF scheme which benefits the whole labour force in order to promote would-be entrepreneurs who form a small minority of the population. Besides, as the household decision-making hypothesis implies, if one member of the household could benefit from salaried employment under the CPF scheme, the spouse would have greater incentive to give a try at self-employment.

The crucial factor which would push graduates into opting for self-employment is, as stated earlier, an increased supply of graduates. Tertiary education is now regarded as both a consumption as well as an investment good, which put it in continual demand. Eventually, many graduates would be working overseas and subsequently starting their own businesses abroad. Fortunately, most of our graduates are bilingual; this makes them more employable and adaptable in East Asia, especially in ASEAN and China. The emphasis on bilingualism should continue. Recently, Malaysia has introduced the subject of Chinese abacus for primary and secondary schools with the objective of making Malaysian students more competitive. Singapore thus faces stiff competition not only from Hong Kong, Taiwan and South Korea but also from Malaysia and Thailand.

At the tertiary level, graduates should be taught that salaried employment is not the only way to make a living or to make a contribution to the country. In other words, we should impart on them the mind-set that self-employment is also desirable and achievable. At the Nanyang Technological University, the Entrepreneurship Development Centre (ENDEC) of the School of Accountancy and Business annually conducts an Entrepreneurship Camp for

A-Level students. The objective is not to impress upon them that salaried employment is the only option. Rather, we seek to impart to them the meaning and rewards of being self-employed. We hope that some of these A-level students will consider self-employment after a successful career.

ENDEC also organizes the World Congress on Entrepreneurship annually with the objective of bringing successful entrepreneurs to share the secrets of their success. This annual gathering of entrepreneurs helps to change the mind-set of many salaried employed Singaporeans to accept that there is much promise in self-employment.

Endnotes

* The database employed in this paper is based on Azlan's M.Bus. thesis. The authors are indebted to Richard Tay and B.C. Ghosh, Azlan's thesis supervisors, for their input in the conduct of the survey.

1 Chan and Chiang (1993), p. 341.

2 For a detailed discussion on the Singapore economy, see Lim and Associates (1988) and Chew (1988).

3 For a detailed discussion on the labour market in Singapore, see Chew and Chew (1991).

4 This issue was examined by Wolpin (1977).

References

Aldrich, J.H. and Nelson, F.D., "Linear Probability, Logit and Probit Models", *Sage University Paper Series on Quantitative Applications in the Social Sciences*, Beverly Hills: Sage Publications, 1976.

Chan Kwok Bun and Claire Chiang, *Stepping Out: The Making of Chinese Entrepreneurs*, Singapore: Prentice Hall, 1994.

Chew Soon Beng, *Small Firms In Singapore*, Singapore: Oxford University Press, 1988.

Chew Soon Beng and Rosalind Chew, *The Singapore Worker: A Profile*, Singapore: Oxford University Press, 1991.

Gill, A.M., "Choice of Employment Status and the Wages of Employees and the Self-Employed: Some Further Evidence", *Journal of Applied Econometrics*, Vol. 3, No. 3, 1988, pp. 229–234.

Lee Tsao Yuan and Linda Low, *Local Entrepreneurs In Singapore: Private and State*, Singapore: Institute of Policy Studies, and Times Academic Press, 1990.

Lim Chong Yah and Associates, *Policy Options for the Singapore Economy*, Singapore: McGraw Hill, 1988.

Neter, J.W.W. and Whitmore, G.A., *Applied Statistics*, Third Edition, Massachusetts: Allyn and Bacon, 1988.

Wolpin, K.I., "Education and Screening", *American Economic Review*, Vol. 67, No. 5, December, 1977, pp. 949–958.

Part 3: The Ethnic Chinese and China

7

Ch'ing China and the Singapore Chinese Chamber of Commerce, 1906–1911

Yen Ching-hwang

In the contest for political power in the overseas Chinese communities during the late Ch'ing period, the efforts of the reformists and the revolutionaries have been well documented.[1] But the role of the Ch'ing government in this battle for the political allegiance of the overseas Chinese has been neglected in the past, partly due to the assumption that its efforts in this regard had been done by its overseas diplomatic establishments. Using the Ch'ing government's relationship with the Singapore Chinese Chamber of Commerce as a case study, this paper is intended to shed some light on this obscure aspect of the triangular contest for overseas Chinese political support in the last decade of Manchu rule.

In Search of a Mechanism for the Control of the Overseas Chinese

The change in the Ch'ing government's emigration policy in 1893 ushered in a new era of close relationship with the overseas Chinese.[2] The lack of a central body handling overseas Chinese affairs left the implementation of the new policy to the individual diplomats concerned. However, what emerged after 1893 was a positive attitude among Ch'ing diplomats to protect the overseas Chinese, and they became more concerned with the well-being of the overseas Chinese.[3] But this policy of forging closer ties with the overseas subjects must have a clear objective – it was either to exploit their economic potential or to acquire their political allegiance to consolidate the rule of the dynasty. In evaluating its new relationship with its overseas subjects, the Ch'ing government did not lose sight of a potential threat coming from the overseas Chinese communities. It was aware of increasing anti-dynastic agitation among the overseas Chinese mounted by the reformists and revolutionaries led by K'ang Yu-wei and Sun Yat-sen respectively.[4] The arrival of the Chinese political refugees in the overseas Chinese communities after 1899 created a new problem for the Ch'ing government. The anti-dynastic agitation reached an intolerable level after the turn of the present century. It was translated into anti-dynastic action exemplified by the revolts in central and south China at the end of the 1900.[5] The Court was quick to identify the source of the threat and took measures to counter the insidious propaganda of its adversaries. An edict issued on 9 March 1901 (19th day of 1st moon of the 27th year of Kuang-hsu) instructed the Chinese ministers (ambassadors) in Europe and America to take immediate steps to defuse the agitations. Suitable diplomats were to be selected to tour the overseas Chinese communities to expose the evil intentions of K'ang's and Sun's gangs, and to persuade the overseas subjects not to lend their support to the conspirators.[6] In response to the edict, the Chinese minister to London, Lo Feng-lu, took prompt action. He instructed his two subordinates, the Chinese Consul-General in Singapore and the Vice Consul in Penang, to quash the anti-dynastic agitation in the local Chinese communities, and then to proceed to tour Australia and Canada for that purpose.[7]

Ch'ing concern for the reformist and revolutionary activities overseas was later expressed in its move to send emissaries to visit overseas Chinese communities. From 1907 to 1912, at least three major missions were sent to tour Southeast Asia where the majority of the overseas Chinese resided. The Yang Shih-ch'i mission of 1907[8], the Wang Ta-chen's mission of 1909,[9] and the Chao Ch'ung-fan's mission of 1911,[10] all attempted to promote industry and commerce among the overseas Chinese, and to induce them to invest in China.[11] But one hidden objective which did not appear in their publicized aims was to defuse the growing influence of the revolutionaries and reformists in the overseas Chinese communities. It was this objective which was condemned by the revolutionaries, and the missions were sometimes met with strong hostility from Sun Yat-sen's supporters.[12] Despite this minor setback, the missions were successful. They succeeded in spreading the message of imperial grace, aroused nationalistic sentiment, and gained support for the dynasty among many overseas Chinese, especially among the rich.[13]

The Chinese diplomats overseas were used by the Ch'ing government to suppress the anti-dynastic elements in the overseas Chinese communities, but they had many constraints. They did not have extraterritorial rights in foreign lands like the foreign diplomats had in China, nor could they apprehend any anti-dynastic ringleaders directly. They had to work through a complex and time consuming extradition procedure before any rebels could be apprehended and duly punished. The kidnapping of Sun Yat-sen in London by the Chinese embassy staff in 1896 created a diplomatic embarrassment for the Ch'ing government, and aroused the suspicion of the British government over the activities of Chinese diplomats in its colonies.[14] Further, Chinese diplomats and emissaries could not build up a sustainable support among overseas subjects. Long-term influence could only be acquired through an influential local organization which could mobilize substantial support when needed. In search of a mechanism for the control of the overseas Chinese, the Ch'ing government found that an institution like the Chinese chamber of commerce was most suitable for that purpose.

Despite its foreign origins, the chamber of commerce as an institution grew rapidly in China at the turn of the present century. Some 800 organizations under the name of chamber of commerce which spread throughout China in the last decade of the Ch'ing rule testified to its dramatic growth.[15] Farsighted Chinese diplomat-reformers at the end of the 19th century saw that much of the strength of Western powers rested with trade and with the activities of merchants, and this prompted some of them to suggest boldly that merchants should rank top among the four classes in the Chinese society, a radical proposal which would lift the lowly merchant's social status above the scholar's.[16] In the eyes of these Chinese mercantilists like Hsieh Fu-ch'eng, the enormous strength and energy of Chinese merchants could be tapped for national purpose if they were organized into an institution like the chamber of commerce.

This belated discovery of the merchants' strength was put into practice when the Ministry of Commerce was founded in 1903.[17] As an instrument to rejuvenate the faltering Ch'ing empire, the Ministry had a mammoth task to use the chamber as a focal point for commercial and industrial activities, and for expansion of China's foreign trade.[18]

The Ministry drafted rules and regulations governing the procedures of establishment, functions and power of the chamber, the power and duties of the leaders, and the chamber's relationship with the Ministry. The rules consisted of 26 articles and 6 supplementary articles which were submitted for approval by the Court.[19] The Court's prompt endorsement enabled the Ministry to move speedily to found main chambers of commerce in major cities and minor ones in regional commercial centres. The first to appear were the Shanghai Chinese Chamber of Commerce and the Canton Chinese Chamber of Commerce in 1904 and 1905 respectively.[20] The founding of these two chambers set in motion the movement of establishing chambers of commerce throughout China and the overseas Chinese communities.

The chamber was not only designed as a means of acquiring new national strength, but also deemed as an instrument for the control of the emerging merchant class. The desire to control this class by the Ministry of Commerce was clearly reflected in the contents of its drafted rules and regulations. The rules required Chinese merchants and traders to register with the chamber in their own locality, and they were to be registered in accordance with their respective trade.[21] They were also required to register official documents with the chamber, including commercial contracts, mortgage documents and land and property titles. All these registered documents were to be stamped by the chamber for official recognition.[22] The legalization of documents gave the chamber additional authority over the members, and it was further conferred the judicial power in settling commercial disputes among members.[23]

The key to the control of the chamber rested with the control of the leadership by the Ministry. Although the rules and regulations empowered the rank and file members to elect directors (*Shang-tung*), the top officers of the chamber, the president (*Tsungli*) and the vice president (*Hsiehli*) were actually appointed.[24] The rules required the president to submit an annual report, and to report directly to the Ministry on important matters relating to commerce.[25] He was also entrusted to protect merchants. He was to act on behalf of the merchants in dealing with local officials and had direct access to the Ministry when necessary.[26] In short, the Ministry saw the president of the chamber as a government appointee carrying out its new policy, and reflecting the opinions of merchants from below. He was to be the protector of merchants and the informant of the Ministry at the same time. In this context, the chamber of commerce as an institution was to be used as an effective mechanism both as a sounding board and as a control panel.

Chang Pi-shih and the Founding of the Singapore Chinese Chamber of Commerce

The Ministry of Commerce was also aware of the importance of the overseas Chinese merchants and their potential role in China's economic modernization. In its drafted rules and regulations, the Ministry stated clearly that chambers of commerce will be established in the major Chinese communities in Southeast Asia, Japan and the United States after they had been widely founded and consolidated in China.[27] But there were no details relating to the power and functions of the proposed overseas chambers and the ways that these chambers should be established. This rather broad statement perhaps only indicates the interest of the Ministry in organizing overseas Chinese merchants into the new institution in the way their counterparts did in China. But the Ministry must have been aware that overseas conditions were different from those in China. Firstly, the overseas Chinese communities were not under the jurisdiction of the Ch'ing government, and the Ministry did not have direct authority over the overseas Chinese. Secondly, overseas Chinese merchants differed in their outlooks and temperament from their counterparts in China, and they could not be easily coerced to form the proposed new institution. They, therefore, needed someone who understood them and commanded their respect and trust to persuade them to organize into chambers of commerce. It was probably because of this consideration that Chang Pi-shih was chosen by the Ch'ing government for the founding of overseas chambers in Southeast Asia.

Chang Pi-shih's direct contribution to the founding of the Singapore Chinese Chamber of Commerce, the first of its kind in the overseas Chinese communities world-wide, was well recognized. The official records of the Singapore Chinese Chamber of Commerce stated as follows:

> Last winter (1905), *T'ai-p'u* Chang Pi-shih was instructed by the Court to investigate commercial affairs in South-east Asia. He and *Ch'ao-chang* Shih Ch'u-ch'ing arrived in Singapore, and used the Thong Chai Medical Institution as his temporary office. He gathered together respectable merchants of both Fukien and Kwangtung origins at the Institution. In his speech, he persuaded them to found a chamber of commerce for the purpose of unity of the entire Chinese community and the promotion of commercial affairs. He donated a sum of $3,000 to set an example for the merchants to follow. Those who attended the meeting were much encouraged by his words and prepared to support the proposed chamber of commerce. From the 22nd day of 11th moon of last winter (18 December 1905) till the 29th day of 1st moon of this spring (22 February 1906), six meetings had been called to draft the constitution for the proposed chamber which consisted of 12 sections ... At the same time, several name books had been distributed to the founding members of various *Pang* (dialect group) who were responsible to recruit members among shop proprietors of their respective *Pang*. More than 600 shop proprietors had signed their names and joined the proposed chamber. On the 22nd day of 2nd moon (16 March 1906), members of various *Pangs* of Fukien and Kwangtung origins gathered to elect Goh Siew Tin and Tan Hun Chiu as Presidents (*Tsungli*), Lim Boon Keng and

nine others as Executives (*Hsiehli*), Teo Sian Keng and 39 others as Committee members (*I-yuan*).[28]

What can be derived from this important record about the founding of the Singapore Chinese Chamber of Commerce is as follows. First, Chang Pi-shih was the driving force behind the founding of the chamber. He personally called the first meeting and donated $3,000 to set the whole thing in motion. Second, with Chang's effort and solid support from Chinese merchants of various dialect groups, the Singapore Chinese Chamber of Commerce came smoothly into existence. Third, the founding date of the Singapore Chinese Chamber of Commerce was on 16 March 1906 of the solar calendar (the 22nd day of 2nd moon of the Ping Wu year of the lunar calendar).

It is important to point out the commonly accepted 15 March 1906 date as the founding date of the Singapore Chinese Chamber of Commerce is a historical error. This is based on the wrong event and the wrong calendar. In the original minutes of the Chamber, the 15th day of 3rd moon was the date that the Chamber's office started to operate temporarily at the Thong Chai Medical Institution.[29] This 15th day of 3rd moon of Ping Wu year was based on the lunar calendar. This was because the lunar calendar was adopted for recording the Chamber's events during the Ch'ing period. After the founding of the Republic in 1912, the solar calendar was slowly phased in. Later, the day of 15th March of the solar calendar was confused for the 15th day of 3rd moon of the lunar calendar.[30] In fact, the 15th day of 3rd moon in which the Chamber's temporary office started to operate at the Thong Chai Medical Institution was not of great significance. However, the general meeting of Chinese merchants held on the 22nd day of 2nd moon of the Ping Wu year in the lunar calendar (16 March 1906) during which the office bearers of the Chamber were elected should be regarded as the founding date of the organization.[31]

At the time when Chang Pi-shih took the initiative to help found the Singapore Chinese Chamber of Commerce, he had already been recruited into the Ch'ing bureaucracy for more than a decade. Since his recruitment as the Chinese Vice Consul for Penang in March 1893,[32] he was a rising star in Ch'ing officialdom, and a credible expert on China's economic modernization. He had often been consulted by top Ch'ing officers like Li Hung-chang and Sheng Hsuan-huai on matters relating to mining, banking and railway construction.[33] His climb up the Ch'ing official ladder achieved a breakthrough in June 1903 when he was granted an imperial audience by the Empress Dowager Tz'u-hsi who consulted him on the strategy of overall economic development for the empire.[34] He was immediately granted a Third Rank

Expectant Director of the Court of Sacrificial Worship (*San-pin ching-t'ang hou-pu*) with the additional honour of a title of Vice President of a Board (*Shih-lang hsien*).[35] In the following month (July 1903), Chang presented an important memorial to the Court outlining twelve points for an overall modernization of China, emphasizing the importance of trade to the nation.[36] Chang's memorial was taken seriously by the Court which had instructed two high-ranking officials to dwell on it and make suitable recommendations. The result of which was the establishment of a Ministry of Commerce.[37] Chang's emergence as a foremost expert on China's economic modernization pushed his political career to the top in October 1904 when he was appointed the Imperial Commissioner for Investigating Commercial Affairs in Foreign Countries as well as the Superintendent of Agriculture, Industry, Railways and Mining of Fukien and Kwangtung.[38] It was probably the second time that an overseas Chinese subject was appointed to such a high position in the imperial bureaucracy and loaded with many honours.[39]

Throughout most of the year of 1905, Chang Pi-shih's main focus of his official activity was in South China, not in the overseas Chinese communities. This was perhaps because the coordination of South China's economic activities required more urgent attention, and after all, the region was the homeland that the majority of the overseas Chinese came from, and any success in the region would automatically attract overseas Chinese merchants to invest in their home provinces. This was why he set up his Canton Bureau in early 1905 as headquarters of his Superintendency of Agriculture, Industry, Railways and Mining of Fukien and Kwangtung.[40] He was busily occupied with the work of gaining the support of local Chinese merchants for the new economic task that the Court had undertaken, and he was also actively involved in organizing the merchants in Kwangtung into the proposed Chinese chamber of commerce, and an ambitious project of building a railway linking Canton with Amoy to facilitate economic activities of both Kwangtung and Fukien provinces.[41]

Although Chang Pi-shih's main bureaucratic activity centred in South China throughout most parts of 1905, he did not lose sight of his responsibility of enticing overseas Chinese merchants to invest in China. When he set up the Canton Bureau in the early part of 1905, he had made clear his intention of protecting returned overseas Chinese merchants in his proclamation which was widely publicized in the overseas Chinese communities.[42] After having achieved initial success of his work in South China, the time was ripe for him to launch a drive for overseas Chinese capital. When he set sail for Southeast Asia at the end of 1905, his main objective was to get Southeast Asian Chinese merchants into Chinese chambers of commerce. The chamber as an institution under Ch'ing influence not only could serve as a focal point for tapping overseas Chinese capital, it could also be utilized as a stronghold for pro-dynastic influence. Further, his network of contacts in overseas Chinese communities must have made him aware of the growing revolutionary and reformist influence in Southeast Asia, especially in Singapore and Malaya.[43] Accompanied by Shih Ch'u-ch'ing, an officer of the Ministry of Commerce, Chang arived in Southeast Asia in early December 1905 to carry out the task. He began in Penang which was his home base where his friends and supporters were around, and were likely to give him their support. He found the atmosphere in Penang conducive for the founding of a chamber of commerce. Before his arrival in the port, the local Chinese merchants had, under the leadership of Lim Kiek Chuan, already organized a commercial organization similar to the proposed chamber of commerce with the name of *Pin-lang-yu shang-wu ch'u* (The Penang Chinese Commercial Association) in September 1903 for the promotion of commerce, and it had the solid support of local Chinese merchants of Fukien and Kwangtung origins.[44] A meeting was arranged for Chang Pi-shih and his aide to speak to the members of the Association. Chang praised the leaders of the Association for their foresight, preached unity and solidarity among the Chinese in Penang, and appealed for support by urging them to convert the name of the Association to the Penang Chinese Chamber of Commerce (*Pin-lang-yu Chung-hua shang-wu tsung-hui*) in line with the rules and regulations set out by the Ministry of Commerce.[45] Even with his new credential as the Imperial Commissioner, Chang found that it was not an easy task to organize promptly a Chinese chamber of commerce on the island. There was no quick result arising from the meeting. This was probably due to the ambivalent political stance of the leadership of the Association.[46] However, Chang's plea to the Penang Chinese merchants probably helped to clear the way for the conversion of the Penang Chinese Commercial Association into the Penang Chinese Chamber of Commerce in January 1907.[47]

Chang Pi-shih was undoubtedly disappointed with the result, but this setback did not deter him from executing his overall plan to organize Southeast Asian Chinese merchants into the proposed new institution. A few days after his abortive attempt in Penang, he left for Singapore to organize a chamber of commerce. He had more success there than he had expected. What made the Singapore Chinese merchants more attuned to the Ch'ing government's proposal than their counterparts in Penang were the following factors: greater need for a Chinese commercial organization, more Chinese educated and China oriented leading merchants, stronger cultural and traditional Chinese identity, and the quest of some Teochew wealthy merchants for leadership status outside the Teochew community. The need for a Chinese chamber of commerce to provide a focal point for Chinese merchants in Singapore was obvious. With the growth of entrepot and international trade in Singapore particularly after the opening of the Suez Canal in 1869,[48] Chinese merchants found themselves handicapped with the lack of a commercial organization which could safeguard their interests. A serious attempt to found a Chinese chamber of commerce (Hua-shang kung-so) was made in February 1896 under the leadership of Seah Liang Seah and Lee Cheng Yan as a result of debates on the amendments to a business bankruptcy legislation which would greatly affect the Chinese business community. But the effort failed for unknown reasons.[49] There were no further attempts to found a Chinese chamber of commerce for almost a decade until Chang Pi-shih's initiative at the end of 1905.

In contrast with the leadership of the Penang Chinese Commercial Association, most leaders of the Chinese Chamber of Commerce in Singapore were born in China and had some forms of traditional Chinese education.[50] Chinese birth and Chinese education helped to mould their China orientation. Chinese birth gave them emotional attachment to their birth place in China. The scenery and people of the village, district and province from which they came invariably stirred their imagination and nostalgia. Traditional Chinese education further strengthened their China orientation. The Confucian values and systems of which they had some experience in Chinese villages helped mould their cultural loyalty towards China rather than to Britain. Further, being discriminated against and sometimes denied leadership status by the British colonial authority in Singapore naturally led them to look to China to seek Chinese informal political power.[51] Some of these leaders were extremely wealthy and were leading merchants in Singapore. Chua Tse Yung, a Teochew, was a leading merchant in sugar, rice and silk import, and his business empire extended from Singapore to coastal China. It was claimed that his annual business turnover reached six million dollars, and his four rice mills in Thailand produced annually more than ten million dollars worth of rice for export, half of each going to Singapore and Hong Kong.[52] Goh Siew-tin, a Fukienese (Hokkien), was another leading merchant in Singapore. He inherited a large fortune and business from his father in 1892, and became a leading trader and ship owner, and he was an important leader of the Fukienese community in Singapore.[53]

Singapore emerged at the end of the 19th and the beginning of the 20th centuries as the bastion of Chinese culture. The Lo Shan She Lecture movement which was to re-assert traditional Chinese values in the overseas Chinese communities was launched in Singapore in 1881; while the Confucian

Revival Movement, a larger scale traditional Chinese cultural movement, was centred in Singapore at the end of the 19th and beginning of the 20th centuries.[54] The convergence of these movements in Singapore placed the island under the spotlight of Chinese cultural revival in Southeast Asia. The movements invigorated traditional Chinese values and customs which rekindled a strong sense of Chinese identity. This led to a wave of China orientation and moved Chinese merchants closer to the Ch'ing government.

Chang Pi-shih's initiative in establishing a Chinese chamber of commerce in Singapore at the end of 1905 also came at an opportune time. The Teochew community, the second largest dialect group in the Chinese community in Singapore, showed ominous signs of split at the turn of the present century. Frustrated by the prolonged monopoly of the social power of the Teochew community by the Seah family, a group of wealthy and powerful Teochew merchants emerged to challenge Seah's hegemony. This group was led by Chua Tse Yung, Tan Hun Chiu and Liao Cheng-hsing.[55] The entrenched position of the Seah family in the Ngee Ann Kongsi, the key social institution in the Teochew community, blocked the social advancement of the group. This was why members of the group were anxious to seek recognition of leadership status outside the Teochew community.[56] Thus, the proposed founding of a Chinese Chamber of Commerce as a key organization for the entire Chinese community in Singapore appealed to them. In fact, the key leaders of this Teochew group, Chua Tse Yung, Tan Hun Chiu and Liao Cheng-hsing became founders and important leaders of the Singapore Chinese Chamber of Commerce.[57]

With favourable conditions and the right mood for the founding of a chamber of commerce in Singapore, Chang Pi-shih adopted a right strategy – to enlist the support of a couple of key merchant leaders in order to produce a chain reaction. Before he left Penang for Singapore, Chang had probably contacted Goh Siew-tin, an old friend and the man who had been close to the Ch'ing bureaucracy, to pave the way.[58] Goh was also an acknowledged leader of the local Fukien community. Chang might also have contacted Chua Tse Yung, who had commanded considerable influence and respect among Teochew merchants, and through them to influence the attitude of the bulk of Chinese merchants in Singapore. Chang Pi-shih's initiative to found a Chinese chamber of commerce was, therefore, taken by many Chinese merchants in Singapore as an official endorsement by the Ch'ing government. This endorsement was much needed in a society where political power was most highly respected. Many Chinese merchants were enthusiastic and prepared to lend support to Chang's proposal. More than 600 shop proprietors and individuals signed up to join the proposed institution on the first instance.[59]

In retrospect, Chang Pi-shih's push for the founding of the Singapore Chinese Chamber of Commerce was crucial, and the establishment of the Chamber would have been delayed without Chang's initiative. Being the first Chinese chamber of commerce linked officially with the Ch'ing government, the Singapore Chinese Chamber of Commerce had the advantage of consolidating its position and setting an example for other overseas Chinese chambers of commerce to follow in the Southeast Asian region.

Ch'ing Government and the Singapore Chinese Chamber of Commerce 1906–1911

The Ch'ing government's initial support for the Singapore Chinese Chamber of Commerce was to legitimize it as the leading organization for the entire Chinese community. Its wish was carried out by its Consul-General in Singapore. At the time when the Chamber came into existence, the Chinese Consul-General was Sun Shih-ting, a career diplomat. Sun left little mark in the diplomatic history of Ch'ing China. He could not be compared with his colourful predecessors such as Tso Ping-lung and Huang Tsun-hsien who proved to be able diplomats as well as Confucian scholars.[60] But Sun must have known the works of both men who had been trying to arouse national consciousness and to cultivate loyalty among the overseas Chinese.[61] Part of Sun's task was to continue Huang's and Tso's works to ensure overseas Chinese loyalty to the dynasty. As a new commercial and social organization, the Chamber had a great potential to be developed into the most powerful body representing the entire Chinese community on the island.

To legitimize the status of the Chamber, Sun was quick to identify issues which could be used to enhance its prestige and authority. Issues which affected the general interests of the Chinese community would give the Chamber credibility as the spokesman for the entire community. Soon after its inception, Consul-General Sun wrote to the Chamber and urged it to participate in the negotiations with the British colonial authority in Singapore over a controversial issue of physical inspection of Chinese immigrants at the quarantine station of the port.[62] The Chamber seized the opportunity, and after an intensive discussion, agreed to participate in the negotiations with the British authority.[63] The actual role of the Chamber in acquiring a satisfactory settlement on the issue was not fully known, but the Chamber was quick to claim credit by issuing a public notice on 20 June 1906, less than two months after it had fully discussed the issue. The notice drew the attention of the Chinese community that some members of the Chamber who were concurrently members of the Po Leung Kuk, a semi-government party for the protection of Chinese women and children, had been informed by the government that it had already agreed to reform the physical inspection of Chinese immigrants arriving in Singapore.[64]

The Ch'ing Consul-General had been consistent to buttress the position of the Chamber in its early stage. A major issue such as anti-opium smoking was passed from the Consul-General to the Chamber. An official letter from Sun urged the Chamber to take up the responsibility on behalf of the entire Chinese community. Although the Chamber decided not to commit itself on the issue, it nevertheless showed the Consul-General's efforts in trying to involve the Chamber on major community issues.[65]

The visits of Ch'ing dignitaries to Singapore provided excellent opportunities for the Consul-General to bolster further the position of the Chamber. In a highly status conscious society like the Chinese community in Singapore, the occasions were manipulated for political purpose. Before 1906, the Thong Chai Medical Institution and the residences of some prominent Chinese were selected as temporary office for the visiting dignitaries.[66] Those selected had the honour of being associated with Ch'ing officials, and felt that their status and prestige in the community had been enhanced. In early July 1906, Prince Tsai Tse and Shang Ch'i-h'eng stopped over at Singapore on their way home from Europe. Tsai and Shang were members of an important mission sent by the Empress Dowager Tz'u-hsi to investigate Western political systems in preparation for a proposed constitution. The mission left China in December 1905, and visited the United States, Russia, Britain, France, Germany and Italy. Tsai and Shang were the advance party returning home. The visiting dignitaries arrived at Singapore in a French ship, and were welcomed by the representative of the Governor with an official guard of honour. They were also met by Consul-General Sun together with about 40 Chinese leaders. Large crowds of Chinese also awaited at the dock to welcome them.[67] During their stopover at Singapore, the Chinese Chamber of Commerce was chosen by the Consul-General as the temporary office for the visitors. The dragon flag was hoisted and a tea party was arranged at the Chamber.[68] Before the arrival of the two Ch'ing dignitaries, Consul-General Sun had shrewdly used the occasion to boost the image of the Chamber. A letter from Sun suggested that the Chamber be used as the envoys' temporary office. The proposal was happily accepted by the Chamber.[69] From then onwards, the Chamber replaced the Thong Chai Medical Institution and private residences as the temporary office for the visiting Ch'ing dignitaries till the fall of the dynasty in early

1912, including Yang Shih-ch'i (1907), Prince Tsun (1909) and Chao Ch'ung-fan (1911).[70]

The strong backing of the Singapore Chinese Chamber of Commerce by the Ch'ing Consul-General was not simply due to his personal enthusiasm, but it was a part of a well-planned policy of bolstering the Chamber as an all-powerful organization in the Chinese community. In the battle for the political allegiance of the overseas Chinese in Southeast Asia, the Ch'ing government was shrewd to place overseas Chinese chambers of commerce under the control of the Ministry of Commerce (after 1907, its name was changed to the Ministry of Agriculture, Industry and Commerce, *Nung-kung-shang pu*). By linking directly with the Ministry, the status of overseas chambers had been elevated above local level. Their leaders were perceived to possess equal status with the Chinese Consul or Consul-General overseas. If the chamber of commerce was to serve as an instrument for the control of the new emerging merchant class in China, the overseas Chinese chamber had an additional political role to play, which was to help the Ch'ing government control the hearts and minds of ordinary overseas Chinese. The chamber was not just a modern commercial guild setting prices and settling business disputes, it had to be all-embracing and even omnipotent. The greater the power the chamber had, the greater the influence the Ch'ing government would command in the overseas Chinese communities. In the contest for influence with the revolutionaries and the reformists in the Chinese community in Singapore, the Singapore Chinese Chamber of Commerce had to be propped up with informal political power from China. The conferring of an official seal (*kuan-fang*) by the throne met this need. Like other Chinese chambers of commerce in China, the official seal was to be used on all official documents of the Chamber, and would carry some weight in dealing with the Chinese authorities in China. The symbolic power of the seal invariably enhanced the power and authority of the Chamber in the eyes of the local Chinese. The arrival of the official seal of the Chamber in Singapore on 14 August 1906 (25th day of 6th moon of 32nd year of Kuang-hsu reign), about five months after the founding of the Chamber, marked an important event in the history of the Chamber. A solemn ceremony was held on 16 August (27th day of 6th moon) in the Chamber's building.[71] A participant of this ceremony, Yeoh Chan Boon, recalled that an elegant glass cabinet was erected in the Chamber's building facing north with a big Chinese character *Chueh* (Imperial palace), and at 6.30 a.m., all office holders of the Chamber, dressed in full mandarin or traditional Chinese costumes, gathered and performed three kneelings and nine kowtowings to the emperor for the imperial grace.[72] The ceremony linked the Chamber with Ch'ing bureaucracy, the Chamber symbolically became a sub-bureau of the Ministry of Commerce, and the office holders of the Chamber also symbolically became minor officials of the Ch'ing government. Many leaders of the Chamber must have been greatly delighted to have acquired this new social status. Overseas Chinese merchants, like their counterparts in China, had always entertained a strong inferiority complex *vis-a-vis* Chinese mandarins because of their traditional lowly social status. Though inflated with new-found wealth and the realization of the great potential influence of that wealth, overseas Chinese merchants had a strong desire for Ch'ing official status. Their purchases of Ch'ing brevet titles indicated their enthusiasm for Chinese informal political power and their desire to be close to Ch'ing bureaucracy.[73]

The Ch'ing government further strengthened the Chamber's authority by granting it the power to issue 'commercial certificates' (*Shang-chao*) which was to protect returning overseas Chinese merchants in China.[74] Probably at the beginning of 1907, the Chamber was empowered to issue the certificate to upright merchant members who would register their certificates with the Chamber's counterparts in the Treaty ports, and through which the returning merchants received protection against extortions or robberies by local bullies or corrupt officials.[75]

The Singapore Chinese Chamber of Commerce did develop close ties with the Ch'ing government in the twilight years of Manchu rule. It was especially important in the economic arena. The Chamber was instrumental in helping the Ch'ing government mobilize overseas Chinese capital in the service of China. It served as an effective channel of communication between the Ch'ing government and the emerging overseas Chinese merchant class. Overseas Chinese merchants for the first time had direct access to the central government and were able to express their wishes without going through a complex diplomatic channel. At the same time, the instructions from the Ch'ing government reached the overseas Chinese merchants in Singapore without unnecessary delays. For instance, the Chamber acted as transmitter of the Ch'ing government for the planned industrial and commercial fair to be held in Nanking in 1910. The Chamber actively promoted the scheme in the local daily Chinese newspaper and sent letters to other Chinese chambers of commerce in Southeast Asia for the same purpose.[76]

The Singapore Chinese Chamber of Commerce also acted frequently as an agent for both private or officially-sponsored companies in China. In August 1906, for instance, the Chamber acted as the agent for the merchant-managed Kiangsu Railway Company, and elected leaders to push for shares among the Chinese in Singapore along the dialect line.[77] In September 1909, the Chamber also acted as the agent to sell stock for the Hupei Rug Company in an attempt to promote Chinese native produce.[78] But the biggest effort made by the Chamber in the mobilization of overseas Chinese capital was to help float the shares of the proposed China Commercial Bank (*Chung-kuo Hua-shang yin-h'ang*). The idea of founding a commercial bank came from an expectant *Taotai* (epistolary designation, *Kuan-ch'a*) named Hsu Ching-ming of P'an Yu district, Kwangtung. Hsu, who obviously had close contacts with overseas Chinese, came up with the big idea of mobilizing overseas Chinese capital for the founding of a commercial bank, an insurance company and a shipping line. In 1906, Hsu obtained support from the Ministry of Commerce by granting him an official status to investigate commercial affairs in Southeast Asia for the purpose of promoting industry in China.[79] Hsu had visited major ports in Southeast Asia, and sounded out support of some wealthy merchants in the region. Hsu returned to China and further obtained strong support from the Shanghai Chinese Chamber of Commerce for his grand scheme. As the scheme gradually crystallized, Hsu proposed to found the China Commercial Bank first, and drew up rules and regulations for the float of shares among overseas Chinese and the Chinese in China. He proposed to float 10 million dollars (*yuan*) as capital for the bank with 2 million shares of 5 dollars each. The main thrust of his float was the overseas Chinese from whom he hoped to raise 8 million dollars (1.6 million shares), while the remaining 2 million dollars (0.4 million shares) would come from the merchants in Shanghai.[80] The headquarters of the proposed bank was to be located in Shanghai, and the regional headquarters in Singapore. The bank would also set up branches in Britain, France, Germany, Russia, the United States and Japan and the major ports in Southeast Asia. The foreign branches would be under the control of the Shanghai headquarters, while the Southeast Asian branches would come under the jurisdiction of the Singapore regional headquarters.[81] To initiate the task of floating the capital for the bank, Hsu also nominated some wealthy overseas Chinese merchants as 'Promotion Director' (*T'i-ch'ang tung-shih*), and for the British colony of Singapore, Goh Siew-tin and Chua Tse Yung, two prominent leaders of the Singapore Chinese Chamber of Commerce were named.[82]

The Singapore Chinese Chamber of Commerce gave the scheme the strongest support. When Hsu Ching-ming arrived in Singapore in the spring of 1907 from the Philippines, he was met by the leaders of the Chamber, and a special meeting was arranged for that purpose. A team for soliciting shares was elected, and it accompanied Hsu to visit four other major cities in the Malay Peninsula of which some 2.3 million dollars worth of shares was claimed to have been promised.[83] To back up the scheme further, the Chamber in 1908 elected Lim Boon Keng and Lin Chu-tsai to accompany the two representatives from the Shanghai Chinese Chamber of Commerce to tour other parts of Southeast Asia for the second round of the share-soliciting.[84] At the same time, the president of the Chamber, Chua Tse Yung, was elected team leader to be assisted by other directors of the Chamber to speed up the soliciting process in Singapore.[85] By September 1908, it was claimed about four to five million dollars worth of shares were promised from Chinese merchants in Shanghai, Luzon (Philippines), Penang, Kuala Lumpur, Perak and Singapore.[86] The Chamber continued to give the proposed bank strong backing through 1909 and 1910, but for various reasons, the proposed bank failed to get off the ground in 1911.[87]

Politically, the Singapore Chinese Chamber of Commerce acted as an ally of the Ch'ing government. It adopted a clear pro-Ch'ing stand. It was instrumental in mobilizing support of the community to show political allegiance to the Ch'ing throne. Its political role in supporting the faltering Manchu dynasty was clearly reflected on occasions of imperial birthdays, visits of Ch'ing dignitaries or other extra-ordinary occasions such as the death of the reigning emperor and the inauguration of the new emperor. Handbills were distributed and a public notice calling for the entire Chinese community to observe the occasion was published in local Chinese newspapers. On a significant occasion such as the inauguration of the new Emperor Hsuan-t'ung at the end of 1908, the Chamber instructed all members of the Chamber to go to the Chinese Consulate-General building to pay homage to the new monarch. The Chamber also called on Chinese merchants to close shops for trading, and to decorate and hoist dragon flags for the auspicious occasion.[88] On the 9th day of 11th moon (2 December 1908), leaders of the Chamber dressed in mandarin robes or traditional costumes and led by the Ch'ing Consul-General, performed a most solemn ceremony of three kneelings and nine kowtowings towards a symbolic throne in the Consul-General's building. Later, various Chinese school students led by their teachers also performed the same homage to the new emperor.[89] On the demise of both Emperor Kuang-hsu and Empress Dowager Tz'u-hsi in November of the same year, the Chamber played the leading role in mobilizing the Chinese in Singapore to show sympathy and to observe the mourning of the deceased Ch'ing rulers. It had used its influence to mobilize a large number of Chinese to observe the mourning and to show loyalty to the Manchu rulers.[90]

In retrospect, the Singapore Chinese Chamber of Commerce did not measure up to the full expectation of the Ch'ing government. It did not become a front organization of the Ch'ing government, nor did it become actively involved in fighting against the reformists and the revolutionaries.

In the growing revolutionary agitation in the Chinese community in Singapore,[91] the Chamber did not seek to curb such agitation or to confront the agitators. At the same time, that the Chamber escaped being a major target of attack by the revolutionary newspapers in Singapore also indicates that it was not considered the main enemy of the revolutionaries.[92]

What made the Singapore Chinese Chamber of Commerce a pro-Ch'ing institution but not an active anti-revolutionary organization is perhaps due to the following factors. Firstly, the death of Goh Siew-tin, a staunch pro-Ch'ing leader in January 1909, deprived the Ch'ing government of a strong supporter within the Chamber.[93] Secondly, although the Chamber was founded by Chang Pi-shih, a high-ranking Ch'ing official and the Chamber was officially linked with the Ministry of Agriculture, Industry and Commerce, it was not a political organization, but essentially an economic and commercial organization. It was to promote commerce and industry, and to protect the interests of the Chinese merchant class in Singapore. This perceived primary role of the Chamber seemed to be shared by the majority of its leaders. Any active participation in the political struggle would be divisive and destructive for the Chamber. Thirdly, the majority of the leaders of the Chamber probably realized that the long-term interests of the Chamber lay not in China, but in Singapore. Therefore, its activities should be focused on local issues, including economic, social and cultural issues.[94] Fourthly, most leaders of the Chamber were wealthy merchants not politicians. Although many of them possessed Ch'ing brevet titles and enjoyed prestige and honour in their relationship with the Ch'ing government, they were not committed politicians, nor did they commit strongly to a political ideology. They were more interested in making money. This led them to take a less committed attitude towards the Ch'ing government politically.

Conclusion

In the battle for political support in the overseas Chinese communities, the Ch'ing government attempted to use the chamber of commerce as a vehicle for political control and for exploiting the economic potential of the overseas Chinese. The Ch'ing government sent a high-ranking official, Chang Pi-shih, himself a prominent overseas Chinese capitalist, to carry out its mission in Southeast Asia. Chang took the initiative to help found the Singapore Chinese Chamber of Commerce at the end of 1905 and through which to influence the founding of other Chinese chambers of commerce in Southeast Asia. The Ch'ing government propped up the Singapore Chinese Chamber of Commerce as the leading economic and social institution in the local Chinese community through diplomatic and political means. The Chamber did emerge in the twilight years of Manchu rule as a pro-Ch'ing organization in the Chinese community in Singapore. It developed close economic ties with China, helping to mobilize overseas Chinese capital in the service of Ch'ing economic modernization. It also acted as a supporter of the Ch'ing government, helping to muster political support for the regime. However, the Chamber did not measure up to the full expectation of the Ch'ing government as a political vehicle. This was due to the untimely death of one of its strongest supporters, the perceived primarily economic role of the Chamber, the local focus of the Chamber, and the nature of merchant leadership. This explains why the Chamber acted as a pro-Ch'ing institution but not as a strong anti-revolutionary organization.

Endnotes

1 See Yen Ching-hwang, *The Overseas Chinese and the 1911 Revolution: With Special Reference to Singapore and Malaya*, Kuala Lumpur: Oxford University Press, 1976; L. Eve Armentrount Ma, *Revolutionaries, Monarchists and Chinatowns: Chinese Politics in the Americas and the 1911 Revolution*, Honolulu: University of Hawaii Press, 1990; Lee Lai To (ed.), *The 1911 Revolution – The Chinese in British and Dutch Southeast Asia*, Singapore: Heinemann Asia, 1987.

2 For a discussion of Ch'ing change in its emigration policy and historical significance, see Yen Ching-hwang, *Coolies and Mandarins: Ch'ing Protection of Overseas Chinese during the Late Ch'ing Period*, Singapore: Singapore University Press, 1985, pp. 249–280; see also Chuang Kuo-t'u, *Chung-kuo feng-chien cheng-fu te hua-ch'iao cheng-ch'ih* (*The Overseas Chinese Policy of China's Feudal Governments*), Amoy: Amoy University Press, 1989, pp. 126–134.

3 See Yen Ching-hwang, *Coolies and Mandarins*, pp. 281–282.

4 For the anti-dynastic agitation mounted by K'ang Yu-wei and Liang Ch'i-ch'iao in the overseas Chinese communities before 1901, see Jung-pang Lo, *K'ang Yu-wei: A Biography and a Symposium*, Tucson: The University of Arizona Press, 1967, pp. 178–183; Ting Wen-chiang (ed.), *Liang Jen-Kung hsien-sheng nien-p'u ch'ang-p'ien ch'u-kao* (*A Draft of Chronological Records of Liang Ch'i-ch'iao*), Taipei, 1959, pp 99–140; Chang P'eng-yuan, *Liang Ch'i-ch'iao yu Ch'ing-chi ko-ming* (*Liang Ch'i-ch'iao and the 1911 Revolution*), Taipei: Chung-yang yen-chiu-yuan, 1964, pp. 81–89; For early anti-dynastic agitation mounted by Sun Yan–sen and his supporters in the overseas Chinese communities, see Feng Tzu-yu, *Hua-ch'iao ko-ming k'ai-kuo shih* (*The Involvement of Overseas Chinese in the 1911 Revolution and the Founding of the Republic*), Taipei: Shang-wu yin-shu kuan, 1953, pp. 1–47; Feng Tzu-yu, *Ko-min i-shih* (*Reminiscences of the 1911 Revolution*), Taipei: Shang-wu yin-shu kuan, 1965, Vol. 1, pp. 4, 17–19, 22–23.)

5 For the analysis of the revolutionary revolt in Waichow, Kwangtung province in 1900, see Harold Z. Schiffrin, *Sun Yat-sen and the Origins of the Chinese Revolution*,

Berkeley: University of California Press, 1968, pp. 214–254; for the reformist engineered revolt in Hankow, Central China in 1900, see Edmund S.K. Fung, "The T'ang Ts'ai-ch'ang Revolt", in *Papers on Far Eastern History*, Canberra: Department of Far Eastern History, Australian National University, No. 1, March 1970, pp. 70–114; Feng, Tzu-yu, *Chung-hua min-kuo k'ai-kuo ch'ien ko-ming shih*, Taipei: Shang-wu yin-shu kuan, 1954, Vol. 2, p. 105; Feng Tzu-yu, *Ko-ming i-shih*, Vol. 1, pp. 128–131.

6 See *Ta Ch'ing te-tsung ching-huang-ti shih-lu* (*Veritable Records of the Emperor Kuang-hsu of the Great Ch'ing Empire*) Ch'ang Ch'un, 1935, Vol. 479, p. 3.

7 *Ibid.*, Vol. 488, p. 6b; "Shih Ying Lo Feng-lu chih wai-pu Ying wai-pu i chu Lo Chung-yao fu Hsin-chin-shan i chieh-hsi tien" (Cable by the Chinese Minister to England, Lo Feng-lu, to the Ministry of Foreign Affairs relating to the obstruction of Lo Chung-yao's tour of Melbourne by the British Foreign Office), in *Ch'ing-chi wai-chiao shih-liao: Kuang-hsu ch'iao* (*Historical Materials on Foreign Relations in the Ch'ing Period for the Kuang-hsu Reign*), Vol. 152 (original), p. 19, or reprint, Taipei: Wen H'ai, 1964, Vol. 5, p. 188.

8 For the details of sending the Yang Shih-ch'i's mission to tour the Chinese communities in Southeast Asia, see *Ta Ch'ing te-tsung ching-huang-ti shih-lu*, Vol. 576 (original), pp. 10b–11a; Chu Shou-p'eng (compiled), *Kuang-hsu ch'ao tung-hua lu* (*The Tung Hua Records of the Kuang-hsu Reign*), Peking: Chung Hua shu-chi, 1958, Vol. 5, p. 91.

9 For details of sending Wang Ta-chen mission to tour Southeast Asia, see the memorial of the Ministry of Agriculture, Industry and Commerce to the Court, in *Cheng-chih kuan-pao* (*Ch'ing Government Gazettes*), Taipei: 1965, Vol. 17, p. 317.

10 For the details of sending this mission, see the memorial of the Ministry of Agriculture, Industry and Commerce to the Court, *Cheng-chih kuan-pao*, Vol. 42, p. 98; see also the cable of the Chinese Ministry of Foreign Affairs to the Chinese Consul-General in Singapore dated 13 February 1911, in "Wai-wu pu shou-fa tien tang" (Cable Records of the Ministry of Foreign Affairs), 3rd year of Hsuan-t'ung Reign (1911).

11 See for instance, in the speech given by roving envoy Chao Ch'ung-fan to a group of about 60 Chinese wealthy merchants in Penang, in which Chao encouraged overseas Chinese merchants to invest in China, and emphasized that they would receive protection from the Ch'ing government, *Penang Sin Pao*, 28 March, 1911, p. 3. (Original newspaper kept in the Chinese Library, National University of Singapore).

12 See for instance, the mission of Yang Shih-ch'i in 1908 met with scathing attacks from the local revolutionary newspaper, the *Chong Shing Yit Pao*. See *Chong Shing Yit Pao*, 9 January 1908, p. 2, 10 January 1908, p. 2; Yen Ching-hwang, *The Overseas Chinese and the 1911 Revolution*, p. 103.

13 See "Memorial of Yang Shih-ch'i to the Court of the 2nd moon of 34th year of Kuang-hsu (March 1908)", *Kuang-hsu ch'ao tung-hua lu*, Vol. 5, pp. 23–26; the same memorial also found in *Cheng-chih kuan-pao*, Vol. 6, pp. 26–29.

14 For a detailed reconstruction of this kidnapping of Sun and its impact, see J.Y. Wong, *The Origins of An Heroic Image: Sun Yatsen in London, 1896–1897*, Hong Kong: Oxford University Press, 1986. For Sun Yat-sen's own account of

this episode, see "Lun-tun pei-nan chi" (My Kidnapping in London), in *Sun Chung-shan ch'uan-chi* (*The Complete Works of Dr Sun Yat-sen*), Vol. 1, Beijing: Chung-hua shu-chi, 1981, pp. 49–86.

15 See Wellington K.K. Chan, *Merchants, Mandarins and Modern Enterprise in Late Ch'ing China*, Cambridge, Massachusetts: Harvard University Press, 1977, p. 213.

16 This view was expressed by Hsieh Fu-ch'eng, a well-known diplomat reformer who was the Chinese minister to Britain, France, Italy and Belgium. He expressed this view in his writings in 1890. See Hsieh Fu-ch'eng, "Ying-chi-li yung shang-wu p'i-fang ti shuo" (British use of merchants for developing undeveloped lands), in Ting Feng-lin and Wang Hsin-chih (eds.), *Hsieh Fu-ch'eng hsuan-chi* (*Selected Works of Hsieh Fu-ch'eng*), Shanghai: Jen-min ch'u-pan she, 1987, p. 297; for an analysis of Hsieh's view, see Hu Chi-ch'uang, *Chung kuo chin-tai ching-chi ssu-hsiang shih ta-kang* (*Outlines of History of Economic Thoughts of Modern China*), Beijing: Chung-kuo she-hui k'o-hsueh ch'u-pan she, 1984, pp. 121–123; Ma Po-huang (ed.), *Chung-kuo chin-tai ching-chi ssu-hsiang shih* (*A History of Modern Chinese Economic Thoughts*), Vol. 1, Shanghai: Shang-hai She-hui k'o-hsueh yuan ch'u-pan she, 1988, pp. 239–242.

17 For the circumstances leading to the founding of the Ministry of Commerce, see Wellington K.K. Chan, *Merchants, Mandarins and Modern Enterprise in Late Ch'ing China*, pp. 161–165.

18 See "Shang-pu chou ch'ien-pan shang-hui cheoh yi chien-ming chang-ch'eng chi" (Memorial from the Ministry of Commerce to the Court relating to the founding of chambers of commerce and the proposed rules and regulations), in *Ta Ch'ing kuang-hsu hsin fa-ling* (*New Statutes of the Great Ch'ing Empire during the Kuang-hsu Reign*), Shanghai: n.d. Vol. 16, pp. 30a–31.

19 *Ibid*., pp. 31–35.

20 For details of the founding of the Shanghai Chinese Chamber of Commerce in May 1904, see Hsu Ting-hsin and Ch'ien Hsiao-ming, *Shang-hai tsung shang-hui shih, 1902–1929* (*A History of the Shanghai Chinese Chamber of Commerce, 1902–1929*), Shanghai: Shang-hai she-hui k'o-hsueh-yuan ch'u-pan she, 1991, pp. 58–59; for the founding of the Canton Chinese Chamber of Commerce, see Wellington K.K. Chan, *Merchants, Mandarins and Modern Enterprise in Late Ch'ing China*, pp. 220–221; Edward J.M. Rhoads, "Merchant Associations in Canton, 1895–1911", in Mark Elvin and G.W. Skinner (eds.), *The Chinese City between Two Worlds*, Stanford: Stanford University Press, 1974, pp. 105–108.

21 See article 18 of the rules and regulations, "Shang-pu chou ting shang-hui chien-ming chang-ch'eng, 24th day of 11th moon of 29th year of Kuang-hsu (11 January 1904)", *Ta Ch'ing kuang-hsu hsin fa-ling*, Vol. 16, p. 33.

22 See article 19 of the rules and regulations. *Ibid.*

23 See article 15 of the rules and regulations. *Ibid*., p. 33.

24 See article 3 of the rules and regulations. *Ibid*., p. 31a.

25 See article 8 of the rules and regulations, *Ibid*., p. 32.

26 See article 7 of the rules and regulations. *Ibid.*

27 See article 25 of the rules and regulations. *Ibid.*

28 See "Hsin-chia-po Chung-hua shang-wu tsung-hui i-shih pu" (Minutes of Committee Meetings of the Singapore Chinese Chamber of Commerce)

(manuscript), Vol. 1, 1906–1909, pp. 1–2.

29 *Ibid.*, p. 3.

30 See "Hsing-chia-po Chung-hua tsung shang-hui shih-chi" (Historical Records of the Singapore Chinese Chamber of Commerce), and Yeoh Chan Boon (Yang Chan-wen), recorded by Liu T'ien-feng, "Chung-hua tsung shang-hui ch'ang-shang shih" (The Vicissitude of the Singapore Chinese Chamber of Commerce), in *Hsin-chia-po Chung-hua tsung shang-hui ta-sha lo-ch'eng chi-nien k'an* (*Souvenir of the Opening Ceremony of the Newly Completed Singapore Chinese Chamber of Commerce Building*), Singapore, 1964, pp. 145, 150.

31 See "Hsin-chia-po chung-hua shang-wu tsung-hui i-shih pu" (manuscript), Vol. 1, 1906–1909, p. 2.

32 Chang was appointed by the Chinese minister (ambassador) for Britain, France, Italy and Belgium, Hsueh Fu-ch'eng, to that position. See Hsueh Fu-ch'eng, "Despatch to the Tsungli Yamen relating to the appointment of the Vice Consul in Penang dated 20th day of 1st moon of 19th year of Kuang-hsu (8 March 1893)", in Hsueh Fu-ch'eng, *Ch'u-shih Kung-tu, tsou-shu* (*Correspondence of My Diplomatic Mission to England, and My Memorials to the Court*), Vol. 2, Taipei, n.d., tz'u-wen, pp. 25a–25b; for circumstances leading to the setting up of the Chinese Vice Consulate in Penang, see Yen Ching-hwang, *Coolies and Mandarins: China's Protection of Overseas Chinese during the Late Ch'ing Period (1851–1911)*, pp. 168–171.

33 See Michael Godley, *The Mandarin-capitalists from Nanyang: Overseas Chinese Enterprise in the Modernization of China 1893–1911*, Cambridge: Cambridge University Press, 1981, pp. 84–90.

34 See *Ta Ch'ing te-tsung ching-huang-ti shih-lu*, Vol. 516, p. 5b; Michael Godley, *op. cit.*, p. 93.

35 Quoting reports from two Chinese newspapers in Singapore and Penang, Michael Godley claims that Chang Pi-shih was named a Vice President of the Board of Trade (Ministry of Commerce). Support for this claim cannot be found in the Ch'ing official records. Chang did not seem to have held that position. Perhaps Chang's entitlement to hold the title of Vice President of a Board was confused by the two local Chinese newspapers, or he was addressed as a Vice President out of respect. See Michael Godley, *op. cit.*, p. 92; *Ta Ch'ing te-tsung ching-huang-ti shih-lu*, Vol. 516, p. 5b.

36 For a thorough analysis of this memorial and its contents, see Michael Godley, *op. cit.*, pp. 97–114; for indirect reference to this memorial, see *Ta Ch'ing te-tsung ching-huang-ti shih-lu*, Vol. 517, pp. 6b, 7a.

37 See *Ta Ch'ing te-tsung ching-huang-ti shih-lu* p. 7a.

38 *Ibid.*, Vol. 535, p. 6b.

39 Another prominent overseas Chinese from Hong Kong, Wu T'ing-fang, was appointed to a high position in Ch'ing bureaucracy before Chang. For Wu T'ing-fang's career, see Linda P. Shin, "China in Transition: The Role of Wu T'ing-fang, 1842–1922", an unpublished Ph.D. dissertation, University of California, Los Angeles, 1970; for his diplomatic career and protection of American Chinese, see Yen Ching-hwang, "Wu T'ing-fang and the Protection of the Overseas Chinese in the United States, 1897–1903", Working Paper No. 12, Centre for Asian Studies, University of Adelaide, 1981.

40 See Michael Godley, *op. cit.*, pp. 115–116.
41 *Ibid.*, pp. 116–117, 157.
42 See *Lat Pau* of Singapore of 3 March, 1905 and the *Penang Sin Pao* of 11 March, 1905.
43 See Yen Ching-hwang, *Overseas Chinese and the 1911 Revolution*, pp. 60–65.
44 See *Penang Sin Pao*, 6 December 1905; for the founding of the Penang Chinese Commercial Association, see Cheng Yung-mei, "Pin-chou Chung-hua tsung-shang-hui chan-ch'ien shih-liao" (Historical records of the Penang Chinese Chamber of Commerce before the Second World War), in Liu Wen-ch'i et. al. (eds.), *Pin-chou Chung-hua tsung-shang-hui tsuan-hsi chi-nien t'e-k'an, 1903–1978* (*Souvenir Magazine of Diamond Jubilee Celebration of the Penang Chinese Chamber of Commerce*), Penang, 1978, p. 77.
45 See *Penang Sin Pao*, 6 December 1905.
46 Most leaders of the Association were Straits born and English educated. Their political allegiance tended to be directed to Britain. In addition, some leaders of the Association like Ng Kim Keng were clearly pro-revolutionary. For details, see Cheng Yung-mei, "Historical Records of the Penang Chinese Chamber of Commerce before the Second World War", in Liu Wen-ch'i et. al. (eds), *op. cit.*, pp. 78–79; Yen Ching-hwang, *The Overseas Chinese and the 1911 Revolution*, pp. 99, 229.
47 The official conversion probably took place in January 1907, and it was officially recognized by the Ch'ing government in February 1907. See the memorial of the Shang Pu (Ministry of Commerce) to the Court dated 19th Day of 12th moon of 32nd year of Kuang-hsu (1 February 1907), in *Shang-wu kuan-pao* (*The Gazettes of Commercial Affairs*), Peking, the Ministry of Commerce, original, 1906–1910, Ting-wei year (1907), Vol. 1, pp. 9–10.
48 See Wong Lin Ken, "Singapore: Its Growth as an Entrepot Port, 1819–1941", *Journal of Southeast Asian Studies*, Vol. 9, No. 1, March, 1978, pp. 56–69; Chiang Hai Ding, A History of Straits Settlements Foreign Trade, 1870–1915, Singapore: The National Muscum of Singapore, 1978, pp. 68–83.
49 See C.F. Yong, "Rivalry between the New and Old Chinese Chambers of Commerce: Contending Elites and Power Struggle within the Chinese Community of Singapore, 1912–1914", in C.F. Yong, *Chinese Leadership and Power in Colonial Singapore*, Singapore: Times Academic Press, 1992, p. 26.
50 For a list of early leaders of the Chinese Chamber of Commerce in Singapore, see "Minutes of Committee Meetings of the Singapore Chinese Chamber of Commerce" (manuscript), Vol. 1, 1906–1909, pp. 2–3; for an analysis of the leadership of the Chamber, see Yong Ching Fatt, "A Preliminary Study of Chinese Leadership in Singapore, 1900–1941", *Journal of Southeast Asian History*, Vol. 9, No. 2, September 1968, pp. 271–275, the same article is also published in C.F. Yong, *Chinese Leadership and Power in Colonial Singapore*, pp. 47–81.
51 For British attitude towards Chinese community leaders in Singapore, see C.F. Yong, *Chinese Leadership and Power in Colonial Singapore*, pp. 291–292.
52 See A. Wright & H.A. Cartwright (eds.), *Twentieth Century Impressions of British Malaya*, London, 1908, p. 715; "Ts'ai Tzu-yung hsien-sheng" (Mr Chua Tse Yung), in P'an Hsing-nung (ed.), *Ma-lai-ya Ch'ao-ch'iao t'ung-chien* (*The Teochews in Malaya*), Singapore: Nan-tao ch'u-pan-she, 1950, p. 195.

53 For a short biography of Goh Siew-tin, see "Wu Shou-chen hsien-sheng" (Mr. Goh Siew-tin), in Su Hsiao-hsien (ed.), *Chang-chou shih-shu lu Hsing t'ung-hsiang lu* (*A Directory of Chang Chou Chinese in Singapore*), Singapore: Ch'iao-k'uang ch'u-pan-she, 1948, p. 59; Yen Ching-hwang, *The Overseas Chinese and the 1911 Revolution*, pp. 273–274; Song Ong Siang, *One Hundred Years History of the Chinese in Singapore*, Singapore: University of Malaya Press, 1967, p. 144.

54 For details about the Lo Shan She Lecture movement, see Yen Ching–hwang, "Overseas Chinese Nationalism in Singapore and Malaya, 1877–1912", *Modern Asian Studies*, Vol. 16, No. 3, July 1982, pp. 399–405; for details of the Confucian Revival movement, see Yen Ching-hwang, "The Confucian Revival Movement in Singapore and Malaya, 1899–1911", *Journal of Southeast Asian Studies*, Vol. 7, No. 1, March 1976, pp. 33–57.

55 For a study of this group, see Yen Ching-hwang, *A Social History of the Chinese in Singapore and Malaya, 1800–1911*, Singapore: Oxford University Press, 1986, pp. 189–190.

56 For a discussion of the power relations in the Teochew community in Singapore at this time, see Yen Ching-hwang, "Power Structure and Power Relations in the Teochew Community in Singapore, 1819–1930", A paper presented at the International Conference on Teochew Studies, held at the Chinese University of Hong Kong, 20–22 December 1993, pp. 28–29.

57 See "Minutes of Committee Meetings of the Singapore Chinese Chamber of Commerce" (manuscript), Vol. 1, 1906–1909, pp. 2–3.

58 Goh Siew-tin acquired a Ch'ing brevet title, *Chih-fu* in1902. In the same year, he was appointed as Acting Chinese Consul-General for the Straits Settlements from January to May. See Yen Ching-hwang, trans. by Chang Ch'ing-chiang, "Ch'ing-ch'ao tsu-kuan chih-tu yu Hsin-Ma hua-tsu ling-tao-ch'en, 1877–1912" (Ch'ing Sale of Honours and the Chinese Leadership in Singapore and Malaya 1877–1912), Appendix 1, in K'o Mu-lin & Wu Chen-ch'iang (eds.), *Hsin-chia-po hua-tsu shih lun-chi* (*Papers on the Chinese in Singapore*), p. 71, the article also published in Yen Ching-hwang, *H'ai-wai hua-jen shih yen-chiu* (*Studies in Overseas Chinese History*), Singapore: Singapore Society of Asian Studies, 1992, pp. 3–43; *Thien Nan Shin Pao*, 22 January 1902, pp. 1–2, 1 May 1902, p. 2, 2 May 1902, p. 7, 4 June 1902, p. 1.

59 See "Minutes of Committee Meetings of the Singapore Chinese Chamber of Commerce" (manuscript), Vol. 1, 1906–1909, p. 1.

60 See Tan Yeok Seong, "Tso Tzu-hsing (Tso Ping-lung) ling-shih tui Hsin-chia-po hua-ch'iao te kung-hsien" (The Contribution of Consul Tso Ping-lung to the Overseas Chinese in Singapore), in Tso Ping-lung, *Ch'in-mien-t'ang shih-ch'ao* (*The Collection of Poems from the Ch'in-mien Hall*), Hong Kong, 1959, pp. 3–4; Chen Mong Hock, *The Early Chinese Newspapers of Singapore, 1881–1912*, Singapore: University of Malaya Press, 1967, pp. 115–121; Yen Ching-hwang, *Coolies and Mandarins: China's Protection of Overseas Chinese during the Late Ch'ing Period, 1851–1911*, pp. 253–266; Cheng H'ai-lin, *Huang Tsun-hsien yu chin-tai Chung-kuo* (*Huang Tsun-hsien and Modern China*), Beijing: San-lien shu-tien, 1988, pp. 369–376.

61 See Yen Ching-hwang, *A Social History of the Chinese in Singapore and Malaya, 1800–1911*, pp. 288–291.

62 See "Minutes of Committee Meetings of the Singapore Chinese Chamber of Commerce" (manuscript), Vol. 1, 1906–1909, p. 13.

63 *Ibid.*

64 See "Shang-hui pu-kao" (A public notice of the Chinese Chamber of Commerce dated 29th day of leap 4th moon of 32nd year of Kuang-hsu), in *Lat Pau*, 2 June 1906, p. 1.

65 See "Minutes of Committee Meetings of the Singapore Chinese Chamber of Commerce" (manuscript) Vol. 1, 1906–1909, pp. 19–20.

66 See Chui Kuei-ch'iang, "wan Ch'ing kuan-li fang-wen Hsin-chia-po" (The visits of Ch'ing dignitaries to Singapore during the late Ch'ing period), in Chui Kuei-ch'iang, *Hsing-Ma shih lun-ts'ung* (*Essays on the History of Singapore and Malaysia*), Singapore: South Seas Society, 1977, p. 93.

67 See *Lat Pau*, 3 July 1906, 4 July 1906.

68 See "Minutes of Committee Meetings of the Singapore Chinese Chamber of Commerce" (manuscript), Vol. 1, 1906–1909, p. 25.

69 *Ibid.*, p. 23.

70 See "Hsing-chia-po Chung-hua tsung-shang-hui shih-chi" (Historical Records of the Singapore Chinese Chamber of Commerce), in *Hsin-chia-po Chung-hua tsung-shang-hui ch'i-shih-wu chou-nien chi-nien t'e-k'an* (*Souvenir Magazine of 75th Anniversary Celebration of the Singapore Chinese Chamber of Commerce*) Singapore, 1982, pp. 57–59.

71 See "Minutes of Committee Meetings of the Singapore Chinese Chamber of Commerce" (manuscript), Vol. 1, 1906–1909, p. 30; "Hsing-chia-po Chung-hua tsung-shang-hui shih-chi", *Souvenir of the Opening Ceremony of the Newly Completed Singapore Chinese Chamber of Commerce Building*, p. 150.

72 Yeoh Chan Boon, a junior director of the Chamber, recalled this event 50 years later. Yeoh recorded wrongly the date of conducting the ceremony as 15 March of 1906, and claimed that date was therefore taken by the Chamber as its inauguration date. See Yeoh Chan Boon, recorded by Liu T'ien-feng, "Chung-hua tsung-shang-hui ch'ang-shang shih", *Souvenir of the Opening Ceremony of the Newly Completed Singapore Chinese Chamber of Commerce Building*, pp. 145-146; "Minutes of Committee Meetings of the Singapore Chinese Chamber of Commerce", (manuscript), Vol. 1, 1906–1909, p. 30.

73 For overseas Chinese desire for Ch'ing honours and the impact of the purchase of Ch'ing titles on overseas Chinese leadership, see Yen Ching-hwang, "Ch'ing's Sale of Honours and the Chinese Leadership in Singapore and Malaya, 1877–1912", *Journal of Southeast Asian Studies*, Vol. 1, No. 2, September, 1970, pp. 20–32.

74 The granting of this "commercial certificate" was initiated by the Singapore Chinese Chamber of Commerce. The original idea was to request the right for the Chamber to issue "Hu-Chao" (visa), but later the name was changed to "Shang-chao". See "Minutes of Committee Meetings of the Singapore Chinese Chamber of Commerce" (manuscript), Vol. 1, 1906–1909, pp. 31, 42.

75 No direct documents relating to the granting of this right to the Singapore Chinese Chamber of Commerce have been found. However, rules and regulations governing the issue of the "commercial certificate" by the Chinese Chamber of Commerce of Surabaya which was based on the Singapore model can be found

in the *Shang-wu kuan-pao*, the request by the Surabaya Chinese Chamber of Commerce was approved by the Ministry of Agriculture, Industry and Commerce on 10 April 1908. See "Ssu-shui shang-hui fa ke hui Hua shang-chao chang-ch'eng" (Rules and Regulations for the issue of the commercial certificate by the Chinese Chamber of Commerce of Surabaya), *Shang-wu kuan-pao*, 25th day of 7th moon of 34th year of Kuang-hsu, Vol. 19, pp. 37–38, the special report section; see also the record of official approval of the Ministry on the 10th day of 3rd moon of 34th year of Kuang-hsu (10 April 1908), *Shang-wu kuan-pao*, 25th day of 3rd moon of 34th year of Kuang-hsu, Vol. 7, p. 5.

76 See the advertisement put out by the Chamber dated 1st day of 8th moon of the first year of Hsuan-t'ung (14 September 1909), *Lat Pau*, 14 September 1909, p. 6, 16 September 1909, p. 13; "Minutes of Committee Meetings of the Singapore Chinese Chamber of Commerce" (manuscript), Vol. 1, 1906–1909, p. 169; for the event and significance of the Nanyang Fair of 1910, see Michael Godley, "China's World's Fair of 1910: Lessons from a Forgotten Event", *Modern Asian Studies* Vol. 12 , 1978, pp. 503–522.

77 Twelve leaders were elected from various dialect groups for the purpose. To push the sale of shares along the dialect line was the most effective way of doing business at the time. See "Minutes of Committee Meetings of the Singapore Chinese Chamber of Commerce" (manuscript), Vol. 1, 1906–1909, p. 31; Michael Godley, *The Mandarin-capitalists from Nanyang*, p. 127.

78 See "Minutes of Committee Meetings of the Singapore Chinese Chamber of Commerce" (manuscript), Vol. 1, 1906–1909, p. 172.

79 See letter from the Chinese Chamber of Commerce of Shanghai to the Singapore Chinese Chamber of Commerce published in *Chong Shing Yit Pao* on 2 October 1907, p. 6.

80 See Rules and Regulations of the Proposed China Commercial Bank, published in *Chong Shing Yit Pao* on 7 October 1907, p. 6.

81 See Rules and Regulations of the Proposed China Commercial Bank, published in *Chong Shing Yit Pao* on 8 October, 1907, p. 6.

82 In addition, Foo Chee Choon of Perak, Loke Yew of Kuala Lumpur, and Wong Ah-fook (Huang P'u-t'ien) of Johore Bahru, were named to represent British colonies in South-east Asia. See *Chong Shing Yit Pao*, 5 October 1907, p. 6.

83 See the notice for floating the shares for the proposed bank put out by the Singapore Chinese Chamber of Commerce, *Chong Shing Yit Pao*, 2 October 1907, p. 6.

84 See "Minutes of Committee Meetings of the Chinese Chamber of Commerce" (manuscript), Vol. 1, 1906–1909, p. 110.

85 *Ibid.*, p. 112.

86 See a report on the founding of the proposed Chinese commercial bank, *Nanyang Tsung-hui Hsin Pao* (*The Union Times*), 24 September 1908, p. 1.

87 See "Minutes of Committee Meetings of the Singapore Chinese Chamber of Commerce" (manuscript), Vol. 1, 1906–1909, pp. 156, 177, Vol. 2, 1909–1912, pp. 22, 79.

88 See the public notice of the Singapore Chinese Chamber of Commerce dated 7th day of 11th moon of the 34th year of Kuang-hsu (30 November 1908), *Lat Pau*, 1 December 1908, p. 8.

89 See a report of this function in *Lat Pau*, 3 December 1908, p. 3.
90 See *Lat Pau*, 18 November 1908, p. 8, 20 November 1908, p. 3.
91 See Yen Ching-hwang, *The Overseas Chinese and the 1911 Revolution*, pp. 100–127.
92 Checking through the *Chong Shing Yit Pao* and *The Sun Pao*, the two main revolutionary newspapers in Singapore during this period, there were hardly any attacks directly aimed at the Chinese Chamber of Commerce. In fact, the *Chong Shing Yit Pao* on some occasions even published the Chamber's economic involvement in Ch'ing China. For instance, it published the Chamber's public notice for the floating of shares for the proposed China Commercial Bank and its rules and regulations. See *Chong Shing Yit Pao*, 2 October 1907, p. 6, 5 October 1907, p. 6, 7 October 1907, p. 6, 8 October 1907, p. 6.
93 Goh Siew-tin died on 25th day of 12th moon of Wu Shen year (16 January 1909), Goh had been the president (*Tsung-li*) of the Chamber since its inception. See "Minutes of Committee Meetings of the Chinese Chamber of Commerce" (manuscript), Vol. 1, 1906–1909, p. 122.
94 Checking through the records of the Chamber during this period, local issues appeared to have dominated the agenda of the Chamber meetings. See "Minutes of Committee Meetings of the Chinese Chamber of Commerce" (manuscript), Vol. 1, 1906–1909, Vol. 2, 1909–1912.

Appendix 7.1

Glossary

Ch'ang Ch'un 长春
Chang Ch'ing-chiang 张清江
Chang P'eng-yuan 张朋园
Chang Pi-shih 张弼士
Ch'ao-chang 曹长
Cheng H'ai-lin 郑海麟
Cheng Yung-mei 郑永美
Ch'ien Hsiao-ming 钱小明
Chih-fu title 知府衔
Chao Ch'ung-fan 赵从蕃
Chong Shing Yit Pao 中兴日报
Chu Shou-p'eng 朱寿朋
Chua Tse Yung 蔡子庸
Chuang Kuo-t'u 庄国土
Chueh 阙
Chui Kuei-ch'iang 崔贵强
Chung-kuo Hua shang yin-h'ang 中国华商银行
Confucian Revival movement 孔教复兴运动
Emperor Kuang-hsu 光绪皇帝
Empress Dowager Tz'u-hsi 慈禧太后
Feng Tzu-yu 冯自由
Foo Chee Choon 胡子春
Fung Edmund S.K. 冯兆基
Goh Siew-tin 吴寿珍
Hsu Ching-ming 徐经明
Hsu Ting-hsin 徐鼎新
Hsieh Fu-Ch'eng 薛福成
Hsiehli 协理
Hsuan-t'ung 宣统
Hu-chao 护照
Hua-shang kung-so 华商公所
Huang Tsun-hsien 黄遵宪
Hupei Rug Company 湖北毡年公司
K'ang Yu-wei 康有为
K'o Mu-lin (Kwa Bak Lim) 柯木林
Kuan-ch'a 观察
Kuan-fang 关防
Kuang-hsu 光绪
Kuang-hsu reign 光绪朝
Lat Pau 叻报
Lee Cheng-yan 李清渊
Li Hung-chang 李鸿章
Liang Ch'i-ch'ao 梁启超
Liao Cheng-hsing 廖正兴
Lim Boon Keng (Dr) 林文庆医生
Lin Chu-tsai 林竹斋
Lim Kiek Chuan 林克全
Liu T'ien-feng 刘天凤
Liu Wen-ch'i 刘问渠
Lo Chung-yao 罗忠尧
Lo Feng-lu 罗丰禄
Lo Shan She Lecture 乐善社讲演
Loke Yew 陆佑
Ma Po-huang 马伯煌
Ministry of Commerce 商部
Nanyang Tsung-hui
  Hsin Pao (The Union Times) 南洋总汇新报
Ng Kim Keng 黄金庆
Ngee Ann Kongsi 义安公司
Nung-kung-shang pu 农工商部
P'an Hsing-nung 潘醒农
P'an Yu 番禺
Pang 帮
Penang Sin Pao 槟城新报
Pin-lang-yu Chung-hua
  shang-wu tsung-hui 槟榔屿中华商务总会
Pin-lang-yu shang-wu ch'u 槟榔屿商务处
Ping Wu year 丙午年
Po Leung Kuk 保良局
Prince Tsun 洵亲王
San-pin Ching-t'ang hou-pu 三品京堂後补
Seah family 佘氏家族
Seah Liang Seah 佘连城
Shang-chao 商照

Shang Ch'i-h'eng 尚其亨
Shang-tung 商董
Shang-wu kuan-pao 商务官报
Sheng Hsuan-huai 盛宣怀
Shih Ch'u-ch'inh 时楚卿
Singapore Chinese Chamber
of Commerce 新加坡中华商务总会
Song Ong Siang 宋旺相
Su Hsiao-hsien 苏孝先
Sun Shih-ting 孙士鼎
Sun Yat-sen 孙逸仙
Surabaya 泗水
T'ai-p'u 太仆
Tan Hun Chiu 陈云秋
Taotai 道台
T'ang T'sai-ch'ang 唐才常
Teo Sian Keng 张善庆
Teochew 潮州
The Sun Pao 晨报
Thein Nan Shin Pao 天南新报
Thong Chai Medical
Institution 同济医院
T'i-ch'ang Tung-shih 提倡董事
Ting Wen-chiang 丁文江
Ting-wei year 丁未年
Tsai Tse 戴泽
Tso Ping-lung 左秉隆
Tsung-li 总理
Tz'u-hsi 慈禧
Tz'u-wen 咨文
Waichow 惠州
Wang Ta-chen 王大贞
Wong Ah-fook
(Huang P'u-t'ien) 黄亚福（黄莆田）
Wong Lin Ken 黄麟根
Wu Chen-ch'iang
(Ng Chin Keong) 吴振强
Wu T'ing-fang 伍廷芳
Yang Shih-ch'i 杨士琦
Yen, Ching-hwang 颜清湟
Yeoh Chan Boon
(Yang Chan-wen) 杨瓒文
Yong, C.F. 杨进发
Yong Ching Fatt 杨进发
Yuan 圆

8

The Founding of the PRC and the Economic Concerns of Singapore Chinese Entrepreneurs

Huang Jianli

The Cold War milieu of international relations and political economy which affected practically every nation on earth until the recent collapse of the Soviet Union had its origins partly in the communist ascendancy of power in China in 1949. The victory of the Chinese Communists over Chiang Kai-shek's Kuomintang was the climax of a long struggle for political power since the late 1920s. The final stage was played out over the battlefields vacated by the Japanese invaders after 1945. The best of Chiang's forces were annihilated in three large-scale military campaigns in North China and his last major line of defence along the Yangtze River collapsed in April 1949. On 1 October, Mao Tse-tung mounted the rostrum at Tiananmen Square to proclaim the founding of the People's Republic of China (PRC), even before Chiang's forces were totally pushed out of mainland China. For the overseas Chinese community, this change in government was driven home in no uncertain terms when Canton, Amoy and Swatow, the three traditional Chinese ports of departure for most of them, fell under communist control by the third week of October.

The end of the decade of the 1940s was therefore an eventful one for Chinese entrepreneurs in Singapore. China was the birthplace for many of them and a country which they still have business dealings with, especially for those involved in trading. The economy of Singapore at that point in time was after all essentially based upon entrepot trade, the import and re-export of goods through a middleman with little or no processing. Industrialization was then at an infant stage, with the manufacturing sector contributing only 16.48% of the employment in 1947. Commerce, on the other hand, directly contributed about 23.23% of the jobs in Singapore, while the trade-related "transport, storage and communication" sector provided 14.82%.[1] Hence, most of the Chinese entrepreneurs whom we are referring to were traders rather than industrialists, although the exact proportion of each has never been ascertained.

This paper therefore proposes to examine the economic concerns of Singapore's Chinese businessmen during the months from October 1949 to the eve of the Korean War when the business environment within which they operated took another dramatic turn. It can be shown that the mental horizons of Singapore Chinese entrepreneurs at this point of time was not just primarily locked on to the 1949 Chinese Communist takeover. They were equally worried, if not more, about some other concurrent issues. By charting their economic concerns at the turn of the decade, we will have a firmer grasp of the mentality of a group of people who played an important role in Singapore's economy and who were poised to make new fortunes during the Korean War boom. This historical investigation of their economic concerns will allow us to make further comments on issues such as the overseas Chinese identity as well as the evolution of Chinese entrepreneurship in Singapore.

The Founding of the PRC

Due to the fact that Singapore Chinese businessmen had usually celebrated the Double Tenth (outbreak of the Republican Revolution against the Ch'ing dynasty on 10 October 1911) as well as Sun Yat-sen's birthday on 12 November, the issue of political affiliation was literally thrust upon them in October 1949 as the first PRC-related problem which they had to tackle. If they had a choice, they would probably have adopted a wait-and-see attitude and held back from any comment or action until the dust of the civil war had settled. But they were swept along by the rapid flow of events and forced to make a stand quickly. Their reactions reflected disunity and indecisiveness within the ranks. The Singapore Chinese Chamber of Commerce (SCCC) which had the reputation of being "conservative" and mainly comprised of "satisfied" and "have" people,[2] had difficulty coming to a consensus. In fact, as a result of the tension caused by the Chinese civil war, the SCCC was by then split into three factions: the pro-KMT conservatives, the leftist sympathizers, and the neutral bystanders.[3] In response to this latest development, the SCCC had to take a majority vote against sending a congratulatory cable message to any Chinese authority but yet simultaneously decided in favour of proceeding to celebrate the occasion of Double Tenth with a cocktail party during which the Kuomintang's flag would be displayed and its Consul-General in Singapore invited.[4] The Singapore Hokkien Association broke rank by holding separate commemorations and dispatching on that day two telegrams urging the Kuomintang leaders to "retire from Chinese state affairs" and pledging their support for Mao's new PRC government.[5] Two months later, it collaborated with the Singapore Kwangtung Association to cable President Truman of the United States to "cease giving any moral and physical aid to those persons claiming authority at Taiwan."[6]

In March 1950, responding to an initiative from businessmen in Hong Kong, these two organizations together with the Kiung Chow Association, Khek Association and Sam Kiang Association dispatched telegrams condemning Chiang Kai-shek for sending aeroplanes from Taiwan to bomb the coastal provinces of mainland China. The SCCC which was also invited to respond in a similar fashion agonized over this issue. When a vote had to be taken at the directorate meeting, it was a tie with nine votes in favour of the dispatch and nine against. The Chairman Tan Lark Sye then decided to end the discussion on this inconclusive note.[7] Such disunity and indecision was a reflection of the difficult choice every overseas Chinese had to make in terms of their own personal political sympathy for the two respective antagonists. However, for those businessmen whose political sentiments were inclined towards the Kuomintang, their decision had probably been made more difficult by the economic attractions of a new stable regime governing a mainland China of more than half a billion people.

Indeed, there were high economic expectations and some early rewards for Singapore as the PRC tightened its grip over China. The trade with China had taken a heavy beating when full-scale military clashes between the Chinese Communists and the Kuomintang first extended into the Yangtze delta and southern provinces of China from mid-1949.[8] But as the situation stabilized towards the end of the year, with the official founding of the PRC, Singapore entrepreneurs were generally flushed with optimism. The naval blockade which the Kuomintang had mounted against the major southern Chinese ports was proving to be increasingly ineffective, especially when the quality of the Kuomintang navy was suspect after its defeat during the defence of the Yangtze River and when the British Royal Navy was rather forthright in protecting British trading vessels running against the blockade.[9] By November, Hong Kong had re-established some trading links with Canton and other Chinese ports and its merchants were reportedly buying exceptional quantities of fruits, dried fish and shrimp, timber, firewood, coconut oil and soap from Singapore, thus pushing up the prices of some items by as much as

25% a week.[10] A substantial portion of these goods was meant for consumption by Hong Kong's own exploding refugee population and the extra British garrison troops, but some were routed to China. Moreover, the Communists were already reviving some of the production lines in cities they had captured, and Shanghainese manufactured goods, such as textiles, aluminium and hot water bottles, were beginning to make their way into Southeast Asia through Hong Kong.[11] With some PRC ports reported to be piling high with goods, Singapore businessmen were looking forward eagerly to and planning for the resumption of direct passenger and cargo service between China and Southeast Asia.[12]

This early optimism, however, could not be sustained. As Table 8.1 below indicates, it took a much longer while for cargo shipping links with China to be re-established. The drastic drop of shipping tonnage from October 1949 continued right into February 1950. A spurt of goods from China came in March 1950, signalling the resumption of direct trade and shipping linkages. However, these ships passing through in March were hardly picking up anything from Singapore and the Federation of Malaya for forwarding to China. A pattern of stable trading was achieved for the following three months from April to June but the volume of incoming and outgoing tonnage never recovered and was only about half to two-thirds of the pre-October 1949 average figures. The eruption of the Korean War in June 1950 boosted the exchanges and these reached a peak in September before they suffered another dramatic plunge with China's direct involvement in the war from December 1950.

Apart from the problem of waiting for a greater number of ships to ply directly between China and Singapore, the Chinese entrepreneurs in the colony were also hampered by their own political caution. Caught in the midst of a communist insurgency campaign fought primarily in the jungles of the Federation of Malaya, their eagerness to seek economic opportunities with the emergence of a new China was heavily dampened by the worry of being associated with anything communist. For example, Lee Rubber Company was one Chinese firm which attempted to resume business dealings with China after the communist takeover. By July 1950 it had sold about 3,000 tons of rubber to the North China Import Corporation at Tientsin. In anticipation of an expansion of business in the future, it approached the British authorities cautiously for permission to send a representative to Tientsin to "set up the machinery for the establish[ment] of terms, conditions of payment, arbitration and other administrative procedures". Due to incomplete documentation, we do not know the exact outcome of this application. But an internal memorandum in the British administration in

Table 8.1: Net Tonnage of Merchant Vessels with Cargo Which Entered from or Cleared for China into and from Singapore/Federation of Malaya

	CHINA	
	Entered	Cleared
1948	**700,471**	**649,707**
1949	**378,063**	**331,080**
January	60,554	47,420
February	39,153	32,598
March	46,582	52,720
April	40,938	36,711
May	56,278	32,906
June	33,896	33,141
July	25,925	25,442
August	26,964	27,174
September	24,610	30,430
October	16,585	8,412
November	1,684	2,080
December	4,894	2,046
1950	**304,195**	**187,817**
January	1,423	5,008
February	3,291	–
March	36,324	2,080
April	16,280	10,965
May	12,138	15,596
June	18,189	15,506
July	28,728	5,189
August	33,561	11,079
September	76,565	50,946
October	25,975	23,500
November	31,760	27,075
December	19,961	20,873

Source: Data extracted from *Colony of Singapore Government Gazette*, 18 March 1949, p. 409; 24 March 1950, p. 423; 2 March 1951, p. 371. These merchant vessels had a minimum net tonnage (with cargo) of 75 tons net register.

response to this request fully justified the caution exercised by Lee Rubber. It noted that "Trade with Communist China [was] still permitted and there [was] thus no economic reason for refusing the facilities asked for ... I agree[d], however, that the facilities should not be given to any person, but only to those who [were] not likely to 'fall' for propaganda while in China. The Special Branch should be considered."[13]

Another example of a business response being held back by political caution was that of Tan Keong Choon who reportedly had become the number one exporter of goods from Singapore to Shanghai during the civil war period until the Communist takeover of the city in May 1949. It was this reputation that led the new People's Republic of China to approach and ask him to resume his trade with Shanghai in early 1950. Tan was excited but his excitement was tempered with caution. He sought advice from his mentor Lee Kong Chien. In the end, he not only wrote to the Trade Department to request permission but, "fearful that any political problem might arise", also took the significant step of applying for "permanent residence in Singapore". It seems that this was one case of "Malayanization" driven as much by immediate economic considerations as by the long term evolution of socio-political attachment to the place of residence. It was only in December 1950, at the height of the Korean War, that he managed to make his way to China. Despite the situation being "very tense", he succeeded in securing some business contracts. But this success proved to be short-lived as the British acting in concert with the United Nations imposed an embargo on the export of rubber to China in 1951 and later extended it to cover other sensitive materials. The embargo was lifted only in 1956 and, in that same year, Tan promptly joined a Singapore Chinese Chamber of Commerce delegation to promote trade with the PRC.[14] That development from the mid-1950s constitutes another story to be told.

In 1949, the spotlight was on Hong Kong. That sleepy British possession became, almost overnight, the critical economic frontier post between the new mainland Communist China and the outside world. At that point in time, like many others, the Singapore entrepreneurs had their eyes on Hong Kong, watching carefully the latter's every contact with its giant neighbour and assessing their own opportunities for economic penetration. In historical and social science analysis, Hong Kong often presents an interesting comparison with Singapore. Hong Kong's rapid transformation from a sleepy backwater town to a vibrant industrialized and export-oriented colony was greatly assisted by the substantial 1949 refugee influx of mainland Chinese (especially Shanghainese) entrepreneurs who brought along their skilled and semi-skilled labourers as well as capital.

From the low of 600,000 people in 1945, Hong Kong's population had increased suddenly to over two million by 1951.[15] Most of the Chinese refugees were not rural peasants. Instead they came mainly from urban areas where they had been soldiers and policemen, professionals and intellectuals, as well as clerks and shop assistants. About 5% of them were identified as businessmen and another 3% as industrial labourers.[16] Many of these businessmen had in fact brought along their own experienced foremen and skilled workers, arriving together in planes chartered by the companies or having travelled *en bloc* overland. At a time when experienced skilled workers were scarce in the colony, these refugee employees came to play a crucial role by helping their bosses start production almost immediately and by training the subsequent batches of skilled hands.[17] The migrating economic elite had also brought along a dramatic infusion of capital into Hong Kong. It was estimated that nearly four to five billion Hong Kong dollars were transferred from China to Hong Kong between mid-1946 and late 1948. The climax of capital flight came with the Communist victory in late 1949 and the total funds entering Hong Kong in the following year were reported to be not less than one billion Hong Kong dollars (an equivalent of about £62.5 million at the current exchange rate of 1:16)[18]

Much of this influx of entrepreneurs, skilled labourers and capital into Hong Kong was generated by push factors closely related to the Chinese civil war. But the Hong Kong colonial government was not sitting about in idleness, it tried its best to be hospitable to the immigrant entrepreneurs.[19] Company laws were amended in 1949 to enable them to acquire immovable property with considerably less red-tape. In the same year, the Import and Export Department was overhauled to form the Department of Commerce and Industry and a new senior staff was appointed to "devote his full time to the encouragement of new industries and the expansion of existing ones" as well as "to advise potential industrialists on factory sites and allied questions". The government also deliberately made available industrial land with an initial lease of about 20 years at a price much cheaper than that of the current market rate. Apparently at the request of the incoming industrialists, the colonial authorities even amended labour legislations to relax the prohibition of women and children working on night shifts.

What about Singapore? Did any of these fleeing entrepreneurs, skilled labourers and "hot" capital find refuge in Singapore in significant quantity? What was the exact impact of the Chinese Communist takeover on the two key factors of production (labour and capital) in the Singapore economy? What in particular caused concern among the local business community? The following discussion on migration, capital movement and overseas Chinese remittances will provide some answers.

Singapore's population as at 31 December 1949 was estimated to be 998,436 of which 774,898 (77.61%) were Chinese.[20] Reflecting the shift from being just sojourners to permanent settlers in Singapore, it was gauged that the share of Straits-born Chinese towards the end of 1949 was already about 66% of the entire Chinese population.[21] In anticipation of high birth rates among the local Chinese population and concerned about problems of housing, employment, food, education and social order, the British colonial authorities had restricted Chinese immigration into Singapore from as early as 1930.[22] In 1949, the security scare of the ongoing communist insurgency in the Malayan peninsula and the current economic recession gave British administrators little grounds to change the existing laws to allow for an influx of refugees from China. But pressure to do so was building up from within the Chinese community. Letters to the authorities and newspapers all urging for a more relaxed or flexible approach towards immigration were evident from the middle of 1949.[23] Lee Kong Chien, for example, made a personal plea on the basis that previous Chinese immigrants had contributed significantly to the economic well-being of the colony.[24] Confronted by these demands, the colonial administration found it necessary to resuscitate the Chinese Advisory Board so as "to assist the Chinese Secretariat in the maintenance of a closer liaison between Government and the Chinese population of the Colony."[25] On 17 September 1949, a special "Immigration Advisory Committee" was also formed to deliberate on appeal cases "which the Immigration Department [could not] decide".[26]

Significantly, all these demands for the admission of more Chinese focused solely on compassionate grounds, especially on parents, children, brothers and sisters of migrants who were already in Singapore. This was in spite of the fact that existing immigration laws also clearly waived restrictions on the admission of "professional and businessmen whose entry [was] to the benefit of the Colony" and "skilled workmen who [could not] be recruited locally".[27] Both the British authorities and local Chinese elites were aware of this special provision. Yet neither party displayed the slightest interest in taking advantage of the ongoing flight of talent and wealth from China. Aw Boon Haw, whose business interest spanned Singapore, Hong Kong and China, spurned a Communist China demand for loan and flew to Singapore on 19 December 1949.[28] But many Shanghainese and Cantonese "Aw's" who were flocking to safe havens were never actively encouraged to come to Singapore. No one was interested in targetting them and skilled labourers as special sources of recruitment, although the laws already provided for their admission. The idea of actively enticing such high value refugees was never publicly or privately raised. There was no sucking in of new resources to expand Singapore's capital base and pool of entrepreneurial talent and skilled labour. This could have been partly due to the fear of having a more crowded field of competitors but surely, in doing so, the Singapore entrepreneurs had also passed up a golden opportunity to enhance their economic strength by selective partnership and recruitment.

Table 8.2: Singapore Chinese Adult Male Deck Passengers from and to China and Hong Kong

	ARRIVALS			DEPARTURES			+/-
	China	Hong Kong	Total	China	Hong Kong	Total	
Whole year 1948	25,876	6,566	32,442	19,237	10,154	29,391	
Whole year 1949	19,165	6,656	25,821	15,811	10,915	26,726	
Whole year 1950	5,383	8,570	13,953	8,267	3,983	12,250	
Jan–Jun 1949	11,628	3,166	14,794	11,296	8,560	19,856	
1949							
July	1,640	507	2,147	1,351	503	1,854	+293
August	1,600	771	2,371	1,163	536	1,699	+672
September	1,900	669	2,569	954	579	1,533	+1036
October	941	678	1,619	435	398	833	+786
November	608	331	939	302	190	492	+447
December	848	534	1,382	310	149	459	+923
1950							
January	282	797	1,079	94	316	410	+669
February	112	475	587	190	210	400	+187
March	881	828	1,709	210	215	425	+1284
April	1,243	1,166	2,409	280	266	546	+1863
May	329	754	1,083	328	275	603	+480
June	—	599	599	416	343	759	-160
July	284	978	1,262	428	477	905	+357
August	523	1,078	1,601	1,591	388	1,979	-378
September	844	732	1,576	1,633	282	1,915	-339
October	721	616	1,337	1,202	510	1,712	-375

Source: These data, sometimes with slight variations, are available from various issues of *Colony of Singapore Annual Report*, *Medical Department Annual Report* and *Labour Department Annual Report*. This table, however, is compiled solely from issues of 1949 to 1951 *Colony of Singapore Government Gazette*. Figures presented here are strictly for Singapore, excluding the Federation of Malaya and "adult males" refers to all men above the age of 12.

In contrast to the massive influx of refugees into Hong Kong when the PRC was founded, the migratory intake of Singapore was almost insignificant. This was especially so for adult male migrants, the category in which entrepreneurs and skilled labourers would most likely be coming from.

Table 8.2 focuses on Chinese adult male deck passengers moving between Singapore and China/Hong Kong by ships, the major form of transportation for most travellers at that time. Hong Kong should be taken into consideration together with China as many were travelling to and from the latter via the former. The table reflects a decline in both arrivals and departures as a result of the political upheaval in China. The surplus of arrivals over departures during the period undertaken by this study was minuscule and clearly there was no sucking in of a significantly wider pool of general adult male refugees from which a good stock of capitalists, skilled and semi-skilled labourers could have been drawn.

New visa regulations for entry into Hong Kong was one issue related to this migratory flow which loomed large in the minds of the Singapore entrepreneurs.[29] In early November 1949, primarily because of the heavy and sudden influx of refugee population, the Hong Kong colonial government introduced laws requiring all visitors to have guaranteed accommodation before issuing a visa for their entry. As noted, there were hundreds who were still leaving Singapore for China and Hong Kong every month. With China in chaos, most would usually languish temporarily in Hong Kong while waiting for transit to the mainland. Only a minority of these travellers from Singapore and the Malayan Federation were merchants "going back for fortunes". Most were said to be "labour or peasant classes people" returning to their homes in China and who had "no acquaintance in Hong Kong" and very concerned about keeping food and accommodation cheap.[30] The new passport procedure of securing lodging guarantee before their arrival in Hong Kong was regarded as a costly and lengthy process for Chinese travellers. And if they were to give up their travel plans, dreams of family reunions would be shattered and the lodging, shipping and travel businesses would be badly hit. It was with these compassionate and economic considerations in mind that the Singapore Chinese Lodging Houses Association spearheaded a campaign to protest against this regulation and propose a security bond system put up by lodging housekeepers to act as guarantees for accommodation. Steamship and travel agencies were goaded into action and the President of Singapore Chinese Chamber of Commerce, Yong Yit Lin, lent support by publicly declaring that he was "extremely interested in the hardship experienced by travellers to China".[31] On the British side, the Secretary for Chinese Affairs, the Chinese Advisory Board and the Controller of Immigration were all dragged into this matter. Eventually these British authorities wriggled out of this public outcry in the classic way of "passing the buck": they decided that nothing could be done at the Singapore end since this was a Hong Kong measure and that the only course of action was for the Hong Kong lodging associations to appeal to their government.[32] This advice was followed, the Hong Kong counterparts managed to put in place a surety arrangement and the whole issue died a natural death in the early months of 1950.

In terms of capital movement, Singapore was also hardly able to benefit from the political crisis in China. There were occasional allegations such as Hong Kong gold flooding into Singapore.[33] But these could not be substantiated as nothing of significance was registered by the Board of Commissioners of Currency for 1949. For the following year of 1950, it reported that currency in circulation increased dramatically by 54% but no mention was made of any major influx of foreign capital. Instead, it attributed the increase to the rising prices of local commodity trade and the local and foreign hoarding of Malayan currency because of its stability.[34] The Registrar of Companies also did not report any unusual business activities. For 1949 and 1950, only three and six Hong Kong companies were set up respectively. As for local limited companies (both privately and publicly listed), figures for the five years from 1946 to 1950 were equally bland: 114, 183, 126, 111 and 125.[35]

Akin to the human migratory pattern, there was also a danger of capital outflow. The ending of the Chinese civil war brought about the anticipation of a new era of stable political and social environment for economic development on both sides of the Straits of Taiwan. Mao Tse-tung was a committed socialist but he had also ridden to power by occasionally soft-selling himself as a social reformist who could accommodate at least temporarily the "nationalist bourgeoisie". For those capitalists who suffered from a natural aversion to Marxism-Leninism, Chiang Kai-shek's Taiwan provided an attractive alternative. Therefore, not surprisingly, upbeat articles discussing the prospects of opening or expanding businesses in mainland China and Taiwan featured prominently in Singapore Chinese newspapers.[36] Whether they succeeded in attracting a capital outflow from Singapore in the long run is a separate development to be tracked. As of February 1950, the colonial administration was happy to declare that "so far as the government [was] aware, it [was] not a fact that a colossal, or indeed any unusual amount of capital [was] going out of this country."[37]

A major preoccupation of the Singapore entrepreneur's mindset at the turn of this decade was in fact the tight British control over the outflow of capital. This issue first exploded somewhat mischievously under the partial cover of humanitarian concern over the further disruption of overseas Chinese family remittances.[38] Lim Soo Gan, President of the Singapore Hokkien Remittance Association as well as of the larger Nanyang Chinese Exchange and Remittance Association was the key mobilizer of business action and public opinion during this protest.

There were two immediate background developments which triggered this remittance outcry. The first one concerned the extension of the civil war to southern China and thus a further reduction in family remittances. This remittance business which revived and flourished from 1946 to 1948 was only about two-thirds of its pre-Japanese invasion strength and was operating under the uncertainties of a fluid, hyperinflation Chinese economy.[39] The breach of the Yangtze River defence and subsequent Communist troop advancements into Kwangtung and Fukien provinces from mid-1949 further strangulated the flow of remittances. Eventually even the clubbed packet service of the Malayan Postal Service Department which catered exclusively for the transmission of overseas Chinese letters, parcel and family remittances had to be suspended on 20 October 1949.[40]

Secondly, the British colonial authorities who had been tightening their control of foreign exchange related to the remittance business every now and then, found it necessary to launch yet another round of clampdown from September 1949 to ensure the success of a recent devaluation of Sterling currency.[41] Inspectors began making their rounds and checking on business accounts. A number of prominent non-Chinese offenders were brought to trial in October and given heavy jail sentences and monetary fines.[42] More than 500 cases of foreign exchange infringement were reported to be under investigation.[43] An atmosphere of persecution therefore hung in the air. Chinese remittance shops were almost in a state of panic as many of them had been remitting money to China and Hong Kong in Hong Kong dollars. Under their charter of operation, they were only allowed to deal in Sterling area currency or Chinese legal tender, and not Hong Kong dollars, up to a maximum value of 45 Malayan dollars per person per month.[44]

Conveniently marrying these two developments together, Lim Soo Gan and his Nanyang Chinese Exchange and Remittance Association which claimed to represent 160 remittance shops with an employment of over a thousand men, orchestrated a campaign which at times gave the misleading impression that the traditional Chinese practice of remitting money back to their relatives in China was now terminated because of the British tightening their control over foreign exchange. An unidentified local business magnate painted the dire consequence of a severe labour drain if the families of these overseas Chinese labourers were denied the money which was desperately needed to meet the deteriorating conditions caused by the raging civil war.[45] When the

SCCC was first lobbied to lend support to the cause, the entire discussion locked on to this humanitarian angle of hardship suffered by the relatives of overseas Chinese as a result of the disruption of family remittances.[46] Petitions were sent to pressure the colonial government to halt the regulatory harassment, allow remittances in Hong Kong dollars and lift the 45 Malayan dollars limit.

The British authorities were rather annoyed. In confidential memoranda, they noted that Lim himself was under investigation for foreign exchange breaches which were not connected with family remittances but apparently did not proceed to make this public.[47] They only openly denied that there were fresh government measures to ban family remittances and emphasized that other obstacles, such as the breakdown in postal services, were responsible for money not getting through.[48] The Secretary for Chinese Affairs confidently declared at a meeting of the Chinese Advisory Board that "rumours of stoppages of remittances to China were all due to misconception."[49] As far as the substance of the policy of foreign exchange was concerned, the British stood firm. The capping of 45 Malayan dollars per person per month continued unchanged and shops could collect remittances in Hong Kong dollars only if their total sales were covered through authorized banks. The remittance shops themselves were still barred from direct remittance in Hong Kong dollars. This remained a privilege for the banks.[50]

The British authorities also went on the offensive to warn the remittance shops against the deliberate delay of remittances as a means of currency speculation.[51] This had apparently become a widespread practice as a means of taking advantage of the hyperinflation during the civil war in China and the corresponding breathtaking devaluation of the Chinese legal tender. Loo Neng, head of the Hainanese Remittance Shops Association in Singapore, admitted readily to such operations. He was then making enough money from his remittance business to open a profitable emporium on Hainan island.[52] The remittance shops were also put on a defensive posture when accusations surfaced about profiteering and the manipulation of remittance exchange rates offered to the public. Lim Soo Gan had to assemble his business comrades and prepare a painstaking explanation that their remittance charges were higher than the official listed exchange rates because of licence fees, transfer charges, handling cost and a necessary reasonable profit margin.[53]

Anyway, with the British clarification of policy at both the public and private levels, the family remittance business was at last able to get moving again at the beginning of 1950. In an effort to secure funds, the new PRC government also played an active part in facilitating this business by stabilizing its new legal tender, setting up "substantial deposit accounts" and arranging for the service of "fixed amount regular remittance".[54] This resumption of family remittances should not be regarded as an alarming new capital outflow from Singapore. It was merely the continuation of a capital movement which had been around for a long time and had come to be accepted as a common right,[55] despite the fact that it was significant enough to affect the rate of capital accumulation and hindered their business expansion and industrialization prospects.[56]

However, as hinted at earlier, the concern of Singapore entrepreneurs over remittances was not exclusively one of overseas Chinese family allowances. It was closely tied in with the larger issue of resisting the foreign exchange control policy of the British Sterling Areas. While the controversy over family remittances abated rather quickly, the problem of foreign exchange control remained in the forefront of the economic attention of Singapore Chinese businessmen. Indeed this battle against general foreign exchange restriction and two other issues, the East Indies trade and the Second Japan-Sterling Area Trade Pact, together hogged the economic outlook of Singapore Chinese entrepreneurs at the point in time when the PRC was founded.

Concurrent Economic Concerns

Foreign currency control was understandably often an area of major concern for businessmen, especially those involved in the import-export trade. The resumption of normal economic activities at the end of the Second World War amidst the general shortage of goods and currency reserves had necessitated the imposition of various commodity and currency controls. Britain, with its far-flung empire and deep involvement in the war, was one of those countries in the postwar period which had tight financial regulations to protect the value of its Sterling and its United States dollar reserve. However, due to fluctuating economic fortunes, it soon suffered a severe drain of its currency reserve and the subsequent shortage of dollars threatened to constrict further its own economy and that of its Sterling Area domains.

Singapore, whose economy was primarily one of entrepot trade, was among those British domains which were badly hit. By about the middle of 1949, the Singapore business community was already asking the British colonial authorities awkward questions about the costs of foreign exchange control, its adverse effects on Singapore's trade, the impact on domestic prices of rubber and tin, the allocation pattern of scarce dollars and such like. Apparently, the comparative Sterling and hard currency prices of Singapore's goods had reached a level that they were no longer competitive when offered to countries which did not "feel the dollar position so acutely". Its trade was being slowly but steadily diverted to countries which "allowed the operation of free sterling markets".[57] The worldwide Sterling-Dollar Crisis eventually reached such a critical proportion that the British Chancellor of the Exchequer in London had no choice but to devalue the Sterling on 19 September 1949 by as much as 30.5%.[58]

However, this devaluation which took effect two weeks before the founding of the PRC did not really soothe the nerves of the Singapore Chinese entrepreneurs. The strong medicine of a devaluation achieved a positive effect of lowering the relative export prices of goods as well as increasing the volume and total value of Singapore's exports. But the British authorities, in their anxiety to hold firm to the new rate of exchange, also tightened simultaneously their foreign exchange control to prevent abuses and currency reserve linkages. As mentioned, inspectors were sent around to scrutinize account books and, from as early as October, public prosecution of foreign exchange infringements with heavy monetary fines and jail sentences began.[59] The Chinese businessmen were deeply worried and reportedly fell into a state of panic.[60]

Initially, their strategy was to submerge their protests against general foreign exchange control under the financial and humanitarian problem of family remittances being temporarily cut off from southern China. However, as that outcry was steadily diffused, the Chinese entrepreneurs were forced to vent their objections more directly and openly. On 26 January 1950, the Overseas Chinese Import and Export Association and the Nanyang Chinese Exchange and Remittance Association jointly mobilized 18 other business organizations to send a memorandum to the British authorities exhorting them to stop the harassment and prosecution of "several hundreds" of businesses for foreign exchange infringements. The Singapore Chinese Chamber of Commerce also quickly assumed the leadership of this protest movement. From January to April 1950, in addition to discussing this issue in its usual monthly directorate gatherings, the SCCC convened two other special meetings with attendance from a wide range of trade representatives, including those from textile, hardware, construction materials, paint, rubber, sago, tea, sugar, rice, sundry, and remittances.[61]

During these meetings, the current crackdown was roundly condemned as unnecessarily harsh. The strict control over foreign exchange was seen as a step which was throttling entrepot trade and general businesses, thereby turning Singapore into a "waste island". It was unanimously agreed that the SCCC should play the leading role in making direct representation to the British and pressing the government into relaxing its control. It was urged that, if possible, Singapore should be treated on a special trading port basis and be freed from being tied to the Sterling currency scheme. It was also proposed that the British authorities should formally establish a "Foreign Exchange Control Advisory Committee" to facilitate feedback from the business community on the drafting and implementation of financial regulations. The Chinese entrepreneurs had therefore reacted much more vigorously over this issue than the economic problems and prospects brought about by the founding of the PRC. This is perhaps to be expected as currency for transaction was the lifeline of all businesses.

On such complaints, the colonial authorities in Singapore had little room to manoeuvre. Foreign exchange control was one issue which had serious worldwide implications and had always been decided within the highest levels of government in London. In reply to local criticisms, the Singapore colonial administrators could only admit readily that its operation of foreign exchange control had affected the economy adversely, but hoped that this would only be of a short term nature and that the stability ensured by remaining within the Sterling area would be one of lasting benefit. They did not respond directly to the 26 January petition from the 20 merchant associations but met with the SCCC representatives to listen to their grouses. Nothing else was offered apart from a pair of listening ears. Even the proposal on forming an advisory committee for matters related to foreign exchange was firmly turned down.[62] Indeed, the whole issue remained unresolved within the period undertaken by this study. In as late as August 1950, the SCCC established yet another sub-committee to study further the impact of foreign exchange control on trade so as to forward more opinions to the British authorities.[63]

Another prominent feature in the economic horizon of Singapore's businesses at the end of the 1940s and the beginning of the next decade was the trade with the islands of East Indies. Coincidentally, the revolutionary change of government in China was paralleled by almost similar developments in Indonesia. Having been given an opportunity to grow during the Japanese Occupation, the Sukarno and Hatta-led Indonesian nationalists resisted the re-imposition of Dutch colonial rule over the East Indies. A full-scale civil war broke out between the Dutch and Indonesian nationalists in 1946 and this ended only in 1949. Giving in to the high cost of war and the rising tide of decolonization across the world, the Netherlands settled for a peace accord and graceful retreat. Sovereignty was returned to the Indonesians and their national flag was hoisted on 28 December 1949.

Singapore's trade with Indonesia was deemed to be in a bad shape in 1949. This was partly because the Singapore Chinese entrepreneurs had been spectacularly successful the year before. Nineteen forty-eight turned out to be an all-time record year when Singapore alone had a trade with Indonesia totalling M$467 million. Much of this came from exporters' success in pouring stocks of inducement consumer goods into small Sumatran ports, a trend which obviously could not continue as it was bound to reduce immediate future demands. As a result, in April 1949, Singapore's overall export to Indonesia dropped drastically to M$8 million, against an average of M$15 million per month in 1948.[64] The British colonial administrators were also keen to put part of the blame on high handling charges and other profit margins which were eroding the competitive edge of Singapore as an entrepot centre. Many places, including Indonesia, were beginning to query Singapore prices.[65]

It was in this context that "very severe criticism" and "heavy fire" spouted from within the business community when Britain signed an Anglo-Dutch agreement in February 1949 to facilitate direct trade of raw materials, foodstuff, technical equipment, iron and steel, motor cars, and textiles between the United Kingdom and the Dutch East Indies. Singapore was not consulted and its businessmen were deeply worried that Singapore's trade would soon suffer from being cut off from such an expansion of direct trade links.[66] They demanded assurances from the colonial administrators that such bilateral pacts would not undermine Singapore's economic position. The Singapore Chinese Chamber of Commerce managed to forge an alliance with the Indian Chamber of Commerce as well as the European Chamber of Commerce and submitted a joint petition to Governor Sir Franklin Gimson. A delegation, comprising representatives from these three Chambers, travelled all the way to London to present their case. After several meetings with key officials and an exchange of letters, they were apparently satisfied that "there was nothing in this trade agreement which would prevent trade flowing through" Singapore.[67]

This storm in the teacup was soon dwarfed by much more serious problems posed by changes to the barter trade system and related foreign exchange difficulties. Traditionally, Singapore's trade with Indonesia, especially its main portion with Sumatra, had been conducted chiefly on a barter basis. In the pre-Japanese Occupation period, the Singapore Chinese Chamber of Commerce played the important coordinating role in maintaining statistics and the settling of outstanding balances. After 1945, however, the system was devolved around individual merchants who created and maintained their own credit balances which did not represent actual currency but might be called "notional" or "artificial" credits for the purpose of the barter trade. Both the Dutch and the British were unhappy with such an arrangement outside of their regular banking system. Both put pressure on merchants to regularize their dealings through established banks, especially when more banking branches were being opened in the Indonesian archipelago. At times, the Dutch authorities would even mount "blockades and seizures" of trading vessels apparently unrelated to smuggling.[68] In 1949, the Dutch government went as far as to order the liquidation of barter balances before 15 April. A debt of M$1.9 million resulting from this liquidation was still unsettled and remained a source of complaint among Singapore Chinese merchants in January 1950.[69]

A total elimination of barter trade was of course difficult to achieve. In recognition of the reality, the United Nations Commissioner for Indonesia announced on 1 November 1949 a new trade agreement between Dutch authorities and the Indonesian Republic which dealt with the barter trade between Sumatra and Singapore. This trade pact aimed at a partial elimination, capping barter exchanges at 30%. The remaining 70% had to be settled by cash deposit at branches of the Hong Kong Shanghai Bank within six days of the landing of the consignment of goods.[70] The Singapore Chinese entrepreneurs were unhappy. They viewed it as an anti-Chinese merchant measure and feared that trade between Singapore and Sumatra would be constricted.[71] As a compromise, they urged the Singapore government to re-negotiate to permit trading on the basis of half barter and half cash and to allow this formula to be extended to all other areas of Indonesia.[72] However, they failed to make any headway and the "30–70" rule remained and was quickly put into operation.[73]

Singapore businessmen involved with the Indonesian trade also suffered a significant blow when their own British colonial authorities tightened up foreign exchange control following their devaluation of the Sterling in September 1949. As noted earlier, a big row was kicked up by the Chinese entrepreneurs first over family remittances to China and then more openly over the adverse effects of foreign exchange control on trade. A large part of the latter outcry arose from problems associated directly with the Indies trade. The majority of merchants whose business books were inspected and found to have infringed financial regulations were those doing business with Indonesia. The British inspectors had regarded the maintenance of notional credit balances in barter exchanges to be in contravention of foreign exchange rules. The Chinese merchants, however, argued in a petition to the Secretary for Chinese Affairs that such outstanding balances in their names would eventually be re-exported to hard currency areas, thereby bringing in more gold dollars into the colony. They were doing something which was "beneficial to the government" and "not, in effect, doing anything that [was] against the law".

In this 22 December 1949 petition, the Singapore Overseas Chinese Importers and Exporters Association which claimed a membership of over 200 merchants "with a very sound standing among the Commercial classes in this colony", urged the British authorities to recognize such barter transactions, spare them from the official banking network and give an assurance that they were not contravening the regulations. Otherwise, trade with Indonesia would become unattractive and this could "work to the detriment of the government itself" and bring about "large scale unemployment in Singapore". It demanded that the authorities should "desist from investigating the accounts of individual merchants ... because all the importers and exporters in this Colony have a feeling of not knowing what [was] right from wrong". They ended their petition on a solemn note: "We would like to live and trade in peace and quiet."[74]

As mentioned, the British authorities in Singapore were not in a position to bend foreign exchange regulations formulated within the broad principles established by London for the larger concerns of the British empire. They ignored such requests and let the situation remain as it was. In the end, it was left to the vagaries of trade to reverse the fortunes of these merchants. The rising demand of consumer goods and escalation in commodity prices, especially rubber which increased some 200% between October 1949 and October 1950, worked to lift the exports of Singapore to Indonesia to about M$14 million per month and imports to more than M$36 million per month.[75]

Apart from the Dutch East Indies trade, Chinese entrepreneurs in Singapore during 1949–50 were also paying close attention to the completion of a new Sterling Trade Pact with Japan which would allow Britain and her domains to export £55 million worth of goods to Japan and import £45 million in return.[76] Japan had been governed since 1945 by the American-dominated office of the Supreme Commander for the Allied Powers (SCAP) and this ended only in 1952. The initial objectives of the Allied occupation was only the demilitarization and democraticization of the Japanese polity. However, with rising tension against the Soviet Union and the likelihood of China turning communist, a policy reversal occurred towards the end of 1947. The new approach was to allow for a limited degree of re-militarization for the purpose of self-defense and, more importantly, to rehabilitate the war-torn economy of Japan. As part of the economic rehabilitation, markets of the United States and the world were opened up slowly for Japanese manufacturers and SCAP's control over the Japanese economy was relaxed steadily. Trade pacts were struck with several regions, floor prices were slowly dismantled, and Japanese private businesses were gradually allowed to deal directly with the outside world without SCAP playing the intermediate and supervisory role.

For the Chinese entrepreneurs in Singapore, the finalization of a new Sterling Area-Japan Trade Pact in the last quarter of 1949 was therefore an exciting economic opportunity. It is true that the ghost of war had still not been completely exorcized. The further liberalization of trade with Japan in fact coincided with the arrival of the seventh and final war reparation payment in the form of more than 300 tons of Japanese machinery being unloaded at the Singapore Harbour Board wharves in November.[77] The Chinese business community was also still demanding the repayment of the M$50 million cash squeezed from them during the war.[78] But at the same time they were certainly looking forward to the prospect of doing extensive business with the new Japan.

The interest of the Singapore Chinese entrepreneurs about this new deal was, however, almost centred exclusively on the issue of import quota. It had been decided by London that £5,004,000 (roughly the equivalent of 42,000,000 Malayan dollars) of the imports under the new trade pact would be given to Singapore, Malaya, Sarawak, and British Borneo. This was about three times the volume of pre-war Japanese imports into the region in 1940.[79] The various business communities were consulted by the British colonial authorities to decide on the sub-division of this share. The Singapore Chinese Chamber of Commerce coordinated the response from within the Chinese business community and helped in shaping the final settlement. Sub-committees were formed, meetings were held and discussions were organized with their counterparts in the Federation of Malaya. In many of these occasions, the exchange of views was often heated and agreement was difficult to reach.[80]

While the import traders were eager about getting a share of the action, three of the largest Chinese manufacturers of rubber goods petitioned the government asking for higher import duties and a quota system to protect the local industry from the dumping of Japanese goods. They argued that the indigenous industry could meet all the local needs and proposed that imports such as canvas shoes as well as bicycle tyres and tubes should be controlled. The proprietor of Shum Yip Leong Rubber Works claimed that the most serious effect of the impending competition would be on the labourers, of which nearly 15,000 workers were said to be employed in Singapore alone in rubber works. Lau Pau Song, an importer in Singapore who had visited Japan recently then, promptly retorted that the manufacturers' fear was groundless as the high cost of living in Japan would make it impossible for it to lower prices to effect dumping. To him, competition in trade should be welcomed by all business circles and, since Japan had imported rubber from Singapore and Malaya, it should be allowed to export its by-products to this region.[81]

Among the import traders themselves, there were other contentious issues. Singapore's three chambers of commerce were unanimous in wanting two-thirds or 67% (M$28 million) of the entire allocation (M$42 million) worth of Japanese imports.[82] In urging a 2:1 formula for Singapore and Malaya respectively, the Malayan Chinese Merchant Association was in agreement with the Singapore proposal.[83] But the Penang Indian Chamber of Commerce was clamouring for a 50% split, half of the allocation going to the Federation of Malaya.[84] The picking of a base year on which to calculate the allocation was yet another bone of contention. So too were the issues of sharing the allocation with exporters as well as reserving something for newcomers in the import trade.[85]

It took nearly half a year before a final settlement was reached and the allocation went into effect only on 1 July 1950. In the end, Singapore secured its two-thirds demand. In terms of product range, the distribution of Japanese imports would be 45% textiles, 20% sundry goods, 15% foodstuff, 15% hardware and construction materials, and 5% cement. As a reflection of the complexities involved in this issue of allocation, it was also decided that the sundry goods portion given to Singapore would be sub-divided, with 80% share going to established import-export firms. The remaining 20% of the Singapore sundry quota would be split among nearly 750 new entrants to the market, each receiving the right of M$4000 imports.[86]

This concentration of attention on the import quota of Japanese goods was overwhelming. Nothing seemed to have been done about facilitating the export half of the trade pact. There might well have been individual Chinese businessmen in Singapore who were actively cultivating export links to Japan, but there must have been so few of them that they had generally gone unnoticed and unreported. As far as organized concerted action was concerned, the Singapore Chinese business community seemed to have made no effort in promoting exports to Japan. This passivity stood in contrast to the more aggressive stance adopted by Japanese businessmen. Soon after SCAP signalled its willingness to relax further its control over private trading, six trading companies in Japan had secured approval by 12 November 1949 from the Japanese Government Screening Committee to send representatives to Malaya on trade promotion trips and one application for entry was already lying on the table of the Singapore authorities.[87] The first businessman from Japan reportedly landed by plane in Singapore on 30 December 1949. Chua Kim Hoay's nationality was not ascertained, but he was of Chinese ethnicity and a trader from Nagasaki. He came to survey the market and to establish contacts with local Chinese business firms.[88] This was the prelude to the waves of Japanese traders and investors who would sweep through Singapore and other parts of Southeast Asia from the mid-1950s to the 1970s. It was an opening act of great significance but one in which the Singapore Chinese entrepreneurs did not then fully comprehend.[89]

Conclusion

A central question perennially raised on the topic of overseas Chinese is their degree of loyalty to and identification with the new place of residence. With regard to the Chinese community in the colony of Singapore and the Federation of Malaya, it is often asked if they still had a "China-orientation" or if they had been "Malayanized". An investigation of such an issue will of course be more productive if a long term perspective is taken. Only then will the process of the evolution of a Malayan consciousness be more thoroughly unveiled. However, it may also be useful if we can occasionally take a snapshot and freeze the development within a single short time span to see if it could tell us anything. Our study of the economic outlook of the Singapore Chinese entrepreneurs from the October 1949 founding of the People's Republic of China to the eve of the Korean War can be used to this effect.

At that point in time, the Chinese business community in Singapore apparently still had a China-orientation. With the change in government in mainland China, they all felt the need to address the issue of political affiliation, especially when the PRC was proclaimed just ten days prior to their traditional annual celebration of the Chinese National Day on 10 October, a date designated by the Kuomintang. However, they were divided in their response. Some were in favour of continuing their backing for the Chiang Kai-shek regime, soon to be exiled in Taiwan, while others voiced support for the new PRC government under Mao Tse-tung. Separate celebrations were organized and different national flags were hung. This split was almost similar to that between the pro-monarchists and the pro-republican revolutionaries within the overseas Chinese community on the eve of the 1911 Republican Revolution.

A China-orientation was also reflected in their concerns expressed over the problems of family reunions and remittances. They pressed the British colonial authorities to relax its immigration rules to allow for an easier admission of refugee parents, children, brothers and sisters of migrants who were already residing in Singapore. And when Hong Kong slapped a visa requirement on Chinese who were departing from Singapore and returning to China via Hong Kong, they also protested loudly. Noise was made again when family remittances to China was further disrupted towards the end of 1949. As discussed, it is true that the latter two instances involved their own pecuniary interests and they were partly using humanitarian and compassionate appeals to further such self-benefits. But, either way, it is undeniable that China was at the forefront of their consciousness.

Indeed, from the economic perspective, many of the Chinese entrepreneurs in Singapore were flushed with early optimism and were watching China closely in anticipation of economic rewards from a new stable regime governing a market of about half a billion people. This rosy expectation did not eventually materialize but they were then certainly watching closely and thinking hard about China in their pursuit of economic gains. In terms of action, however, they were hampered partly by their own political caution.

A common explanation for the overseas Chinese eventually changing their orientation from China to the host society has been China's turning communist and the consequent cutting off of nearly all the ties from overseas Chinese communities. This may well be true after 1957 when Mao increasingly socialized the Chinese economy and fell back on self-reliance and autarky. At least from 1949 to 1950, however, the PRC remained very keen in tapping the resources and skill of overseas Chinese and, as noted, was making special effort to restore family remittances to its normal level. In other words, the pull factor was still there. What in fact hindered most the renewal of Singapore-China economic exchanges during this period were logistical problems and, more importantly, the internal pressure arising out of the local communist insurgency in peninsula Malaya.

The Malayan Emergency from June 1948, the resultant British anxiety and the security measures they implemented, as well as the psychological fear among Chinese entrepreneurs of being seen as political suspects due to communications or other associations with the new PRC regime, all had a heavy dampening effect on business contacts with China. Apart from writing in to the British colonial administration to request endorsement, businessman Tan Keong Choon even felt the need to apply for Singapore permanent residentship before departing to seek business in China. Therefore, a China-oriented economic proposal actually prompted him to take a further step in his Malayanization. A move towards localization and a dilution of his China identity was deemed necessary before he could proceed with his China business venture. Given the timing of this act, it was not a spontaneous espousal of political commitment to his new place of residence. Instead, it was most likely a shrewd, economically-motivated move. On the one hand, he was eager to make a business trip to the new China to reap the maximum economic benefits from his ancestral and ethnic links as well as from his previous business connections. On the other hand, he saw the need to neutralize the danger of possible British deportation and ensure his safe passage back to Singapore which was his main base of economic operations. He was striving to have the best of both worlds.

The China-orientation of these Singapore Chinese entrepreneurs from 1949 to 1950 must also be further discounted when the larger picture is considered. The 1949 Chinese Communist takeover was not the only item which hogged their economic horizon at the turn of the decade. They were deeply concerned with three other matters: the foreign exchange clampdown, the East Indies trade and the Sterling Trade Pact with Japan. Their reactions towards foreign exchange restrictions was understandably the most vigorous as currency movement was their economic lifeline. Due to geographical proximity and the development of close economic ties over the years, the East Indies had by 1949, if not earlier, become a region of critical importance to them. Hence, proposed changes in trading arrangements and other problems naturally aroused their deep concerns. Moreover, they were equally attentive and hopeful about gaining from the new American policy of rehabilitating the Japanese economy and reconnecting it to the outside world. China was therefore only one of their areas of concerns. Their orientation had stretched beyond their ancestral homeland over into Southeast Asia where they had settled and built up their business network and had reached over into re-emerging Japan.

This study of their four major economic concerns from 1949 to 1950 can also be used to ponder over the entrepreneurial quality of Singapore Chinese businessmen. Literature on "entrepreneurship" seldom provide a neat, concise and yet all-encompassing definition for the term. Generally speaking, an entrepreneur is at least someone who will take initiative and maximize his opportunities, organize his business practices along new lines, have an eye for capital formation and the development of entrepreneurial skill as well as seek new markets. Given what has been discussed about their economic outlook, the Singapore Chinese businessmen of 1949–50 did not seem to measure up very well to this set of criteria.

First and foremost, instead of taking the initiative to prise open further economic opportunities, a great deal of their time and energy was expended on reacting to and fighting a rearguard action against changes in their politico-economic environment. They fought vigorously against the Hong Kong visa requirement, a further downturn in overseas Chinese family remittances, another clampdown on foreign exchange infringements after the Sterling devaluation, and new trading arrangements for the East Indies trade. Yet, in all of these instances, practically nothing was achieved. The authorities just lent a listening ear and deftly sidestepped their demands.

During these protest actions, it is to their credit that these businessmen acted together in a fairly united manner despite the divergence in business interests and the occasional disagreements. However, their channels and methods of dissent also showed that they were still operating through the traditional trade and clan associations which had been around since the turn of the century. They principally relied upon these long-established business and community organizations as well as the time-honoured leadership of the Singapore Chinese Chamber of Commerce to raise their protests. There was little entrepreneurial effort to organize themselves along different lines and to seek new alliances.

These Singapore Chinese businessmen of 1949–50 also do not measure up very well to the criterion of capital formation and the development of entrepreneurial skills. Despite the obvious flight of capital out of China, they did not make any significant concerted effort to tap this attractive source and expand their capital base. Instead, they exerted themselves forcefully on the British colonial authorities, accusing them of tightening foreign exchange controls and strangulating the flow of overseas Chinese family remittances back to China. They seemed much more interested in ensuring the continuation of capital leakage rather than an expansion in capital formation, notwithstanding that this stemmed partly from their humanitarian concerns over family needs.

As for skill development, the China crisis provided an opportunity for Singapore to tap into the pool of refugee entrepreneurs as well as skilled and semi-skilled labourers streaming out of China. However, apart from the reunion of family members, the Singapore Chinese business community did not even lobby the colonial government for any selective population intake. During that period, there was in fact still a regular outflow of Chinese from Singapore back to China and Hong Kong. And when Hong Kong imposed a new visa requirement to cope with its exploding refugee population, the Singapore Chinese entrepreneurs ironically protested vigorously about this disruption of a labour outflow from Singapore. This misplaced priority and negligence to encourage a selected useful labour inflow was made all the more notable by the fact that immigration regulations in operation then actually had a special clause providing explicitly for an easier entry of professional businessmen and skilled labourers into Singapore.

Yet another glaring lack of entrepreneurship was their failure to actively scout for new markets. They joined hands to protest against several negative developments as a result of the Chinese Communist takeover. However, apart from some individual exploratory contacts, they did not put in any coordinated effort to organize trade or business promotion trips to China. This failure with regard to the new China market might well be accounted for by the dampening effect of political caution caused by the communist insurgency on the Malayan peninsula. No such excuse, however, could be summoned for their lopsided concern in the new Sterling Trade Pact with Japan. Here, they spend enormous amounts of time and energy almost exclusively on how to allocate among themselves and other business communities the quota of Japanese imports into Singapore and Malaya which had already been fixed by the pact and the London authorities. But nothing was discussed about the export quota and no noticeable effort was made to organize export promotions to Japan. This stood in sharp contrast to the Japanese traders who at this time were just beginning to knock on the doors of Singapore and who were eventually to play a critical role in transforming the political economy of Singapore and the rest of Southeast Asia.

All these shortcomings have perhaps been put across in too harsh a manner. One must remember after all that we are looking at the thinking and actions of the Singapore Chinese businessmen only over a very short span of time and we have chosen a period which happened to be exceptionally tumultuous. It would be wrong to pass a damning judgement on their overall entrepreneurial credentials. At the most, what we can say is that, looking back with the advantage of hindsight, these businessmen during the few critical months of 1949–50 were apparently overwhelmed by dramatic changes in their politico-economic environment and their entrepreneurial flair was then certainly not at its best.

Endnotes

1 S.C. Chua, Chief Statistician and Superintendent of Census, *Report on the Census Population of 1957*, Singapore: Government Printer, 1964, Table 15.7 which contrasts the 1957 census with that of 1947, p. 84. Data also available in Garry Rodan, *The Political Economy of Singapore's Industrialization: National State and International Capital*, London: Macmillan Press, 1989, p. 46.

2 Oral history transcript of Mr Tan Ee Leong, p. 8. Oral History Department, Singapore, 1980. Interview conducted in English by Jannie Lim Poh Hoon. Reference No. A00003/21.

3 Lim Choo Hoon, "The Transformation of the Political Orientation of the Singapore Chinese Chamber of Commerce, 1945–1955", *Review of Southest*

Asian Studies, Vol. 9, 1979, pp. 30–34 discusses the Chinese Civil War 1945–50 as a whole and has not examined the SCCC's specific reactions towards the October 1949 Communist victory. A more useful account on this issue is Chui Kwei-chiang, *Hsin ma hua-jen kuo-chia jen-t'ung ti tsuan-hsiang, 1945–1959 (The Changing National Identity of Singapore and Malayan Chinese, 1945–1959)*, Singapore: South Seas Society, 1989, pp. 287–288.

4 "Minutes of the 19th Meeting of the 25th SCCC Directorate", 30 September 1949, *Straits Times*, 10 October 1949, p. 1 and 11 October 1949, p. 1. The Kuomintang as a political party in Malaya and Singapore was proscribed by the British for the third time in May 1949 but this did not stop its supporters from celebrating the Double Tenth. See C.F. Yong and R.B. McKenna, *The Kuomintang Movement in British Malaya, 1912–1949*, Singapore: Singapore University Press, 1990, pp. 218–222 and C.F. Yong, "Some Thoughts on the Creation of a Singaporean Identity among the Chinese: The Pre-PAP Phase, 1945–1959", *Review of Southeast Asian Studies*, Vol. 15, 1985, p. 53.

5 *Straits Times*, 11 October 1949, p. 1; Chui Kwei-chiang, *Hsin-ma hua-jen kuo-chia jen-t'ung ti tsuan-hsiang*, pp. 252–253.

6 *Straits Times*, 23 December 1949, p. 4.

7 "Minutes of the 1st Meeting of the 26th SCCC Directorate", 28 March 1950.

8 See the decline in cargo shipping from mid-1949 in Table 8.1.

9 *Straits Times*, 7 November 1949, p. 3 and 12 November 1949, p. 3. As for the United States, its policy makers were still in a mood of disengagement from Chinese affairs and were most reluctant to offer assistance to American blockade runners. As a result, Mr Hans J. Isbrandtsen who operated ships of the Isbrandtsen Line, partly from Singapore through their agent Wah Hin & Co., openly accused the US Secretary of State, Dean Acheson, of "callously waiting for the loss of American lives". See *ibid.*, 3 December 1949, p. 3.

10 *Ibid.*, 29 November 1949, p. 5 and 12 December 1949, p. 6. *Nanyang Siang Pau*, 20 October 1949, p. 4, 25 October 1949, p. 4, 8 November 1949, p. 4 and 26 November 1949, p. 4.

11 CO 717/182/52928/4, *Review of Chinese Affairs*, November 1949, p. 3; *Nanyang Siang Pau*, 13 November 1949, p. 9.

12 *Nanyang Siang Pau*, 2 November 1949, p. 4 and 9 November 1949, p. 6.

13 File SCA 153/50, CSO 3840/90 on "Lee Rubber Co., Ltd: Application for Permits".

14 Oral history transcript of Mr Tan Keong Choon, pp. 50 and 59–60. Oral History Department, Singapore, 1981. Interview conducted in Mandarin by Mr Lim How Seng. Reference No. A000052/24.

15 Wong Siu-lun, *Emigrant Entrepreneurs: Shanghai Industrialists in Hong Kong*, Hong Kong: Oxford University Press, 1988, p. 3; Theodore Geiger and Frances M. Geiger, *The Development Progress of Hong Kong and Singapore*, London: Macmillan, 1975 edition, pp. 65 and 68.

16 Wong Siu-lun, *Emigrant Entrepreneurs*, pp. 23–24.

17 *Ibid.*, pp. 65–66; Theodore Geiger and Frances M. Geiger, *The Development Progress of Hong Kong and Singapore*, p. 69.

18 Wong Siu-lun, *Emigrant Entrepreneurs*, pp. 43–44.

19 The following discussion is based on *ibid.*, pp. 24–25 and 90.

20 *Colony of Singapore Government Gazette*, 24 March 1950, pp. 425–426.

21 See the lengthy discussion by Mr John Laycock and the Colonial Secretary's concurrence in *Proceedings of the First Legislative Council, Colony of Singapore*, 1949, pp. B436–440 and B443. This share of Straits-born Chinese was an increase over the 1947 Census figure of 59.9%, see *ibid.*, p. B391. For an overview of the demography of Singapore from 1824–1980, see G. Shantakumar, "The Demography of Singapore: A Selective Survey of the Scholarly Literature", in Basant K. Kapur (ed.), *Singapore Studies: Critical Surveys of the Humanities and Social Sciences*, Singapore: Singapore University Press, 1986, pp. 243–302.

22 In 1930 the British put into force the Immigration Restriction Ordinance which was later updated by the Aliens Ordinance (1933). Shipping registration, quota limitation, and landing fees were imposed on Chinese immigration into Singapore and Malaya, while Britons and Indians who were British subjects were spared. The effect on adult male immigrants, against whom the legislation was primarily aimed, was dramatic. Their intake dropped from 158,000 in 1930 to 14,000 in 1933. See Mary Turnbull, *A History of Singapore, 1819–1975*, Singapore: Oxford University Press, 1977, pp. 137–138.

23 See correspondence, notes and newspaper extracts in File CSO 7812/48 on "Questions Asked by Mr C.C. Tan and Mr Tan Chin Tuan Regarding Immigration" and File SCA 183/49, CSO 4856/49 on "Entry Permits from China for the Families of those Residents in Singapore".

24 *Nanyang Siang Pau*, 17 October 1949, p. 5.

25 *Proceedings of the First Legislative Council, Colony of Singapore*, 1949, p. B385.

26 Extracts of the first and second meetings of the reconstituted Chinese Advisory Board, 15 July and 5 September 1949, and news clipping of *Straits Times*, 17 September 1949, in File SCA 183/49, CSO 4856/49 on "Entry Permits".

27 The six categories of aliens to whom entry permits would be more readily issued were listed in the set of May/June 1949 correspondence and notes in File CSO 7812/48 on "Questions Asked by Mr C.C. Tan and Mr Tan Chin Tuan".

28 *Straits Times*, 19 December 1949, p. 1; CO 717/182/52928/4, *Review of Chinese Affairs*, December 1949, p. 7. Aw himself was a Nanyang businessman rather than an indigenous Chinese entrepreneur. Partly because of his ownership of Chinese newspapers in Hong Kong and Singapore, the British authorities were monitoring him rather closely, see the long exchanges in CO 717/183/52928/26 "Political Development: Aw Boon Haw".

29 The following discussion is based mainly upon correspondence, internal memorandum, extracts of Minutes of Meeting of the Chinese Advisory Board, and newspaper extracts in File SCA 302/49 on "Hong Kong Immigration Regulations". It has been supplemented by Minutes of the 21st Meeting of the 25th SCCC Directorate, 28 November 1949, as well as various issues of *Straits Times* and *Nanyang Siang Pau*.

30 Letter from the Singapore Chinese Lodging Houses Association to the Secretary for Chinese Affairs, dated 2 December 1949, in File SCA 302/49 on "Hong Kong Immigration Regulations". It is most unlikely that the majority of these returnees from mid-1949 to 1950 were merchants as suggested in Chui Kwei-chiang, *Hsin-ma hua-jen kuo-chia jen-t'ung ti tsuan-hsiang*, p. 262.

31 *Sin Chew Jit Poh*, 28 Nov 1949, in File SCA 302/49 on "Hong Kong Immigration

Regulations".

32 Memo from Deputy Controller of Immigration to Secretary for Chinese Affairs, dated 7 December 1949, and letter from Secretary for Chinese Affairs to Singapore Chinese Lodging Houses Association, dated 17 December 1949, in *ibid.*

33 *Nanyang Siang Pau*, 11 November 1949, p. 5; CO/717/182/52928/4, *Review of Chinese Affairs*, December 1949, p. 8.

34 *Annual Report of the Board of Commissioners of Currency*, 1950, pp. 3–4.

35 *Annual Report of the Registrar of Companies*, 1949, pp. 2 and 4; 1950, pp. 1–2 and 4.

36 For examples, see *Nanyang Siang Pau*, 16 November 1949, p. 3, 17 November 1949, p. 3 and 21 November 1949, p. 4.

37 *Proceedings of the First Legislative Council, Colony of Singapore*, 1950, p. B22. This general statement issued on 22 February 1950 made no explicit mention of China.

38 The following discussion is based mainly upon correspondence, memoranda, notes and newspaper extracts in File SCA 263/49, CSO 5901/49 on "Remittances to China".

39 Kua Bak-lim "Hsin-chia-p'o ch'iao-hui yu min-hsin-yeh yen-chiu" *(A Study of Remittance and Credit Business in Singapore)* in Kua Bak-lim and Ng Chin-keong (ed.), *Hsin-chia-p'o hua-chu-shih lun-chi (A Collection on the History of Singapore Chinese)*, Singapore: Nanyang University Alumni Association, 1972, pp. 188–189.

40 *Annual Report of the Postal Service Department, Malaya*, 1949, p. 8; *Nanyang Siang Pau*, 19 November 1949, p. 5.

41 For the earlier two rounds of major tightening in October 1946 and October 1948, see discussion in Kua Bak-lim, "Hsin-chia-p'o ch'iao-hui yu min-hsin-yeh yen-chiu", pp. 183–187. However, Kua's treatment of events from 1949 to 1950 was scanty.

42 *Straits Times*, 8 October 1949, p. 7 and 28 October 1949.

43 *Nanyang Siang Pau*, 28 October 1949, in File SCA 263/49, CSO 5901/49 on "Remittances to China".

44 These restrictions were clearly restated in the memorandum of the Deputy Controller of Foreign Exchange, dated 21 November 1949, in *ibid*. The 45 Malayan dollars limit was much less than the prewar limit of 250 Malayan dollars and was first imposed from March 1946. See Kua Bak-lim, "Hsin-chia-p'o ch'iao-hui yu min-hsin-yeh yen-chiu", pp. 175–176 and 183.

45 *Nan Chiau Jit Pao*, 26 October 1949, in File SCA 263/49, CSO 5901/49 on "Remittances to China".

46 "Minutes of the 20th Meeting of the 25th SCCC Directorate", 28 October 1949.

47 Undated draft memo and the 21 November 1949 memo from the Deputy Controller of Foreign Exchange, in File SCA 263/49, CSO 5901/49 on "Remittances to China".

48 *Straits Times*, 19 November 1949, p. 7; *Nanyang Siang Pau*, 19 November 1949, p. 5.

49 Extract of the Minutes of Meeting of the Chinese Advisory Board, 9 December 1949, in File SCA 263/49, CSO 5901/49 on "Remittances to China".

50 Memorandum from the Deputy Controller to the Controller of Foreign Exchange,

dated 21 Nov 1949, and letter from the Deputy Controller of Foreign Exchange to the Secretary for Chinese Affairs, dated 25 November 1949, in *ibid.*

51 Warnings from the British colonial administration as reported in *Nan Chiau Jit Pao*, 24 and 27 November 1949, in *ibid.*

52 Oral history transcript of Loo Neng, pp. 38–39, Oral History Department, Singapore 1982. Interview conducted in Mandarin by Cai Rong Hua. Reference No A000208/11.

53 *Chung Shing Jit Pao*, 11 Dec 1949, reporting on an anonymous letter addressed to the Singapore Hokkien Remittance Shops Association, and *Nanyang Siang Pau*, 31 January 1950, news about an informal meeting of the Nanyang Chinese Exchange and Remittance Association, in File SCA 263/49, CSO 5901/49 on "Remittances to China". A hint of such irregularities can also be found in CO 717/182/52928/4, *Review of Chinese Affairs*, December 1949, p. 7.

54 News extracts of *Nan Chiau Jit Pao*, 31 December 1949, 18 January 1950, 20 January 1950 and 26 January 1950; *Ta Kung Pao*, 18 January 1950; *Sin Chew Jit Poh*, 22 January 1950, 25 January 1950, 7 February 1950 and 1 March 1950, in File SCA 263/49, CSO 5901/49.

55 For a general understanding of the extent and importance of pre-1949 overseas Chinese family remittances from Singapore and elsewhere, see Hsia Ch'eng-hua, *Chin-tai Kwang-tung-sheng chiao-hui yen-chiu, 1862–1949 (A Study of Contemporary Overseas Chinese Remittances to Kwangtung Province, 1862–1949)*, Singapore: South Seas Society, 1992. With regards to overseas Chinese remittances for direct investment purposes, the representative work is Lin Chin-chih, *Chin-tai hua-chiao t'ou-tzu kuo-nei ch'i-yeh k'ai-lun (An Outline of Contemporary Overseas Chinese Investments)*, Amoy: Amoy University Press, 1988.

56 Garry Rodan, *The Political Economy of Singapore's Industrialization*, p. 42. He offers this insight without substantiating. The topic of capital accumulation and transfer of surpluses to industrial projects in pre-independent Singapore is one area which requires further research.

57 *Proceedings of the First Legislative Council, Colony of Singapore*, 1949, pp. B147–149, B191, and B388–389; CO/717/183/52928/24, *Federation of Malaya Monthly Newsletter*, Vol. 8 (16 August–15 September 1949), pp. 1–2.

58 *Straits Times*, 20 September 1949, p. 1 and 3; CO/717/183/52928/24, *Federation of Malaya Monthly Newsletter*, Vol. 9 (16 September–15 October 1949), p. 13.

59 *Straits Times*, 8 October 1949, p. 7 and 28 October 1949.

60 "Minutes of the 1st Meeting of the 26th SCCC Directorate", 28 March 1950; "Minutes of the Special Meeting of the 26th SCCC Directorate", 19 April 1950; Correspondence, memoranda, notes and news extracts in File SCA 263/49, CSO 5901/49 on "Remittances to China".

61 "Minutes of Meetings of the SCCC Directorate", for 28 October 1949, 28 November 1949, 28 January 1950, 28 March 1950, 19 April 1950 and 28 April 1950.

62 *Proceedings of the First Legislative Council, Colony of Singapore*, 1950, pp. B19–20.

63 "Minutes of the 6th Meeting of the 26th SCCC Directorate", 28 August 1950.

64 *Proceedings of the First Legislative Council, Colony of Singapore*, 1949, pp. B190–191; See also the data in CO/825/74/4/55404, *Singapore Political Report*,

Vol. 11, November 1949, Appendix.

65 *Proceedings of the First Legislative Council, Colony of Singapore*, 1949, pp. B190–191.

66 *Ibid.*, pp. B147–150.

67 *Ibid.*, pp. B388–389; *Colony of Singapore Annual Report*, 1949, p. 13.

68 Correspondence in File SCA 3/50 on "Foreign Exchange Control Restrictions".

69 *Straits Times*, 30 November 1949, p. 4, reports that the Singapore Overseas Chinese Importers and Exporters was asking the Secretary for Economic Affairs to put pressure on the Indonesian authorities on this issue; *Ibid.*, 5 January 1950, p. 7, notes that eight major Chinese import and export firms had sought help from the SCCC to release this money frozen by the Dutch. They were Messrs Heng Hong Hung, Chin Lam Hoe Kee, Chin Ah Co., Chek Guan Trading Co., Tong Hua Co., Hoe Hin Co., Tai Seng Co., and Ban Hin Leong Co.

70 CO/825/74/4/55404, *Singapore Political Report*, Vol. 11, November 1949, Appendix, p. 6; *Straits Times*, 1 November 1949, p. 1 and 29 November 1949, p. 5.

71 "Minutes of the 20th Meeting of the 25th SCCC Directorate", 28 October 1949.

72 *Straits Times*, 12 November 1949, p. 4.

73 *Ibid.*, 29 November 1949, p. 5; 22 December 1949, p. 4.

74 Letter from the Singapore Overseas Chinese Importers and Exporters Association to the Secretary for Chinese Affairs, dated 22 December 1949. The Secretary merely forwarded it to the Colonial Secretary on 4 January 1950 for information. Apparently, no further action was taken. See File SCA 3/50 on "Foreign Exchange Control Restrictions".

75 *Proceedings of the First Legislative Council, Colony of Singapore*, 1950, pp. B342–343.

76 *Straits Times*, 18 October 1949, p. 1, 17 November 1949, p. 5 and 23 November 1949, p. 3. There was an earlier Sterling Area-Japan trade pact which operated from mid-1948 to mid-1949 but this was apparently on a trial basis and was of a limited scale.

77 *Ibid.*, 30 November 1949, p. 7.

78 *Ibid.*, 19 December 1949, p. 7.

79 CO/717/183/52928/24, *Federation of Malaya Monthly Newsletter*, Vol. 11, (16 November–15 December 1949), p. 13; *Straits Times*, 17 November 1949, p. 5 and 23 November 1949, p. 5. Detailed trade figures for 1939 indicate that the value of imports from Japan into this entire region then totalled Straits dollars $12,480,458 (Singapore's share was $10,678,456) while the value of exports to Japan was $64,256,851 (Singapore's share was $42,871,247), see H. North-Hunt, Registrar-General of Statistics, *Malaya: The Foreign Trade of Malaya for the Year 1939*, Singapore: Government Printing Office, 1941, pp. 16, 20, 22 and 46–49.

80 "Minutes of Meetings of the SCCC Directorate", 28 November 1949 and 15 December 1949; *Straits Times*, 3 December 1949, p. 4.

81 *Straits Times*, 26 November 1949, p. 1.

82 *Ibid.*, 29 November 1949, p. 5.

83 *Nanyang Siang Pau*, 4 December 1949, p. 10.

84 *Straits Times*, 2 December 1949, p. 4.

85 *Ibid.*, 29 November 1949, p. 5.
86 "Minutes of the 5th Meeting of the 26th SCCC Directorate", 31 July 1950.
87 *Straits Times*, 12 November 1949, p. 4. Approval had also been given to send trade promotion representatives to Iraq, Iran, Egypt, Ceylon, India, Pakistan, Burma, Siam and Hong Kong.
88 *Ibid.*, 30 December 1949, p. 4. The headline of this newspaper story is "Chinese is First Japan Trader".
89 For the important role to be played by Japanese in the political economy of Singapore and other members of the Association of South-East Asian Nations, see Kunio Yoshihara, *The Rise of Ersatz Capitalism in South-East Asia*, Singapore: Oxford University Press, 1988, passim. In his discussion about Chinese businessmen in the more recent years, the author avoids using the term "entrepreneur" even though he agrees "one might argue that the term 'entrepreneur' is more neutral and better suited to academic writing". He prefers to call them "capitalists" and postulates them as "ersatz" or fake capitalists, see pp. 1–4. On the labelling and conceptualizing of Chinese businessmen in historical and contemporary Singapore as "entrepreneurs", see for example Chan Kok Bun and Claire Chiang See Ngoh, *Stepping Out: The Making of Chinese Entrepreneurs*, Singapore: Prentice Hall, 1994.

9

China's Economic Modernization and the Ethnic Chinese in ASEAN: A Preliminary Study

Leo Suryadinata

Introduction

With the introduction of the Four Modernizations by Deng Xiaoping, both skills and capital were required to modernize China. However, China was lacking in these resources. Therefore it began to look overseas. This paper examines briefly China's strategies to obtain these resources, one of which has been to secure the assistance of ethnic Chinese from all over the world. How successful has the strategy been? What has been the response of the ethnic Chinese and respective governments in the ASEAN states? What are the profiles of these Chinese who have invested in China? Are they loyal to Southeast Asian countries? These are some of the questions which this paper attempts to answer.

China's Four Modernizations and the Ethnic Chinese

It is a well-known fact that during the Cultural Revolution between 1966 and 1969, both the Chinese economy and education encountered a major setback. Even after the Cultural Revolution officially ended, the Gang of Four was still in control. China witnessed a continuation of the old policy which caused the further decline of the economy. The ill-treatment of the Chinese intellectual class and the "returned overseas Chinese" forced many educated Chinese to leave the PRC.

The Gang of Four fell from power on 4 October 1976. However, Deng Xiaoping was not immediately in control of the government. It was Hua

Guofeng and Ye Jianying who were temporarily holding the key positions. Deng re-emerged for the third time in July 1977, first sharing power with Hua Guofeng, and eventually dominating the Chinese political scene. Deng introduced the Four Modernizations Programme, that is, agriculture, industry, technology and the military, in order to modernize China by the end of the 20th century.[1] To implement such a programme, China required trained people and capital. But the Chinese educational system during and after the Cultural Revolution failed to produce sufficient numbers of highly skilled professionals who could help China modernize.[2]

The Deng Xiaoping group considered the ethnic Chinese outside China as the source for both skilled professionals and capital. It is not surprising that once he was in power, he immediately announced the new "Overseas Chinese Policy" which has the following objectives:

1. Beijing would like to reduce, if not stop, the departure of "domestic overseas Chinese" intellectuals;
2. It is also eager to attract ethnic Chinese professionals to participate in the modernization of China;
3. Beijing would also like to secure more remittances and investments from the ethnic Chinese;
4. Lastly, Beijing hopes that the ethnic Chinese would serve as a bridge in unifying mainland China and Taiwan.

Due to time constraints and limited information available, this paper will focus on the first three points. The above needs to be examined in order to gauge whether or not China has achieved its policy objectives. One can assess the policy during the two periods, i.e. during the Cold War Period (1977–1989) and the post-Cold War period (1990–).

First let us look at the departure of the returned overseas Chinese. Between 1949 and 1966, there were approximately 500,000 returned overseas Chinese in mainland China.[3] However, many of them left China during the Cultural Revolution because of mistreatment. According to *Min Bao Yuekan*, (*Ming Bao Monthly*) in Hong Kong, in 1973 more than 50,000 overseas Chinese left China.[4] This figure does not include those who left China without permission. By the end of 1976, there were only 100,000 returned overseas Chinese in mainland China.[5]

Most publications in Hong Kong published in the early 1980s maintain that the domestic overseas Chinese continued to apply for exit permits even after the moderate policy towards them was in place. The most common complaint was that the policy was not really implemented. The ultra leftwing idea – the distrust of the domestic overseas Chinese – continued to prevail. Mu Chang, a writer who specializes in commentary on the overseas Chinese problem, maintained that the overseas Chinese continued to be barred from joining the army, the Communist Youth League, the Communist Party, top universities and important agencies. They were even excluded from important meetings and functions.[6] Many agencies and institutions refused to employ persons with an overseas Chinese background although they had been instructed by the top leaders to accept them.

It should be pointed out that the returned overseas Chinese never lost their overseas Chinese identity. In the past, the overseas Chinese were granted special treatment because of their different standards of living and lifestyle, and during the Cultural Revolution this was used by the "revolutionaries" for discriminating against them. The overseas Chinese were considered reactionaries and they were hunted by the "revolutionaries". Since their identities were properly recorded, they could be easily identified.[7] Thus even after the Cultural Revolution, many complained that they were still identified as such and hence faced discrimination. Apart from the political factor, economic considerations have also played its part. The living conditions in China after the so-called "Ten Years Disaster" had declined and the overseas Chinese wanted to go to Hong Kong, Macao, the ASEAN states and the West in search of a better life.[8]

According to some reports, the returned overseas Chinese in general received better salaries, especially those living in major cities. However because of inflation, many still complained that the salaries were insufficient. However, the single most important factor to cause discontent had been the bitter experiences during the "Ten Years Disaster". A large number of professionals and intellectuals (both overseas Chinese and non-overseas Chinese) lost their confidence in the political system and were afraid of the emergence of a second "Ten Years Disaster". According to an incomplete survey of 17 provinces, between January 1979 and January 1980, more than 10,000 intellectuals (mostly university graduates) left China; many were still in Hong Kong.[9] According to another report, after the fall of the Gang of Four, in Guangdong alone, several hundreds of thousands of returned overseas Chinese and their families applied to leave China.[10] However, after 1981, the Chinese leaders announced that these ex-domestic overseas Chinese would be welcomed back and the agencies or institutions concerned were instructed to re-employ them. Those encouraged to return were restricted to "intellectuals" (*Zhishifenzi*) who were defined as those whose qualifications would be higher than that of primary school teachers.[11] It was hoped that this new appeal would attract some Chinese intellectuals to re-enter China, but it seems that the new policy did not stop the brain drain from China.

In fact, a lot of non-overseas Chinese intellectuals had also applied to study overseas. Many were approved as China realized that modernization required Chinese professionals. According to US sources, there were at least 65 to 70,000 Chinese students in the United States before the Tiananmen affair.[12] These Chinese students will be crucial to China's modernization. However, it was reported that many refused to return to the PRC. This was especially the case after the Tiananmen affair. These Chinese students, most of whom were graduate students and highly skilled professionals, preferred to stay overseas.[13]

However, with the end of the Cold War, the introduction of the open door policy of China, and the improvement in the treatment of intellectuals and professionals, some Chinese intellectuals may have been attracted to return to the PRC. There is no figure available as yet on the new returnees. It is possible that those who were unable to adapt to life outside China would have returned to China eventually. However, some observers have noted that more "overseas Chinese" felt that they would be treated better in China as foreigners compared to "returned overseas Chinese".[14]

Apart from skilled manpower, capital is needed to modernize China. It should be noted that China attempted a two-prong policy in order to get both foreign loans and investment: one source being the West and Japan and the other the ethnic Chinese.

How successful is China in getting the overseas loans from Japan and the West? According to one source, before the end of 1979, the Bank of China had signed various loan agreements with a number of Western countries amounting to US$27.586 billion in letters of credit, of which loans from the UK, France, Italy, Canada, Sweden, Australia and Belgium amounted to US$11.845 billion.[15] In 1980, the Bank of China signed loan agreements with Norway and West Germany. Therefore up to 1980, China had an accumulated letters of credit of about US$12.4 billion.[16] However, due to the readjustment of the economic plans, most of these letters of credit were unused.

Apart from getting loans from Western countries, it was important to attract foreigners and the ethnic Chinese to invest in China. According to an official source, between July 1979 (i.e. the announcement of the Joint Venture Regulations) and December 1981, the PRC approved 40 joint venture projects (*Zhongwai Heying Qiyue*) with a total value of US$1.8924 billion, of which foreign capital accounted for US$0.8748 billion.[17] The United States was the largest investor, contributing 50%; Hong Kong second, contributing 33%; and Japan was third, with a contribution of about 7.5%. The above were classified as "Joint Industries" in which China provided a certain proportion of capital to match the foreign capital.[18]

There is another kind of investment which is classified as "Joint Venture Companies" (*Zhongwai Hejuo Jingying*) in which China provides the site rather than the capital, and the terms of investment included more liberal capital.[19] The total investment under this category is about US$1.8 billion, numbering 400 projects. The largest number of projects has been in Guangdong, which had 360 projects with a value of US$1.5 billion. The rest are located in Beijing, Fujian, and Shanghai.[20] Most of these investments are in the form of hotels, restaurants, residential property, transport and the food industry. It was reported that 90% of the investors were Gangow Tongbao (Hong Kong and Macao residents) and "overseas Chinese" (*Huaqiao*).[21]

According to a survey, between 1979 and the end of 1991, direct foreign investment in China amounted to US$26.885 billion, of which US$13.932 billion were capital from Hong Kong and Macao, accounting for 51.82% of the total investment.[22] Taiwan capital accounted for 9.29%, and "overseas Chinese" capital, presumably from Southeast Asia and other areas, accounted for 5.57%.[23] During the first quarter of 1992, there were 3,837 newly registered foreign companies in China, of which 2,560 were from Hong Kong, 480 from Taiwan and 113 from Macao.[24]

However, in the officially published Chinese statistics, there is no separation between the investment from Hong Kong and Macao and that from the so-called overseas Chinese. Therefore it is very difficult for us to know the percentage of the "overseas Chinese" investment, especially that of the ASEAN Chinese. Most of the work done has been based on educated guesses. Most of the studies assumed that Southeast Asian Chinese invested heavily in Hong Kong, moving into mainland China from there.

I have not conducted in-depth research but it seems that Southeast Asian Chinese capital in the past was often considered as *Nanyang Bang* (Southeast Asian Clique) which tended to be differentiated from the Hong Kong, Macao and Taiwan capital. In those years, the *Nanyang Bang* was not influential; only in the last 10 years has one begun to see the emergence of the *Nanyang Bang* in Hong Kong. The most well-known are perhaps Robert Kuok of Malaysia who bought over the major share of the *South China Morning Post*, the First Pacific Company owned by Liem Sioe Liong (Sudono Salim) of Indonesia, and the Lippo Group owned by Li Wenzheng (Mochtar Riady)'s family, also from Indonesia. These *Nanyang Bang* companies have invested in mainland China in recent years (although Robert Kuok entered China much earlier than the others), in the initial period, the *Nanyang Bang* has not been successful in moving into Hong Kong and mainland China. One may therefore argue that in the early period, it is questionable if the amount of ASEAN Chinese investment in China was larger than that from Hong Kong, Macao and Taiwan Chinese. One of the major reasons was political, because most of the ASEAN states were still suspicious of the PRC. It was also true that in the 1980s, economic opportunities were not yet available in mainland China.

The situation changed during the 1980s, especially after the end of the Cold War. Many Chinese MNCs from the ASEAN states began to invest in China. As noted earlier, it is still difficult to know the amount of investment in China originating from the ethnic Chinese in ASEAN. However, the perception of the ASEAN governments which are dominated by indigenous groups is that ASEAN Chinese have been investing tremendously in China, especially in the South from where most of the ethnic Chinese came.

At this juncture, one can pose a question as to the importance of Chinese investment from Hong Kong, Macao, Taiwan and Southeast Asia. It has been assumed that the amount has been very large and constitutes a crucial part of capital investment in China. However, many argued that in terms of the amount, it still forms a small part of China's total investment.[25] One writer maintained that up to 1991, foreign capital (both Chinese and non-Chinese) only accounted for 3–5% of China's total investment.[26]

Where did the foreign investment come from? According to the Chinese sources, in 1991 the contracted investment in China doubled that of previous years. Singapore (2.1%) was the fifth largest investor in China, after Hong Kong/Macao (61.8%), the United States (9%), Japan (8.1%) and Taiwan (2.5%).[27] But the Singapore figures are much smaller compared to those of Hong Kong/Macao.

In the first 9 months of 1992, Singapore's investment in China was reported to have exceeded the total amount invested over the last 13 years.[28] The amount continued to increase and there were more joint projects with China.[29] However, one has to point out that Singapore's investment in the PRC as of 1992 only constituted about 2% of its total overseas investment. Most of Singapore's ventures were still concentrated in Malaysia (22%), Hong Kong (12%), New Zealand (11%), Australia (7%), US (4%) and Taiwan (3%),[30] and Singapore has now become the largest investor in Indonesia.[31] Other ASEAN countries such as the Philippines and Thailand have also been investing in the PRC in recent years. As for Singapore, direct investment in China from these countries did not create any domestic outcry. Apparently, "Chinese phobia" in Singapore is not as strong as in some other ASEAN states. In Indonesia, on the other hand, there is still a lingering suspicion of Beijing. Jakarta fears that Indonesian capital may go to China, to the detriment of the Indonesian economy where capital is badly needed. Not surprisingly, Indonesia has recently been monitoring investment by its nationals in the land of the dragon.[32] It was reported that the Indonesian Chinese have increased investments rapidly in the last two years in China since the re-establishment of ties between Jakarta and Beijing.

There is no doubt that direct foreign investment has increased since 1992 and it may account for a larger percentage in China's investment. Nevertheless, it still remains a small percentage compared to China's total investment. Nevertheless, the direct foreign investment is still very important because China needs the capital badly. More important is perhaps various skills (including management skills) which are being transferred by the ethnic Chinese to China. Both capital and skills are contributing significantly to China's modernization programmes.

Responses of Ethnic Chinese Entrepreneurs and ASEAN Governments

With the isolation of China by the West after the 1989 Tiananmen affair, it seems that more attention was paid by the PRC towards ethnic Chinese capital. Many ethnic Chinese entrepreneurs themselves also felt that this was the time for them to invest in mainland China, following the Chinese in Taiwan and Hong Kong.

The Chinese communities, especially businessmen, saw it as a golden opportunity to expand their businesses. However, it is incorrect to say that the revival of ethnic networking was *merely* a response to Beijing's policy towards the ethnic Chinese. It was *mainly* a response to the new environment – the general revival of ethnicity in the world, the end of the Cold War, and the new economic opportunities provided by China. The new situation enables the ethnic Chinese in general to capture the new opportunities to promote their businesses. One can also see this as part of the globalization process of ASEAN Chinese businesses. It is also interesting to note that many entrepreneurs are now openly using the informal ethnic Chinese networks.

A case in point is the Chinese Chamber of Commerce and Industry in Singapore which took the lead in holding an international convention of World Chinese Entrepreneurs in August 1991. The convention had been planned for two years,[33] presumably soon after the occurrence of the Tiananmen affair. Singapore's Senior Minister Lee Kuan Yew was invited to give a keynote address at the convention. It is interesting to note that Lee stressed the importance of the ethnic links in promoting Singapore's development. He noted that:

> Our world is increasingly interdependent. Trade, investments, travel are also no longer impeded by oceans or mountains or national boundaries. Singaporeans now need to go international. Chinese entrepreneurs overseas will be valuable contacts in these countries. Ethnic and cultural empathy facilitates rapport and trust.[34]

However, he did not confine himself to the promotion of ethnic Chinese links but included reference to other ethnic links (e.g. Indians). He said that other Asians overseas, especially Indians, can help Singaporeans break into markets abroad.

> Singapore also welcomes those of you who are interested in expanding to Southeast Asia. Singapore is a convenient base camp for trade and investments, especially joint ventures, in the region. Useful links can grow out of meetings such as this.[35]

Nevertheless, due to the large number of ethnic Chinese in Singapore, Lee stressed the importance of ethnic Chinese links. He also noted that "as Chinese we are affected by the future of China".[36] He also suggested that China's modernization would benefit from the experience of the "Chinese overseas", namely the examples set by Hong Kong, Taiwan and Singapore.

The emphasis on ethnic links in Southeast Asia is often interpreted as an appeal to create networks based on one racial group excluding the others. In multi-racial Southeast Asia, this approach has been criticized by indigenous politicians, especially those from Indonesia and Malaysia, although the two countries are not free from "racial" exclusiveness – for instance their differentiation between the so-called *bumiputra/pribumi* (indigenous populations, i.e. non-Chinese) and *non-bumiputra/non-pribumi*. Nevertheless, since the state is defined in indigenous terms, ethnic categories favouring the indigenous population, not immigrant ethnic groups are considered as "natural".

When the convention was held in Singapore, some Indonesian government officials and the press were very critical.[37] In fact, many conglomerates, for instance Liem Sioe Liong, William Soeryadjaya (Tjia Kian Liong) and Ciputra (Tjie Tjing Hoa), were absent from the convention, probably due to pressure from the Indonesian government.

When the Second Convention of World Chinese Entrepreneurs was held in November 1993 in Hong Kong, some media in the ASEAN states were equally critical as it was geared for one ethnic group. In addition, many saw this as being linked to China's efforts to attract ethnic Chinese capital –

the Chinese authorities had organized a sight-seeing tour in the Zujiang Delta.[38]

Lee once again was invited to be one of the keynote speakers at the convention. By this time, Lee had discovered that some ASEAN states were concerned with ethnic Chinese networking and investment in mainland China. He advised that ethnic Chinese who come from "certain sensitive ASEAN countries should take care that their investments in their own countries do not diminish as a result of their China investments."[39]

He warned that increasing investment by "overseas Chinese" in China could affect race relations in some ASEAN countries. "If relations turn sour between any ASEAN country and China, those ethnic Chinese who have invested in China will be accused of disloyalty".[40]

It is interesting to note that there are two views regarding the role of the ethnic Chinese in Southeast Asia in China's development. One view is represented by Lee who sees that China after the end of the Cold War is no longer aggressive and is merely interested in economic development. According to this view there is ample opportunity for cooperation between China and the Southeast Asian countries. Ethnic Chinese can serve as a link (*guanxi*) or a bridge between China and this region: Southeast Asians can invest in China through the ethnic Chinese while China can also invest in the region through them. The assumption here is that in an interdependent world, no country can afford to adopt an isolationist stance and an attitude of mutual hostility.

However, there is another view which sees China as a possible hegemon. China is a major power and has overlapping claims with five Southeast Asian countries over the South China Sea.[41] While agreeing to cooperate with China, this view stresses that attention has to be paid to regional solidarity among Southeast Asian countries, especially among the ASEAN states. According to this view, China is using the Southeast Asian Chinese to modernize the country. Its links with the ethnic Chinese in Southeast Asia might be used by a strong China to influence, if not control, Southeast Asia. Therefore, the ethnic Chinese should not be drawn too close to China. To make them loyal to the ASEAN states, the policy of assimilation should be continued. Some Indonesian military and Malay nationalist leaders, for instance, hold this view. The strategy used is to create more "growth triangles" among the ASEAN states. In addition, liberal regulations on foreign investments are being introduced so that ASEAN countries can compete with China for foreign investments.

A few ASEAN states have been concerned with the possible establishment of the "Great Chinese Economic Zone" (*Da Zhonghua Jingji Quan*) which would involve the so-called "overseas Chinese networks". According to some, China is the core of this economic zone and other areas where the ethnic Chinese reside are part of this zone. (The proposal was made by some academics in Hong Kong and Taiwan, but the PRC, understandably, did not endorse this concept because it knew its negative implications.[42])

Indonesia and Malaysia, for instance, feared that this "Great Chinese Economic Zone" concept would involve the Chinese in the ASEAN states, which may have a negative impact on their nation-building process.[43] In fact, some Chinese entrepreneurs and politicians in these countries voiced their concern with the concept which may put them in a very difficult position.[44]

The first view appears to be gaining. Many observers, including those who were suspicious of China, have admitted that China is developing rapidly and offers great economic opportunities. These observers also believe that China, as an Asian country, will find it mutually beneficial to be involved in the ASEAN regional development and to accept the international rules of the game. This cooperation will promote regional stability. At the same time, the Southeast Asian states, especially ASEAN, are supposed to put their own houses in order so as to compete with China for investment and market. For many ASEAN countries, China is both an opportunity and a challenge.

Profiles of Ethnic Chinese Investors

There are many ethnic Chinese entrepreneurs who have invested in mainland China in recent years. However, there are no comprehensive studies on the subject as yet. Due to lack of information and time constraint, I shall only identify 25 major ethnic Chinese investors from five ASEAN states – therefore it is far from comprehensive.[45]

From Indonesia, the most well-known taipan who invested in China is Sudono Salim (Lin Shaoliang), followed by Eka Tjipta Widjaja (Oei Ek Tjong), Mochtar Riady (Li Wenzheng), Suhargo Gondokusumo (Go Kah Hien) and Hendra Rahardja (Tan Tjoe Hien); from Malaysia, Robert Kuok Hock Nian (Guo Henian) or the Kuok brothers, Lee Ming Tee, and Lim Goh Tong (Lin Wutong); from the Philippines, Lucio Tan (Chen Yongjai), John Gokongwei (WuYihui), Tan Yu (Zheng Zhouming), George S.K. Ty (Zheng Shaojian), Henry Sy Sr (Shi Zhicheng), and Jose Yao Campos; from Singapore, Lee Seng Wee (Li Chengwei), Kwek Hong Png (Guo Fangfeng), Ng Teng Fong (Huang Tingfang), Wee Cho Yaw, Lien Ying Chow, Ong Tjoe Kim and Khoo Teck Puat; from Thailand, Dhanin Chiaravanont (Xie Guomin), Mongul Kanjanapas (Huang Ziming), Chatri Sophonpanich (Chen

Youhan) and Boonsoong Srifuengfung (Zheng Mingru).

If we examine the above ethnic Chinese entrepreneurs, we can draw the following conclusions:

Most of these ethnic Chinese entrepreneurs are first generation, i.e. born in China but migrated to Southeast Asia during the 20th century. Many received some Chinese school education either in mainland China or have no formal education. Many are still members of Chinese clan associations. Those who were second generation (i.e. born in Southeast Asia) are culturally still "Chinese" in the sense that they received a Chinese education either in China, Hong Kong or locally. Even if they are English-educated they have also been to Chinese school prior to English school. Their command of the Chinese language (not necessarily Mandarin) and their association with the Chinese community are two important ingredients for their success in their businesses. In China they have an edge over those who do not read or speak Chinese.

Nevertheless, it should also be pointed out that these Chinese entrepreneurs are multinationals. Their businesses have not been confined to the countries where they live. In fact they have business links (even branches) of their companies in the ASEAN region, Hong Kong, Taiwan and the United States. It is also interesting to note that many Chinese entrepreneurs have established cooperation with Chinese entrepreneurs in other countries.

It is incorrect to say that these Chinese entrepreneurs have mainly invested in mainland China. Many spread their investment in the region and in Western countries. They moved into mainland China in recent years because of business opportunities there. But it only represents part of their total investment.

Ideologically, before the end of the Cold War, some were pro-Beijing and others were pro-Taipei but ideological differences have become irrelevant since the end of the Cold War. When there was an economic opportunity in China, these ethnic Chinese entrepreneurs made use of it to trade and invest in mainland China.

It has been argued that ethnic Chinese investment in China is based on their primordial sentiments and "Chinese patriotism". This is perhaps the case with the first generation Chinese in the ASEAN states. Being born in China and culturally still "Chinese", there is a certain nostalgic factor in their investment. However, for those Chinese who were not born in China, this primordial sentiment is very weak, if not completely absent. Nevertheless, no matter which generation, ethnic Chinese entrepreneurs/businessmen are profit-oriented. If there is no profit to be made in mainland China, it is difficult to imagine that they would invest in their ancestral land. In fact, one can point to the fact that before China's open door policy, the number of Chinese entrepreneurs who invested in China was very small indeed. The dramatic increase in their investment only occurred after the new economic policy was introduced and there were more opportunities to make money.

Examining the Chinese tycoons who have invested in China, only about 25 can be identified. Many names such as William Soeryadjaya (Tjia Kian Liong), Ciputra (Tjie Tjing Hoa) and Sofjan Wanandi (Liem Bian Khoon) of Indonesia, Loh Boon Siew and Lee Loy Seng of Malaysia are conspicuously absent from the list. The number of Chinese taipans in ASEAN is much larger and it is interesting to ask why many of them did not follow the trends. Perhaps, some of them have lost command of the Chinese language and cannot deal with the mainland Chinese, others are due to political reasons – they do not want to be identified too closely with the PRC. Some taipans may also feel that they are unfamiliar with the system in China and are hence reluctant to move in.

The Chinese who invested in China appear to be in property developments, tourist industries, banking and other types of services. Some (such as two Malaysian tycoons) were reported to have secured lottery licences from Chinese local governments but it is doubtful that the central government would allow the operation of the lottery or casino.

It should also be pointed out that the ethnic Chinese did not consist of entrepreneurs alone. Most of these Chinese who invested in China are multinationals. Their businesses are no longer confined to one ASEAN country. In many ways, they are similar to other MNCs. However, unlike other MNCs, the ethnic Chinese MNCs are relatively new. They also tended to use the ethnic networks in expanding their businesses. Their links with China may or may not be strong, depending on the economic opportunities.

Their links with China may or may not be a problem depending on China's relations with the ASEAN states. When the relations are good, these links will not be a problem. But when the political relations are at odds, the links will become an issue.

Conclusion

There is no doubt that the PRC after the re-emergence of Deng Xiaoping has introduced a new policy in order to secure support from the ethnic Chinese. During the initial period, the policy was not very successful. Although it managed to improve the conditions of the "returned overseas Chinese" and hence arrested the trend of an "overseas Chinese exodus" from China, there are still many Chinese students/intellectuals who have not returned.

As to investments from "Chinese overseas", initially there was a significant volume mainly from the Chinese in Hong Kong, Macao and Taiwan rather than the ethnic Chinese in ASEAN. However, since the late 1980s after the end of the Cold War, more ethnic Chinese saw the great economic opportunity in mainland China and started to invest there. However, their investment share is still quite small compared to the Chinese in Hong Kong, Macao and Taiwan. It should be noted, nevertheless, that the PRC has benefitted not only from the ethnic Chinese investment but also from their experience and skills, which are needed for China's modernization.

The opening up of China has posed a challenge to the ASEAN countries not only with regard to foreign investment but also to the ethnic Chinese. Some countries which had introduced an assimilationist policy felt that economic necessity has forced the government to relax such a policy. The ethnic Chinese were thus allowed to go to China and to be exposed to Chinese culture again. Some governments dominated by indigenous groups feel that the ethnic Chinese may be re-sinicized and that this could retard their nation-building process. This could create tension in the future if relations between China and the ASEAN states sours.

The rise of China has also posed a dilemma for some ASEAN countries which define nation in both racial and cultural terms rather than cultural terms alone. Adjustments by both China and ASEAN may be necessary in order to maintain political stability and economic development in the future.

Endnotes

1 *Jing Bao* (Hong Kong), 10 August 1980, p. 18.
2 Michael Lindsay, "The People's Republic of China in 1974", mimeo., 1974.
3 Stephen Fitzgerald, *China and the Overseas Chinese: A Study of Peking's Changing Policy 1949–1970*, Cambridge: Cambridge University Press, 1972, p. 69.
4 Ai Zhichun, "Wu yi xi wei gui: tan dalu huaqiao zhengce" (Scarce Goods Are Expensive: A Note on Mainland China's Policy towards the Overseas Chinese), *Ming Bao Yuekan* (Hong Kong), Vol. 12, No. 10, October 1977, p. 9.
5 *Ibid.*
6 *Jing Bao*, No. 43, 10 February 1981, pp. 22–23.
7 For this argument, see *ibid.*; also *Jing Bao*, No. 50, 10 September 1981, pp. 34–35.
8 *Jing Bao*, No. 19, 10 February 1979, p. 5.
9 *Ibid.*, No. 50, 10 September 1981, pp. 34–35.
10 *Ibid.*, p. 34.
11 *Jing Bao*, No. 46, 10 May 1981, p. 24.
12 According to the US statistics, up to 1987, the US Immigration has issued 62,007

student visas to PRC students. Leo A. Orleans, *Chinese Students in America: Policies, Issues and Numbers*, Washington D.C.: National Academy Press, 1988, p. 88.

13 According to one source, only 10% of the students would return to the PRC.

14 Mu Chang, for instance, observed that "there are two kinds of overseas Chinese: the 'live ones' (*huo qiao*) who stayed abroad and became wealthy and the 'dead ones' (*si qiao*), those who were once patriotic and returned to China. They were given very different status and received quite different treatment. See *Jing Bao*, Vol. 56 (March 1982), cited in Michael R. Godley, "The Sojourners: Returned Overseas Chinese in the People's Republic of China", *Pacific Affairs*, Vol. 62, No. 3, Fall 1989, p. 351.

15 "Zhongguo dui wai touzi de sishou", *Meizhou Jingji Pinglun* (*Hong Kong Economic Weekly*), 24 August 1981, p. 12.

16 *Ibid.*

17 Ma Hong, (ed.), *Xiandai Zhongguo Jingji Shidian*, Beijing: Zhongguo Shehui kexue chubanshe, 1982, p. 380.

18 *Ibid.*

19 *Ibid.*, p. 383.

20 *Ibid.*

21 *Ibid.*, p. 384.

22 Lin Jingzhi, "1979–1992 Haiwai huaren zai Zhongguo dalu touzi de xianzhuang ji qi Jinhou fazhan qushi" (The Present Stage of Overseas Chinese Investment in China and Their Future Trends: 1979–1992), *Huaqiao Huaren Lishi Yuanjiu*, No. 1 (1993), pp. 2–3.

23 *Ibid.*

24 *Ibid.*, p. 12.

25 Lin Jingzi, *op. cit.*

26 Prof Lin Jingzhi made this point to this author.

27 See Appendix 9.1 for the relevant information.

28 "Investors Pumped $790m into China in First 9 Months of Year", *Straits Times*, 23 December 1992.

29 In China, Singaporeans committed investments amounting to about US$411 million in 224 projects in the first quarter of 1993, making them among the top 10 investors there. In 1992, a total of US$990 million was committed for 742 projects. *Straits Times*, 14 January 1994.

30 *Business Times*, 22 September 1992.

31 In Indonesia, Singapore was the top foreign investor last year with approved investments totalling US$1.33 billion in more than 42 projects. *Straits Times*, 14 January 1994.

32 *Kompas*, 6 April 1993; *Bisnis Indonesia*, 5 April 1993.

33 "Welcome Address by Mr Tan Eng Joo", in *A Global Network: 1st World Chinese Entrepreneurs Convention*, Singapore: Singapore Chinese Chamber of Commerce and Industry, 1992, p. 19.

34 "Keynote Address by Senior Minister Mr Lee Kuan Yew at the Official Opening of the World Chinese Entrepreneurs Convention 10 August 1991", in *A Global Network*, p. 23.

35 *Ibid.*

36 *Ibid.*
37 For instance, the report in *Tempo*. The author also heard that some Indonesian ministers expressed their displeasure over the "racial conference".
38 See for instance "Para Taipan Sedunia, Bersatulah!" (Taipans of the World, Unite!), *Tempo*, 27 November 1993, pp. 22–24.
39 "SM Lee: Be Sensitive to ASEAN Feelings", *Straits Times*, 23 November 1993.
40 *Ibid.*
41 See for instance, Mark Valencia, "The Spratly Islands: Dangerous Ground in the South China Sea", *Pacific Review* Vol. 1, No. 4, 1988, pp. 438–443; Chang Pao Min, "A New Scramble for the South China Sea Islands", *Contemporary Southeast Asia*, Vol. 12, No. 1, June 1990, pp. 20–39.
42 Reported by Hong Kong Chinese press, republished in *Lianhe Zaobao* (Singapore), 2 December 1993, p. 27. ("'Da Zhonghua Jingji Quan' de Gouxiang shou zhiyi")
43 Jusuf Wanandi, "Cina Raya dan Cina Perantauan", *Tempo*, 20 November 1993, p. 69.
44 See for instance, a Malaysian MP, Weng Xijie's statements in a recent seminar held in Singapore. Reported in *Lianhe Zaobao*, 9 January 1994, p. 9.
45 See Appendix 9.2 on "Ethnic Chinese Tycoons and Their Investments in the PRC".

Appendix 9.1

Sources of Direct Foreign Investment* in China, 1979–1991
(Contracted investment, US$ million)

	1979–85	1986	1987	1988	1989	1990	1991	Cumulative Total	Cumulative % share
National total	**16,660.71**	**3,330.37**	**4,319.12**	**6,190.70**	**6,294.09**	**6,986.32**	**12,421.73**	**56,203.04**	**100.0**
HK, Macau	10,628.96	1,773.43	2,364.66	4,161.20	3,733.95	4,257.67	7,834.51	34,754.38	61.8
US	2,177.01	541.48	361.48	384.30	645.89	365.68	555.29	5,031.13	9.0
Japan	1,628.63	282.82	386.29	370.60	515.38	478.46	886.05	4,548.23	8.1
Taiwan	n.a.	n.a.	n.a.	n.a.	n.a.	n.a.	1,392.34	1,392.34	2.5
Singapore	192.54	140.76	79.84	136.90	147.65	106.91	155.21	959.81	2.1
UK	378.30	51.69	28.56	56.40	33.26	121.23	131.97	801.41	1.7
Germany	162.06	55.58	139.64	69.20	159.60	47.34	565.29	1,198.71	1.5
France	262.47	11.92	73.80	32.90	17.55	12.72	14.38	425.74	1.4
Italy	137.43	91.59	19.42	22.90	63.34	10.52	21.78	366.98	0.8
Canada	74.31	91.01	34.30	39.50	49.11	30.87	21.78	340.88	0.7
Australia	105.23	31.57	47.44	17.40	83.66	17.83	44.04	347.17	0.6
Netherlands	4.70	0.30	0.10	153.30	17.70	27.40	16.87	220.37	0.5
Thailand	40.34	3.21	4.53	41.70	56.80	2.53	108.27	257.38	0.4
Switzerland	22.94	25.00	57.14	38.70	11.79	27.79	19.96	203.32	0.4
Philippines	46.94	3.81	30.50	15.50	4.70	10.73	17.44	129.62	0.2
Austria	0.00	90.11	0.90	3.40	9.41	6.45	8.12	118.39	0.2
Belgium	52.76	0.30	1.67	0.60	21.15	6.06	0.70	83.24	0.1
Denmark	6.53	42.62	0.57	0.50	0.00	0.00	0.06	50.28	0.1
Ex-USSR	0.00	0.00	0.00	0.00	3.07	8.35	22.04	33.46	0.1
Other	739.56	93.17	6688.28	645.70	720.08	1,447.78	94.38	4,428.95	7.9

* This includes all kinds of foreign investment – equity and cooperative JVs, wholly owned enterprises, joint offshore oil exploration, leasing, compensation, and processing and assembly.
Sources: MOFERT, BC calculations.

Appendix 9.2

Ethnic Chinese Tycoons and Their Investments in the PRC

Only the following information is provided: Name, dialect group if relevant, place and date of birth, education, major companies and business, investment in China.

Indonesia

Liem Sioe Liong (Lin Shaoliang, alias Sudono Salim) 林绍良

Hockchia (Fuqing), born in China on 16 July 1916, migrated to Indonesia in 1936. Received little formal education. Associated with Suharto's family. Leader of the Salim Group which is involved in banking (Bank Central Asia), real estate, a cement plant (Indocement), import-export. The group has also controlled First Pacific Company (Hong Kong), UIC (Singapore) and Hegemayer (Holland). His sons (including Anthony Salim) help run his business empire. **Investment in China**: Yuan Hong Industrial Park in Fujian, real estate (Fujian?), noodle factory (Shenzhen and Fujian), light industry, Rongqiao Hotel, residential projects. Total investment in China: unavailable.

Li Wenzheng (better known as Mochtar Riady in Indonesia) 李文正

Henghwa (Xinghua), born in Malang on 12 May 1929 (one source says in China). Educated in Chinese school in Java and university in China. Leader of Lippo Group. Involved in banking and real estate. Business extended to Hong Kong, the US and Australia. His Western university-educated sons help run his business empire. **Investment in China**: infrastructure development in Fujian, airport construction and highway with Fuzhou Municipal Government, tourist resort in Fujian. Total investment in China: $170 million.

Oei Ek Tjong (Huang Yicong, alias Eka Tjipta Widjaya) 黄奕聪

Hokkien. Born in Quanzhou, China in 1922, migrated to Ujung Pandang when he was 9 years old. Educated in Chinese school in Indonesia. Founder of the Sinar Mas Group which has more than 400 affiliated companies, ranging from fiinance, paper manufacturing, plantations, palm oil and hotels. His Chinese-educated second son Oei Hong Leong was in Singapore and now in Hong Kong/China, running his business in mainland China. **Investment in China**: paper manufacturing in Shanghai, cooking oil in Fujian/Liaoning/ Shanxi. Total investment: approx. $250 million.

Go Kah Hien (Wu Jiaxiong, alias Suhargo Gondokusumo) 吴家熊

Hokkien. Born in 1925 (1924?) in Nanan, Fujian. Migrated to Indonesia in 1941. Founder of the Dharmala Group which has been involved in finance, import-export, real estate and the food industry. It has now expanded to Malaysia, Singapore, Thailand and China. His California University-educated son (Suyanto) is believed to run the group's day-to-day activities. **Investment in China**: Office properties and hotels in Fujian. Total investment: not known.

Tan Tjoe Hien (Chen Zixing alias Hendra Rahardja) 陈子兴

Hokchia. Born in 1943 in Makassar (Ujung Pandang). Received Chinese school education. Founder of the Harapan Group, involved in hotels, real estate and the banking business in Indonesia, Singapore and Hong Kong. Encountered financial difficulty in 1987 but re-emerged five years later. Investment in China: Shopping centres in Fuzhou. Total amount of investment: unknown.

Sources: Leo Suryadinata, *Indonesian Chinese Culture and Society* (in Chinese), Singapore: Singapore Society of Asian Studies, 1993, pp. 17–51; *Apa dan Siapa: Sejumlah Orang Indonesia 1985–1986*, Jakarta Grafiti Pers, 1986; Feature articles in *Lianhe Zaobao* (Singapore), 9 September 1992 (on Oei Ek Tjong), 24 October 1992 (on Tan Tjoe Hien); Willy Lim Laoho, "Filipino Reactions to Philippine Chinese Investments in China: An Exploratory Survey", *China Currents* (Manila), Vol. 4, No. 4 (October–December 1993), p. 4; Bambang Soesatyo, "Raksasa Ekonomi Baru Dari Timur", *Info Bisnis*, October 1993, p. 30; Chen Jinli, "Yinni Libao wenzha wenda", *Zibenjia*, No. 25 (October 1993), pp. 50–59; "75 Pengusaha Terkaya ASEAN", *Warta Ekonomi*, 28 February 1994, pp. 3654.

Malaysia

Robert Kuok (Kuo Hock Nian, or Guo Henian) 郭鹤年

Hokchew (Fuzhou). Born on 18 May 1921 in Johor Baru, educated in both Chinese and English schools in his birth place and Singapore. Inherited parents' business and together with his brothers he developed it into a business empire involving the sugar industry and other agricultural products, real estate, shipping, insurance. Entered partnership with Lim Sioe Liong. Known as Asia's Sugar King. Expanded his company to ASEAN states, Hong Kong and mainland China. **Investment in China**: property developments in Beijing (including World Trade Centre), Shanghai, Liaoning, petrochemicals in southeastern coast. Amount of investment: $1,000 million.

Lee Ming Tee 李明治

Not much known about this figure. A Malaysian, owner of Allied Corporation, active in Singapore. Recently he has been active in mainland China. **Investment in China**: property development in Liaoning and Shandong. Amount of investment: approx. $26.4 million.

Note: Information on Malaysian Chinese investment in mainaland China is sketchy. Very few tycoons in Malaysia have invested in China. Lim Goh Tong of the Genting Berhad and Tan Chee Yioun (Vincent, born in 1952?) of the B & B Enterprise Sdn Bhd are reported to have secured lottery licences; Lim Kim Hong (not much known about this person) is reported to have invested $2.9 million in a power generation project. See Willy Lim Laohoo, *op. cit.*, also "75 Pengusaha Terkaya ASEAN", *op. cit.*, Edmond Terence Gomez, *Political Business: Corporate Involvement of Malaysian Political Parties*, Townsville: James Cook University of North Queensland, 1994, pp. 28, 284.

Philippines

Lucio C. Tan (Chen Yongjai) 陈永裁

Hokkien. Born in Amoy (Fujian) in 1934. Came to the Philippines at the age of 9. Received local Chinese education. Boss of fortune Tobacco Corp., Asia Brewery, and owner of The First Malayan Bank. Moved into property business. Associated with President Marcos. **Investment in China**: properties, established a branch of his Allied Banking Corporation in Xiamen (Amoy). Amount of investment: unknown.

John L. Gokongwei Jr (Wu Yihui) 吴奕辉

Hokkien. Born in Cebu in 1926 (one source says that he was born in Amoy but came to the Philippines at the age of 12). His father was China's honorary consul in Cebu in the late 1930s and early 1940s. Left school at the age of 12. Founded Universal Corn Products Corp., and Consolidated Food Corp. Boss of Universal Robina Corp. He is in the property and food business as well as in banking. **Investment in China**: several infrastructure projects in Xiamen (Amoy). Amount of investment: unknown.

Tan Yu (Zheng Zhouming) 郑周敏

Hokkien. Born in Bicol, Luzon in 1930 (one source says in Fujian, came to the Philippines at the age of 5.) Received four years of Chinese education. Founder of Asiaworld Group. Its operation covers Taiwan (one says that the company is now based in Taiwan), South Korea, Canada and the US. Involved in property, agriculture and commerce. His daughter (Emilia Roxas) and son (Elton) are managing his business. **Investment in China**: acquired land-use rights in Xiamen. Amount of investment: unknown.

George S.K. Ty (Zheng Shaojian) 郑少坚

Hokkien. Born in Yongcun (Fujian), migrated to the Philippines at young age. Son of a businessman who sold flour. Received some Chinese education. Boss of Metropolitan Bank and Trust Company, which has branches all over the world. Also moved into the property market. **Investment in China**: has signed an agreement with the Agricultural Bank of China for the establishment of a joint venture bank in Shanghai. Amount of investment: unknown.

Henry Sy (Shi Zhicheng) 施至成

Hokkien. Born in Jingjiang (Fujian) in 1923, came to the Philippines at young age. Father owned a small grocery store. Boss of Shoe Mart (SM) chain stores. Also moved into finance and investment. **Investment in China**: building an over-100-hectare industrial-commercial complex in Xiamen. Amount of investment: unknown.

Jose Yao Campos (Yao Julie) 姚祖烈

Date and place of birth unknown, but grew up in Quezon province. About 70 years old. Founded Unilab. Supported Marcos. Expanded to California. He has migrated to Canada but still controls the company. **Investment in China**: building a pharmaceutical factory in Guangdong. Amount of investment: unknown.

Note: In addition to the above Chinese tycoons, there are three more less well-known Chinese businessmen from the Philippines who were reported to have invested in China: Go Tong (Gotesco) Group, in condominiums; Leonardo Ty, in MSG plant and paper factory; John Ng, in steel mill and apartelle. See Willy Lim Laohoo, *op. cit.*, p. 6. The information on these tycoons is taken from *Zibenjia*, June 1992, pp. 72–101; Zhu Xingfu, *Jinre Filibin*, Shishi Chubanshe, 1991, pp. 196–203.

Singapore

Lee Seng Wee (Li Chengwei) 李成伟

Hokkien. Third son of Lee Kong Chian, who was son-in-law of Tan Kah Kee. Born in Singapore in 1927, educated in Hua Chong and Western university? The largest shareholder of Overseas Chinese Banking Corporation (OCBC). Still owns a lot of plantations in Malaysia. **Investment in China**: unknown.

Kwek Hong Png (Guo Fangfeng) 郭芳枫

Hokkien. Born in Tongan (Fujian) in 1912. Received little formal education.

Came to Singapore in 1928 (1930?). Ten years later established Hong Leong Co., involved in finance and property. Has three sons who are now running the business. **Investment in China**: property development, amount of investment: $210 million. (Passed away in early November 1994.)

Ng Teng Fong (Huang Tingfang) 黄廷芳

Hokkien. Born in China in 1928. Came to Singapore at young age. Received little formal education. Have been investing in property since the 1950s. Established Far East Organization. Became well-known developer. Expanded his business to Hong Kong and established Tsim Sha Tsui Properties Ltd and Sino Land. His son Robert Ng is in charge of the business in Hong Kong. **Investment in China**: property development in Xiamen, Fuzhou and Guangzhou. Amount of investment: not known.

Wee Cho Yaw (Huang Zuyao) 黄祖耀

Hokkien. Born at Jingmen (Fujian) on 10 January 1929. Went to Kuching (Sarawak) with his mother in 1937. His family later migrated to Singapore. Educated in Chung Cheng and Hua Chung High Schools for a year, graduated from St Andrew's School. In 1965 his father established the United Chinese Bank, later the name was changed to United Overseas Bank (UOB). Wee Cho Yaw developed the bank and diversified its business. Under his leadership, UOB has become one of the largest companies in Singapore. **Investment in China**: industrial and commercial properties in Xiamen, established a UOB branch in Shangai and Guangzhou. Amount of investment: unavailable.

Lien Ying Chow (Lian Yingzhou) 连瀛洲

Teochew. Born in Chaoyang (Guangdong) in 1905, migrated to Singapore in 1919. Received little formal education. Active in politics prior to the Second World War. In 1949 established Overseas Union Bank (OUB). Later OUB was developed into a group and was involved in property. **Investment in China**: Mandarin Hotel in Shanghai, two bank branches in Beijing and Senzhen. Amount of investment: not available.

Ong Tjoe Kim (Wang Ziqin) 王梓琴

Hokkien. Born in Zhangzhou (Fujian) in 1911. Migrated to Indonesia in 1926. Received some Chinese education. Began to work at the age of 16. Worked for department store, and later set up his own. Re-migrated to Singapore and in 1957 established Metro in Singapore. Metro later became a major department store chain. It also moved into the property market in

Singapore and Malaysia. **Investment in China**: It was reported that in 1992 Ong's company had a joint venture with Shanghai municipal government to build houses. Amount of investment: unavailable.

Khoo Teck Puat (Qiu Deba) 邱德拔

Hokkien. Born in 1917 in Singapore. Son of rice businessman. Graduated from St Joseph's College in Singapore. Goodwood Park Hotel, Central Properties Ltd. **Investment in China**: property development in Fujian and Guangdong. Amount of investment: unavailable.

Note: It should be noted that in recent years, government companies have been involved in various major development projects in China such as Suzhou and Shandong. In fact, this should not be considered as merely "ethnic Chinese" projects. The information on various tycoons is taken from *Zibenjia*, June issue 1992, pp. 72–101; No. 21 (June 1993) pp. 70–76; "75 Pengusaha Terkaya ASEAN", *op. cit.*, Willy Lim Laohoo, *op. cit.*, p. 4.

Thailand

Dhanin Chiaravanont (Xie Guomin) 谢国民

Teochew. Born in Thailand in 1939. Son of a leading businessman. Education unknown but received an honorary doctorate degree from Agricultural University in mainland China. Boss of the Charoen Pokphand Group. Active in the poultry industry. It also expanded to textile and other areas. **Investment in China**: motor vehicle manufacturing in Henan and petrochemicals in Zhejiang, probably the largest Thai Chinese investor in mainland China. Amount of investment: unavailable.

Mongul Kanjanapas (Huang Ziming) 黄子明

Born in Puning (Guangdong) in 1920. Migrated to Thailand when he was young. Education unknown. Major shareholder of the Bangkok Land and Tanayong. Active in the property business. His two sons, Anant and Keree, assist him in his business. **Investment in China**: Moved into mainland China towards the end of 1992 on a large scale. Signed contracts with Beijing municipal government to re-develop some areas and modernized Friendship Stores. Amount of investment in China: $2.86 billion.

Chatri Sophonpanich (Chen Youhan) 陈有汉

Teochew. Born in Bangkok in the 1930s (?). Son of Chin Sophonpanich, the founder of the largest bank in Thailand, the Bangkok Bank. Educated in Hong Kong (?). Chatri has succeeded his father and is now in charge of the

Bank. It has become a multinational bank with branches in many countries. **Investment in China**: opened a few branches in China, including Swatow, Xiamen and Guangzhou. Amount of investment: unavailable.

Boonsoong Srifuengfung (Zheng Mingru) 郑明如

Born in Fensheng, Guangdong. Date unknown. Migrated to Thailand at young age. His brother Kiarti (Zheng Liang Ying), who was the manager of the Quangdong Bank in Bangkok, was the one who started the Bangkok Metropolitan Bank in 1949. Boonsoong helped him in the bank. In the 1950s they started forming joint ventures with foreign companies such as Thai Asahi Glass, Thai Caustic Soda and Goodyear (Thailand). Kiarti died and Boonsoong together with his nephews run the business. In 1992 Boonsoong began to move into mainland China. **Investment in China**: building a hotel in Beihai (Guangxi), and passenger car manufacturing in Chongqing. Planned to establish a joint venture bank in Hainan. Amount of investment: unavailable.

Note: It was reported that Kitti Dumnerchanwanit invested in Guangdong (in paper products) for $1 billion and Wong Chong-po (of Thailand) invested in Beijing and Guangdong (in property development) for $5.4 billion. See Willy Lim Laohoo, *op. cit.*, p. 4. The information on Thai tycoons is taken from *Zibenjia*, No. 21 (June 1993), pp. 76–82; "75 Pengusaha Terkaya ASEAN", *op. cit.*, Yoshihara Kunio, *The Rise of Ersatz Capitalism in South-East Asia*. Kuala Lumpur, 1988, pp. 191–199.

10

The Ethnic Chinese, The Philippine Economy and China

Theresa Chong Carino

Introduction

China's economic boom has energized ethnic Chinese capital and fuelled economic dynamism in the region. In this overall scenario, some see the ethnic Chinese as providing the intra-regional network that has become "China's secret weapon". From this perspective, ethnic Chinese capital is seen as an extension of China's economy and its economic penetration of the region. On the other hand, if we see ethnic Chinese capital emanating from Southeast Asia as essentially Southeast Asian capital, then it can be seen as contributing to the rapid integration of the Chinese economy with that of the region and as a means of penetrating the potentially vast China market for Southeast Asian products. Outside of Hong Kong and Taiwan, Southeast Asian capitalists have been the most active in investing in China in recent years. This has elicited some expressions of concern from Southeast Asian political leaders. From Kuala Lumpur to Manila, politicians have raised questions about Southeast Asian Chinese loyalty as they actively invest in China – an activity perceived as bleeding much needed capital from Southeast Asian countries.[1]

Until very recently, China has been regarded by the Philippines mainly as a competitor for investments and markets. To some extent, the re-directing of Taiwanese investments away from the Philippines to southern China in recent years gives credence to this perspective. Nevertheless, the unprecedented economic boom that China is now experiencing is rapidly reshaping its trade and investment patterns and demands a closer examination of how the Philippines can derive benefits from expanding economic linkages with an increasingly prosperous neighbour through its ethnic Chinese minority.

Recent moves by the Ramos administration indicate that Philippine political leaders are beginning to take serious stock of the role ethnic Chinese capital can play in the economic recovery of the Philippines. There have been transparent attempts to harness and mobilize the economic resources of the Chinese Filipinos by the Ramos administration in the last two years. While their investments in China may be considered by some as "capital flight" from the Philippines, there are increasing indications that the Philippine government also recognizes the long term value of having Philippine investments in China. Not only can the ethnic Chinese help in the market penetration of China, they have already amply demonstrated that through informal networks and joint ventures, they have been able to draw investments to the Philippines from China, Taiwan and Hong Kong as well as ASEAN countries.

Harnessing Philippine Chinese Capital for Development

The potential contribution of Chinese Filipino big business in developing the Philippine economy has been highlighted since President Fidel Ramos brought the so-called "six taipans" with him to China during his state visit there in April 1993. While in Beijing, Ramos pointedly made the announcement that six of the wealthiest Chinese Filipino capitalists, who were among his entourage, had agreed to form a consortium that would invest in infrastructure projects in the Philippines. Included among the six were Alfonso Yuchengco, Lucio Tan, John Gokongwei, Henry Sy, George Ty and Andrew Gotianun. All are tycoons involved in fast expanding conglomerates that include banks, real estate companies, department store chains, hotels, food and beverage companies, communications and power generating corporations.[2]

According to newspaper accounts, the six had first met in January 1993 at the initiative of President Ramos and had been persuaded to jointly invest in priority projects that would include power and energy, telecommunications, transportation, roads and tourism. The six finally agreed on 20 April to pledge 100 million pesos each to the consortium that would invest in infrastructure projects beginning with a new airport at Sangley Point and the expansion of the Ninoy Aquino International Airport. Reports revealed that the president had played on the sense of patriotism and nationalism of the six tycoons.[3]

In this particular case, the Ramos administration must be given credit for having successfully brought together businessmen who have been and continue to be rivals in business. By timing the announcement of the consortium's formation with his visit to Beijing on 27 April, Ramos was signalling to his Chinese hosts that he expects the Chinese Filipinos to be loyal first and foremost to the Philippines. The formation of the consortium was presented as a testimony of loyalty from the Chinese Filipino "taipans". It was also a clear challenge to the Chinese Filipinos to re-invest their capital in the Philippines. On the other hand, by bringing them with him on his visit to China, Ramos was also signalling his intention to use the ethnic Chinese as a bridge in improving economic relations between China and the Philippines.

The Rise of Chinese Filipino Big Business

The moves by the Ramos administration to harness ethnic Chinese capital for infrastructure projects in the Philippines represents an acknowledgement of the considerable economic power the ethnic Chinese have amassed. The last 10 years have seen the emergence of formidable conglomerates headed by Chinese Filipinos and this despite the fact that the Philippine economy has undergone one of the worst crisis since the end of the Second World War. It is estimated that the Chinese in the Philippines own or control at least 8,500 enterprises in the country.[4] According to the latest study by Ellen Palanca, 354 of the top 1,000 corporations in the Philippines are owned or controlled by Chinese Filipinos (based on a 1990 sample).[5] In comparing this with a 1980 sample, Palanca has found that the Chinese Filipino share among top corporations has remained relatively constant. It was 33% in 1980 and 35% in 1990.[6] In contrast, the share of non-Chinese Filipinos dipped from 50% in 1980 to 34% in 1990. Palanca attributes the drop in the share of non-Chinese Filipinos to closures and migration – possible indicators that there was more capital flight on the part of the non-Chinese Filipinos as compared to the Chinese Filipinos during the political and economic tumult of the mid-80s.

This data ought to be reassuring for the Philippine authorities for it indicates that contrary to impressions, the ethnic Chinese in the Philippines have continued to invest their money in the Philippines even through the most difficult times. As a matter of fact, there is evidence that despite the poor overall performance of the Philippine economy over the last three years, Chinese Filipino enterprises have been growing and expanding. Enterprises that began in the retail business have diversified into realty development, car assembly and food chains, to name a few.[7]

In terms of size, Chinese Filipino firms tend to be smaller than the top Filipino corporations but they have been diversifying rapidly and expanding within the country. Significantly, Chinese Filipino companies are fast becoming industry leaders. For instance, Jollibee Foods Corporation, a fast-food chain owned by Chinese Filipinos has more than 100 branches nationwide and has become the largest Filipino-owned fast-food chain in the industry. It even overtook McDonald's (Philippines) in 1990 by netting gross revenues of 1.2 billion pesos and has become the market leader of food chains in the country. In the last five years, it has set up six subsidiaries in Brunei and Indonesia.[8]

In the field of banking, 9 out of 26 private, domestic commercial banks in the Philippines are owned by Chinese Filipinos, controlling almost 39% of the total assets.[9] These include Metrobank (George Ty), Rizal Commercial Banking Corporation (Alfonso Yuchengco), Equitable Bank (George Go), the Allied Bank (Lucio Tan), China Bank (Peter Dee), the Philippine Bank of Communications (Ralph Nubla), Philippine Trust (Emilio Yap), Philbanking (Domingo Lee) and Producers Bank (now the First Bank, owned by Henry Co).

Four out of the nine banks have risen to rank among the top ten in the country. Metrobank, controlled by George Ty, is now the country's biggest private commercial bank in terms of assets, ranking third only to the state-controlled Philippine National Bank and the Land Bank of the Philippines.[10] Beyond that, the bank has grown into a huge conglomerate with subsidiaries in finance, insurance, manufacturing and car assembly. Its gross revenues were 8.15 billion pesos in 1992 and it earned a record net income of 1.23 billion pesos making it one of the most profitable banks in the country.[11]

Conditions for Chinese Filipino Success

In tracing the rise of Chinese Filipino conglomerates, it may be useful to investigate some of the political conditions that have made their development possible over the last two decades. In retrospect, while the martial law regime of Ferdinand Marcos has been blamed for much of the present ills of the Philippine economy, in many ways, it provided important conditions for the rise of ethnic Chinese capital in the Philippines. The most significant turning point for the Chinese in the Philippines was the Presidential Decree (LOI 270) of 1975 that opened the door to citizenship for the majority of the ethnic Chinese. Until then, the Chinese had always lived with the possibility of deportation and expulsion. As "aliens", they had been barred by legislation from engaging in retail trade, from owning land and from practising a wide variety of professions.

The granting of Philippine citizenship in 1975 to many Philippine Chinese opened up areas of economic activity from which they had earlier been barred. It gave them a sense of security which was further enhanced by the perception that the Marcos regime was sympathetic to the Chinese. On his part, Marcos seemed to have fully understood the value of cultivating the political and hence the economic support of the Philippine Chinese community. Having abolished Congress in 1972, his policies towards China and the Chinese went uncontested and fostered an unusually close relationship between him and the leadership of the Philippine Chinese community.[12]

The acquisition of Philippine citizenship allowed ethnic Chinese entrepreneurs to operate beyond the confines of Chinatown and the network of the ethnic Chinese core community. It certainly furthered the integration of the Philippine Chinese at all levels, opening up economic opportunities no longer circumscribed by ethnicity.

In the last two decades, Chinese Filipinos have, in rapidly increasing numbers, attended mainstream schools and universities, joined the professions and actively engaged in a wide range of economic activities well beyond the walls of Chinatown. With the integration of the Chinese Filipinos into the mainstream, it should not be surprising that five out of the six "taipans" identified by Ramos have never been active members or leaders of the Federation of Filipino Chinese Chambers of Commerce and Industry, long considered the repository of economic and political power within the core Chinese community. All of them have taken great pains to stay out of the political limelight and to maintain a low profile (with the possible exception of Lucio Tan who aspired to the leadership of the "Federation"). Of the six, three are known to have closer links with mainland China than with Taiwan, while two are essentially neutral in relation to China-Taiwan politics. Only one has had any noticeably close ties with Taiwan, a further indication of the increasing drift away from the traditional norm associated with Chinese business leaders in the Philippines.[13]

Challenging the "Old Rich"

The rapid growth and diversification of Chinese Filipino owned corporations in the last few years have posed challenges to the traditional or "old rich" in the country. Quite a few of the newly formed conglomerates have assets that are climbing close to the levels of traditional giants such as San Miguel and

Ayala Corporations. The assets of J.G. Summit which is controlled by the John Gokongwei group was recently estimated at 18 billion pesos. This is almost one third of the capital of the Ayala conglomerate and one fourth of San Miguel's.[14]

The Gokongwei conglomerate is into food products, textiles, banking, sugar refining, power generation, department stores and more recently, telecommunications. John Gokongwei is known to be a stockholder in San Miguel Corporation but he has thus far been effectively prevented by the Sorianos from sitting on its Board of Directors. In his latest venture into telecommunications, he is pursuing plans to put up an international gateway facility that will bite into the market share of PLDT (Philippine Long Distance Telephone Company), which has hitherto monopolized telecommunications in the Philippines.[15]

In the area of real estate development, Chinese Filipino companies have entered the field with a vengeance. Many have been active in the development of the Ortigas area in downtown Metro Manila that now seeks to rival Makati (developed by the Ayalas) as the financial centre of the Philippines. In recent months, the Gotianuns (one of the six "taipans") who own Filinvest Company, outbid the well-established Ayalas for the development of the Alabang Stock Farm.[16] More spectacular has been the taking over of a majority stake in Philippine Airlines (PAL) by Lucio Tan who amassed his fortune from tobacco and who now heads a conglomerate that includes hotels, breweries, farms and real estate. In the PAL takeover bid, Tan was able to gain majority control of PR Holdings, the consortium that acquired 67% of PAL from the government in late 1992.[17] He succeeded in ousting Antonio Cojuangco from the chairmanship of PAL but was blocked from assuming full control of PAL by the government. What was revealing about the controversy over the PAL takeover bid by Tan was the inability of the Ayalas, Sorianos and Cojuangcos combined to buy him out of the company. At one stage, Tan had offered to sell his stake at PAL for five billion pesos but his rivals were unable to raise the amount he demanded.[18] The liquidity of Chinese Filipino capital has been difficult to match.

To a large extent, the Chinese Filipinos engaged in big and medium-scale business in the Philippines today represent an emerging class of Filipino entrepreneurs who are independently wealthy (that is, not dependent on foreign capital), whose assets are extremely liquid, and whose economic activities while posing challenges to the old landed elites (the majority of whom are Chinese-mestizos or Spanish-mestizos), are in many ways stimulating the Philippine economy. The penchant for diversification (not unusual in an economy subject to the risks and uncertainties of political instability and rapid structural change) among Chinese Filipino entrepreneurs has driven them not only into highly varied economic activities but also into different geographical areas in the country. It has been reported, for instance, that Henry Sy, a name now synonymous with shopping malls in the Philippines, is investing or has plans to invest in Tagaytay, Iloilo, Cebu and Davao.[19] Lucio Tan, on the other hand, has been reported to have plans of developing an industrial estate in Northern Mindanao and agro-industrial farms in Northern Luzon.[20] Other Chinese Filipino entrepreneurs have diversified into the development of beach resorts and tourist facilities that are expected to boost the country's tourism industry.[21] All these are expected to stimulate other investments and economic activities in areas outside Metro Manila.

The economic dynamism of Chinese Filipino entrepreneurs has no doubt helped to bolster investor confidence. Numerous tie-ups between Philippine Chinese groups and investors from other Asian countries have been reported. The Federation of Filipino Chinese Chambers of Commerce and Industry (known as "the Federation") has announced that its main concern for the next few years is to attract foreign investors to the Philippines.[22] That its target is the ethnic Chinese network in the region is clear from its self-imposed task of translating investment policies and brochures into Chinese. Numerous trade missions have been sent to ASEAN countries in pursuit of its goal. The "Federation" has also hosted international business gatherings that have drawn ethnic Chinese entrepreneurs from the region to the Philippines.

The economic success of the Philippine Chinese has definitely raised their stake in the development of the Philippine economy. There is little doubt that the Chinese Filipinos consider the economic recovery of the Philippines as essential to their own political and economic interests. The six "taipans" needed very little persuasion to form a consortium that will aid the government in its infrastructure projects. The name chosen for the consortium (Asia's Emerging Dragon Corporation) and the choice of Alfonso Yuchengco (known for his intensive advertising campaigns on the Philippines as the next "dragon economy") as head, reveal the aspirations many Chinese Filipino entrepreneurs have for the country.

Investments in China

It is in this light that one has to assess the issue of Chinese Filipino investments in mainland China. In some quarters, including the Philippine press, Chinese

Filipino investments in China have been described as capital flight and even regarded as downright "unpatriotic" acts.[23] From a more dispassionate perspective, one may argue that much of Chinese Filipino investments in China have been economically motivated with spates of investment coinciding with downturns in the Philippine economy. Given the secrecy with which such activities have been shrouded, it is difficult to arrive at an accurate assessment of the levels of investments in China originating from the Philippines. Besides, investments made through Hong Kong subsidiaries are often difficult to trace.[24] Nevertheless, it is probably safe to say that in comparison to other ASEAN countries, Philippine investments in China have been relatively limited and inconspicuous.[25] Investments from the Philippine Chinese have never reached high enough levels to spark international media interest.

While the data is incomplete and difficult to come by, there is evidence that some Philippine Chinese had already begun to invest in China since the turbulent years following 1983 when the Philippine economy began its downward spiral. During the economic crisis of the mid-80s and the political turmoil surrounding the demise of the Marcos regime, quite a number of Chinese Filipinos invested in mainland China. This period coincided with the rapid liberalization of the Chinese economy, a more stable polity (compared to the Philippines) and certainly better prospects for more profitable returns on investments. The development of Xiamen as a special economic zone in China also provided additional allure for the Philippine Chinese, most of whom still have relatives in Fujian Province. Some of the big names in Chinese Filipino business circles responded to the relatively attractive incentives offered by China. Among them were Leonardo Ty, the Gotesco Group, Lucio Tan, Henry Sy, John Gokongwei and George Ty.[26]

Investments have been varied and although more than 50% have been concentrated in Fujian Province, they have not been confined to it. Chinese Filipinos have invested in Shanghai, Beijing, Tienjin and as distant as Yunnan Province. In the last three years, both push and pull factors have contrived to draw capital from the Philippines to China. The remarkable growth in China's economy has naturally drawn businessmen and investors from the region like a magnet. Chinese Filipino business has responded no differently and to date, they are known to be involved in manufacturing, real estate development, hotels and banking. Those who have invested argue that China's incentives for foreign investments are very competitive and hence very attractive. Its booming economy promises both short and long term profits that are difficult to bypass. Besides, the Chinese in the Philippines, like many ethnic Chinese in Southeast Asia, are acutely aware that cultural affinity and kinship ties with Chinese on the mainland are distinct advantages in doing business with China – something they ought to capitalize on.

The push factors compelling Chinese Filipinos to bring capital out of the Philippines have been particularly strong in the last three years. Foremost among them has been the spate of kidnappings of ethnic Chinese for ransom by crime syndicates linked to disgruntled sectors of the Philippine military. Although the Chinese are not the only targets of these kidnap gangs, the number that has been victimized has been disproportionately high, eliciting much alarm from the Philippine Chinese community.

The kidnappings peaked in 1992 and in the face of the government's seeming ineptitude in stemming the tide, many Chinese Filipinos felt compelled to join a mass rally of some 18,000 people in February 1993 to prod authorities into taking more drastic measures. A total of 113 groups and associations, mainly Chinese Filipino in composition, participated in the mass rally.[27] The rash of kidnappings have abated somewhat but not sufficiently to give the ethnic Chinese a greater sense of personal security. In fact, an international school run by Filipinos has been set up in Xiamen specifically to cater to the educational needs of Chinese Filipino children sent there for security reasons.

It is important to note that many of those who have sent their children and some of their capital abroad tend to regard these as temporary measures. Some Chinese schools have reported that students who took leave to go abroad during the rash of kidnappings in 1992 have returned to enrol in 1993. Among Chinese Filipinos there is considerable expectation that the situation can and will improve. Understandably, there have been cases of families migrating to Canada and the United States but few have completely severed their ties with the Philippines. Given improved conditions, it is very likely some of these families will return to set up base again in the Philippines.

In addition to the threat from kidnap gangs, Chinese Filipino business like all other Philippine business has also been adversely affected by the acute power shortage that plagued the country over the last two years. While the worst is now over, the power crisis was particularly daunting to business and has simply added to the impulse to invest elsewhere.

Compounding the prevailing sense of uneasiness and insecurity among the Philippine Chinese have been the very mixed signals that the Ramos administration has been sending to the Chinese community. Soon after the President's visit to China where he announced the administration's intention of tapping Chinese Filipino capital for much needed infrastructure projects, press releases were made to the effect that the six "taipans" were being investigated for tax evasion. The Philippine press has particularly focused on the case of Lucio Tan whose Fortune Tobacco Company is alleged to have cheated on corporate taxes to the tune of billions of pesos.[28] Given his earlier reputation of having been a Marcos crony and his more recent association with the presidential candidacy of Ramon Mitra (who opposed and lost to Ramos in the 1992 presidential elections), the public impression was that the moves against him were politically motivated. The high degree of publicity surrounding the Bureau of Internal Revenue's charges of tax fraud against Lucio Tan sent political ripples through the Philippine Chinese community, arousing fears of a campaign targetting the minority community.

It should be understood that in the Philippines, the ethnic Chinese have been conditioned by historical experience to regard public investigations into their finances by government agencies as indirect attempts at extortion. As a matter of practice, ethnic Chinese businessmen have tended to jealously guard against public disclosures of their real wealth and conscientiously avoided any kind of publicity. By publicizing tax evasion charges against Lucio Tan and singling him out, the administration wittingly or unwittingly sparked fears that other ethnic Chinese would follow as targets of investigation.

In an apparent attempt to allay these fears, influencial presidential advisor, Jose Almonte, has publicly reassured the Chinese that the tax campaign measures will be evenly applied among the business sector. The president himself with the key members of his cabinet took pains to hold a two-hour dialogue with Chinese Filipino business leaders in October to reassure them that the government was not being anti-Chinese in its policies. This has not been completely convincing and some Chinese believe that the campaign against corporate tax evaders has to cut across ethnic boundaries to prove the government's claims.

Reactions to Chinese Filipino Economic Power

Reactions from Filipinos towards the rise of ethnic Chinese big business has been ambivalent and mixed. Some politicians and bureaucrats still regard the wealthy Chinese as "milking cows" and take every opportunity to approach the Chinese for financial contributions to various causes. In the general elections of 1992, all presidential candidates except one were known to have approached the Chinese for campaign contributions. Despite the fact that most of them as Filipino citizens can now participate directly in politics as voters and as candidates, many Chinese Filipino businessmen still feel the need to protect their interests by contributing to the campaign chests of various political parties. A common practice has been to contribute to all as a safeguard against potential retributions from winning candidates whom they might have missed supporting.

Obviously, crime syndicates, in targetting the Chinese, share this view of the Chinese as "milking cows". The preference of the ethnic Chinese for secrecy, their dislike for publicity and the cultural propensity to avoid legalistic entanglements have added to the vulnerability of the Chinese. Kidnap syndicates operate on the understanding that the Chinese are less likely to report kidnappings in their desire to avoid public disclosure of their situation and particularly, their wealth and economic status, and therefore the most likely to comply with the demands of the kidnappers. Moreover, the extreme liquidity of Chinese Filipino assets or at least their capacity to mobilize large amounts of capital at short notice have contributed to their being favoured targets by criminals.

On the whole, reactions to ethnic Chinese economic success in the Philippines have been a mixture of envy and admiration. While there remains residual prejudices against the Chinese and some reservations about their political loyalties, there is also grudging admiration for their economic prowess. There is no doubt that the economic success of Hong Kong, Taiwan and Singapore (known as the "dragon economies") and the more recent economic achievements of China have increased respect for the Chinese. Nevertheless, the Chinese Filipinos are not yet fully accepted or integrated in Philippine society and there are still voices raised against the "Chinese control" of the Philippine economy. There are not infrequent references to the existence of "Chinese cartels" which are resented by the Filipino majority. The fact that many of the ethnic Chinese are engaged in business has also meant that they interact with the Filipino majority as employers. The division between employer and employee along ethnic lines is a sensitive issue and labour unions are known to have been more critical or resentful of Chinese-owned firms.

On the issue of Chinese Filipino investments in China, an exploratory investigation has shown that more than 50% of the sample agreed that capital should be re-invested in the Philippines rather than in China.[29] Nonetheless, such views have been muted and both the political authorities and influential economists have cited the advantages of having Philippine investments in China. Bernardo Villegas, head of the think tank Communications Research Center of the Philippines, has been quoted as saying that "capital flight to China must be regarded as an investment in the future".[30] He has also urged the forging of strategic alliances between Chinese Filipinos and their business counterparts in Taiwan and Hong Kong as a way of boosting trade between the Philippines and China. In this respect, he sees the Chinese community as an asset to the country.

It is clear that the present administration sees the importance of mobilizing ethnic Chinese capital for Philippine economic recovery. While the Philippine government would rather see capital re-invested in the Philippines, it also recognizes that Chinese Filipino investments in China can be productive in the long term especially if it will enable the Philippines to have access to a slice of the China market. There is recognition of the advantages the ethnic Chinese can provide in the expansion of economic relations with China and the ASEAN economies.

The challenge to the Philippine government is how it intends to further integrate the ethnic Chinese minority into its larger social, economic and political fabric. This will require skilful handling. Quite apart from allaying fears of the Chinese that they are being targetted or squeezed by big politicians, the idea of an alliance between Chinese big business and the state will itself be a sensitive issue. There will be questions raised about the creation of a "Ramos-Chinese conspiracy" to control the Philippine economy.

For ethnic Chinese business, especially big business, it poses a major dilemma. Should they align themselves with the government, they run the risk of being too closely identified with the ruling oligarchy. Their fortunes will wax and wane with the fortunes of the ruling administration. Should they avoid this role, then they may be accused of non-cooperation or of being unpatriotic. The "six taipans" walk the thin line of having to cooperate with the present administration without necessarily being completely identified with it.

Conclusion

As in other parts of Southeast Asia, the lingering sense of political and social insecurity has contributed to the mobile and liquid character of ethnic Chinese capital in the Philippines. Combined with the push factors, there have been pull factors that have drawn some of them to invest in China in recent years. Through their informal networks, they are playing a significant role in integrating the Philippine economy with the rest of the region. Some of the traditional communal organizations, especially clan and hometown associations have been re-invigorated and function as informal business networks.

The dynamism of Chinese Filipino business will be a vital stimulant to the Philippine economy. Most noticeable has been their intensive activities in finance and real estate. While only one-tenth of the Chinese Filipinos among the top 1000 corporations were engaged in finance and real estate (compared to half in manufacturing and a third in trade) in 1990, they accounted for one-fourth of the finance sector.[31] Among the "six taipans", five already own banks and the sixth has plans to buy one. Obviously, the ethnic Chinese in the Philippines will be a vital source of domestic capital for the development of the economy. By attempting to tap these resources for infrastructure development, the Ramos administration has made a wise move. To ensure that the Chinese Filipinos will continue to re-invest in the country, it will have to step up its efforts in ensuring public security and in providing a political environment in which their ethnicity does not become an issue.

Endnotes

1 See *Time*, 10 May 1993, where the Chinese diaspora was dubbed China's "secret weapon". Negative reactions to ethnic Chinese investments have also been cited in Willy Laohoo, "Filipino Reactions to Philippine Chinese Investments in China: An Exploratory Survey", unpublished paper presented at the conference *China, Taiwan, the Ethnic Chinese and the Philippine Economy* organized by the Philippine Association for Chinese Studies at the Ateneo De Manila University, November 1993.

2 Reported in "Six Chinese-Filipinos Team Up: Consortium Announced in China", *Manila Chronicle*, 28 April 1993, p. 1. See also "Local Taipans to Build Airport", *Manila Chronicle*, 29 April 1993, pp. 1 & 7.

3 Booma Cruz, "Yuchengco Chosen Consortium Head", *Manila Chronicle*, 30 April 1993, pp. 1 & 6.

4 This figure has been cited in the *Overseas Chinese Economy: Yearbook 1992*, Taipei, 1993, p. 219.

5 Ellen Palanca, "The Economic Position of the Chinese-Filipinos among the 1990 Top 1000 Corporations in the Philippines", unpublished paper presented in Manila at the conference *China, Taiwan, the Ethnic Chinese and the Philippine Economy* organized by the Philippine Association for Chinese Studies at the Ateneo De Manila University, November 1993.

6 *Ibid.*

7 For reports on this, see *Manila Chronicle* issues for 28 June 1993, 26 August 1993 and 21 October 1993. Also, *Manila Bulletin*, 12 August 1993.

8 "Jollibee to Expand Abroad", *Manila Chronicle*, 28 June 1993 and "Jollibee reports P622 m Sales", *Manila Chronicle*, 4 November 1993.

9 Go Bon Juan, "Ethnic Chinese in Philippine Banking", unpublished paper presented at the conference *China, Taiwan, the Ethnic Chinese and the Philippine Economy* organized by the Philippine Association for Chinese Studies at the Ateneo De Manila University, November 1993.

10 Reported in "Metrobank No. 1 in Resources", *Manila Chronicle*, 21 August 1993, p. 9.

11 This is based on figures provided in the Metrobank's Annual Report for 1992 (p. 8). Refer also to the news item "Metrobank Group Pays P4.04 b Taxes", *Manila Chronicle*, 28 April 1993.
12 For the linkages see Theresa C. Carino, "Leadership and Organization among the Chinese in the Philippines: Continuity and Change", *Asian Culture*, No. 15, June 1991, Singapore.
13 Since the Second World War, Philippine Chinese leaders have been closely allied with the Guomindang Party and it is widely known in the minority community that election to the leadership of major communal organizations requires the party's *imprimateur*. Lucio Tan has been on the Board of Directors of the Federation of Filipino Chinese Chambers of Commerce and Industry for more than a decade but his bid for leadership has always been blocked by pro-Taiwan factions in the organization. None of the other "taipans" have been active members of the Federation.
14 See "Awaiting J.G. Summit", *Manila Chronicle*, 23 May 1993, p. 14.
15 See "Gokongwei asks FVR to Support Digitel's IGF Bid", *Business Star*, 9 August 1993, p. 14.
16 "Filinvest Land Poised to Become McDonald's of Housing Industry", *Manila Chronicle*, 1 November 1993, p. 19.
17 Refer to "Tan Wants P5 b for PAL Stake", *Manila Bulletin*, 23 January, 1993, p. 1 (Business Section). According to sources close to him, Lucio Tan sold two buildings in Hong Kong in order to buy his stake in Philippine Airlines.
18 *Ibid.*
19 Refer to reports "Sy, Floirendo Eye Ind'l Estate", *Philippine Daily Globe*, 24 September 1991, p. 9 and "Smooth Sailing for RP's Favorite Retailer", *Manila Chronicle*, 29 August 1993, p. 11.
20 "Lucio Tan's Ind'l Estate Rising", *Philippine Daily Globe*, 14 June 1991 and "Tan Plans Big Piggery Projects", *Manila Bulletin*, 27 April 1992, p. 9.
21 Reported in "Ever Gotesco Group Sets Diversification", *Manila Bulletin*, 12 August 1993, p. 4.
22 "Chinese Chamber Vows to Attract Investors", *Manila Chronicle*, 5 April 1993, p. 11.
23 In the report "Jolly Six Giants", *Philippine Daily Inquirer*, 30 April 1993 the six taipans were described as being "unpatriotic" for having invested in China.
24 Refer to the study of Willy Laohoo, *op. cit.*
25 In comparing figures of ASEAN investment in China, the Philippines has consistently lagged behind Thailand and Singapore. It was ahead of Indonesia and Malaysia between 1984 and 1991 but since 1992, the Philippines has invested the least in China. Refer to the tables in Yong Pow Ang's article "Singapore's Investment in China" in this book.
26 Willy Laohoo, *op. cit.*
27 In *Tulay*, 8 March 1993, pp. 8 & 9.
28 See "A Taxing Dilemma", *Asiaweek*, 20 October 1993, pp. 57–62.
29 Willy Laohoo, *op. cit.*
30 Villegas was quoted in *Manila Bulletin*, 29 March 1993, p. 7, (Business Section).
31 Ellen Palanca, *op. cit.*

11

Recent Developments in the Political Economy of China-Malaysia Relations

Ho Khai Leong

In June 1993, Malaysia's Prime Minister Mahathir Mohamad led a 290-member delegation to the People's Republic of China (PRC). Later he described this as "the most successful delegation" he has led in his twelve-year-old administration.[1] Much was achieved by this visit, and it is possibly the most encouraging and significant sign of the changed relations between China and Malaysia. This visit in effect picked up the momentum which the Prime Minister himself had set in motion in 1985 with his first visit to China. From that first visit, he was already convinced that economic issues should be the basis of a bilateral relationship.[2] The end of the Cold War, the demise of the Malayan Communist Party, the commitment shown by the PRC government in economic reform, and more importantly, the rush by ASEAN states to invest in China, have all contributed to the accelerated development of economic relations between China and Malaysia in recent years.

One of the more interesting effects related to this development is the increased volume of investment by Malaysian Chinese in China. While difficult to trace, it is believed to be growing substantially. Such a general trend is parallel to the enthusiasm shown by the ethnic Chinese in the ASEAN region. In that regard, the Malaysian Chinese investment interest in the mainland is not unique. This phenomenon, however, is more complicated and politically sensitive in multi-ethnic Malaysia. This paper attempts to look at the development of economic relations between the two countries and, with special reference to the Malaysian Chinese investment in China, some of the political implications that have arisen. It will also discuss the potential policy problems involved in Sino-Malaysian economic relations.

The Development of Sino-Malaysian Economic Relations

There is long history of trading links between Malaysia and China. As far back as the early 15th century, there had been recorded contacts between China and Peninsular Malaya. Trade was to boom in the 19th century as a flood of migrant workers left their homeland for the "South Seas" to make their fortunes. Many then returned home with cash and goods. Even in the troubled times of the 1940s when the Chinese Communists took control of China and the Malayan Communist Party (MCP) was actively involved in political insurgency in colonial Malaya, the trade links were still there and these were maintained throughout the 1950s. In 1957, the newly formed Alliance government of Malaya chose to continue the British policy of trading with China despite ideological differences. China-made goods and merchandise (mainly foodstuff, herbs, medicines and textiles) were allowed into the country. In return the Chinese government bought raw materials such as rubber and tin. In general, trade was done through a number of companies which were granted approval to import such goods.[3]

One of the outstanding features that characterized the relationship during the 1950s and 1960s was the way in which trade was conducted through third countries and non-governmental agencies. Since both China and Malaysia did not recognize each other, commercial transactions remained unofficial. Places such as Hong Kong and Macau were used as intermediaries for these transactions. The trade balance, however, had always been in China's favour. Although trade had no offical status, it paved the way for a rapid increase of two-way trade during the following years.

One can argue that the obstacle to economic relations between the two countries during this period is the absence of formal channels and diplomatic relations. Diplomatic relations between China and Malaysia were non-existent before Tun Razak's visit in May 1974. Why was it so difficult for the two countries to establish diplomatic relations? The limitations imposed upon Sino-Malaysian relations can be analysed systematically in terms of two sources of pressure.

First, the PRC had been active in supporting revolutionary movements throughout Southeast Asia. For instance, the North Kalimantan Unitary State Revolutionary Government in North Kalimantan, the Malayan National Liberation League and the Malayan Communist Party (MCP) in Malaya and Singapore were three organizations which received public Chinese support after 1965. The Malayan National Liberation League was even invited to establish a permanent diplomatic mission in Beijing in January 1966. "The Voice of the Malayan Revolution" began regular radio broadcasts in 1969.

On 29 April 1975 the Chinese Communist Party sent a congratulatory note to the MCP when it celebrated its 45th anniversary. As far as the Alliance government was concerned, the Communist insurgency constituted a serious threat to regime stability and legitimacy. In the light of the PRC's open support for the MCP, the Malaysian government certainly had reason to doubt the sincerity of the PRC in its pursuit of diplomatic and economic relations.

The second source of pressure is the question of dual nationality and the allegiance of the Malaysian Chinese. A large number of ethnic Chinese residing in Malaya during the 1950s and 1960s were non-citizens. Their cultural and ethnic ties with the mainland had always been viewed with suspicion by the local population. Although the Malayan Chinese Association (MCA) attempted to obtain citizenship for many non-citizen Chinese, the question of dual nationality and political allegiance remained a largely unresolved issue.[4] The situation was not helped by the fact that the PRC did not have a consistent and clear policy on the status of Chinese residing overseas.

These two sources of pressure clearly constituted major obstacles to the establishment of diplomatic relations between the two countries. As Leo Suryadinata observes, "Not surprisingly, prior to the establishment of diplomatic ties, Malaysia insisted on negotiating with the PRC on two major issues: the national status of the ethnic Chinese and the Malayan Communist Party. On the first point, Beijing guaranteed that it recognized single nationality for the ethnic Chinese, but on the second issue, China only agreed not to interfere in Malaysian domestic affairs and not to carry out subversion."[5]

While both these factors contributed to the stagnation of political relations between the two countries, China's closed-door policy of the 1950s and 1960s also contributed to the problem. During the Maoist period the Chinese economy was inward-looking in its orientation. It advocated a policy of self-reliance aimed at reduced dependence on world markets. For example, during the 1950s and 1960s, the total value of foreign trade was only about 2% of the gross national product (GNP).[6] Certainly the policies practised by the PRC government were not very conducive to or encouraging of trading with the outside world. Only in 1978 did China drastically change its view on foreign trade and investment. Chinese economists and politicians had argued vigorously that China should participate in the world market and foreign trade should not be shunned – instead it should be regarded as a means for filling gaps in domestic development. In short it was acknowledged that foreign exchange for imports should be valued and export expansion encouraged. These changes, which are important components of China's post-Mao reforms, provided the impetus for China's opening to the outside world.

In general, the political atmosphere of the 1950s and 1960s made impossible any major development of Sino-Malaysian links. A turning point in the bilateral relations occurred in 1974 when Malaysia became the first ASEAN state to open diplomatic relations with China. Malaysia's then Prime Minister Tun Abdul Razak visited China in May 1974 and issued a Joint Communique with Premier Chou En-Lai at the end of his visit. In the Joint Communique, the emphasis was on the "mutual recognition and the establishment of diplomatic relations".[7] No mention was made of trade relations.

Despite that, available data showed that trade volumes, while still remaining relatively low, had began to pick up. But investment was still almost non-existent. In order to meet the demand for greater volume of trade, the Malaysian government appointed the government-owned PERNAS (*Perbadanan Nasional* – National Corporation) as the main agent for China trade. PERNAS was registered as a public company in November 1969 under the Companies Act of 1965. It was responsible for a number of tasks, among them making the arrangements for Malaysians to go to Canton (Guangzhou) twice a year to order their goods at the trade fair.[8]

In the late 1980s, China's open-door policy and its commitment to economic reform began to have an impact on the ASEAN countries' perception of the Communist giant. In November 1985, Prime Minister Mahathir led a large delegation to visit the PRC, and this was a turning point in Sino-Malaysian economic relations. During the visit, both parties signed various agreements, the most important being the Avoidance of Double Taxation Agreement. What followed was a series of important events which include the Sino-Malaysia Direct Flight Agreement (1986) and Sino-Malaysia Trade Agreement (1988). The PRC's Premier Li Peng also visited Malaysia in 1991.

In the early 1990s, Singapore led the way on investment in China, and thus began a surge of ASEAN investment. With the disbanding of the MCP in 1989, the Malaysian government appeared to have resolved the issue of China's supporting revolutionary movements. The political huddle was finally cleared for economic relations to take off.

The only question that remains now is the allegiance and loyalty of the Malaysian Chinese. While doubts have always been raised by the radical factions of the Malay community, the ethnic Chinese in Malaysia have always been committed in their duty to the Malaysian state. Practically all Malaysian

Chinese leaders have made public declarations pledging the total allegiance of the Chinese community to the Malaysian state. After all, Malaysia has been independent for 27 years, and the younger generations of the Malaysian Chinese population have been "localized" and "assimilated". While there may still be lingering doubts, the argument of disloyalty certainly is not convincing. When investment in China by the Southeast Asian region began to grow, the prime minister, as a policy initiator, became the first to call for more trade with China. Economic considerations, it seems, for government officials at least, have finally outweighed the doubts of Malaysian Chinese allegiance.

In summary, the factors that led to closer economic relations between China and Malaysia are both internal and external. China's economic reform under Deng Xiaoping and its open policy have certainly contributed to the large volume of investment pouring in from the Asian states, and in that regard, Malaysian investment in China is not an exception. Malaysia's need to maintain its impressive economic performance and its increased emphasis on sustained economic growth have made it necessary to diversify and to invest elsewhere. China's attractively huge market and its potential have prompted Malaysia to expand economic relations with the mainland.

Mahathir's Visit to China in June 1993

One of the most significant events that has improved Sino-Malaysian relations is Mahathir's second visit to China in June 1993 when he paid a 10-day official visit, heading a 290-member delegation, comprising four Cabinet ministers and at least 150 businessmen. It is the biggest Malaysian mission to China since the two countries established diplomatic relations in 1974. Prime Minister Mahathir toured several factories in the light industry field in the Shanghai and the Shenzhen Special Economic Zone in Guangdong province. The delegation met Chinese Premier Li Peng who appeared in public for the first time after a seven-week illness. One of the major outcomes of the trip was the large number of agreements reached between the two countries. A total of 36 memorandums of understanding (MOU) were signed. These will make Malaysia's investments in China reach an estimated RM8.2 billion, according to officials in the International Trade and Consumer Affairs, if all the MOUs are implemented.[9] The trip secured RM1.494 billion worth of business contracts. About RM280 million of the deals were for the export of Chinese goods into Malaysia, while the remaining RM1.15 billion represented the total value of investments for joint venture projects already agreed on or under negotiation.[10] The issue of direct trade between the two countries was also discussed.

Prime Minister Mahathir expressed preference for an expansion of direct bilateral trade with China over indirect dealings through third countries. He was quoted as saying, "Trade with third countries in goods originating from Malaysia cannot be regarded as trade with Malaysia as such trade already appears in the records of our trade with such countries."[11] Obviously direct trade and investment would be far more efficient than having to operate through a third party. It is likely that direct trade with China will increase in the future.

It was obvious that Mahathir's official visit to China has particular importance *vis-a-vis* the prospects of Sino-Malaysian political as well as economic relations. The visit to China was described by Mahathir as a "leap forward" in Sino-Malaysian relations.[12] China had been viewed with mistrust as it had a long history of actively supporting the banned Malayan Communist Party. It was only in December 1989, when the MCP, partly under pressure from Beijing and partly in acknowledgement of the futility of its armed struggle in the post-Cold War era, decided to sign a peace accord with the Malaysian and Thai governments in Haadyai, Thailand, that matters took a turn for the better. Mahathir's visit, therefore, had helped to clear some of the misgivings which had retarded the relations between the two countries.

The trip was also seen as a move by Malaysia to marshal support for the idea of the East Asia Economic Caucus (EAEC). China's Premier Li Peng explicitly endorsed the idea. But the most significant objective and outcome of the trip was Malaysia's effort to foster economic ties with the Chinese, including technical cooperation and joint venture projects.

The desire to strengthen trade ties is expressed by both sides. The chairman of China's Standing Committee of the National People's Congress (NPC), Qiao Shi, visited Malaysia in July 1993 and he expressed Beijing's desire to strengthen economic ties with Malaysia. A Chinese consulate in Kuching was proposed to facilitate trade. China also agreed to allow Malaysian Airlines System (MAS) to increase its Kuala Lumpur-Beijing-Guangzhou flights from the current six a week to eight in 1994 and to twelve in 1996.[13]

Since 1986, a few major trade agreements have been signed between the two countries. Some of the trade agreements include the Avoidance of Double Taxation Agreement, the Shipping and Aviation Agreement, the Trading Agreement, the Investment Guarantee Agreement, and the Economic Trade Joint Committee Contract.

In the past few years, there were also many Chinese delegations led by high-level officials visiting Malaysia in search of investment. Many of them had the authority to give instant approval to proposals which they considered attractive and beneficial. The Tianjin Municipal People's Government Foreign Investment Committee delegation which visited the country in May 1993 was such a delegation.[14]

In general, reciprocal visits of government officials and high-ranking officials between China and Malaysia have been on the increase in the past few years. Official trade delegations and friendly financial delegations sent by their respective governments have also exchanged visits, further promoting the economic cooperation between the countries. The Annual Spring Guangzhou Trade Fair is an attraction to Malaysian Chinese businessmen, and the Federation of Malaysian Chinese Chamber of Commerce organizes annual trips for members to attend. Apart from economic delegations, there have been numerous visits made by cultural, religious, juristic, military and journalists' and writers' delegations from both sides.

Sino-Malaysian Trade Patterns

Since the signing of the Bilateral Trade Agreement in April 1988, trade between China and Malaysia has grown rapidly. Two-way trade increased from RM1,647 million in 1987 to RM4,446 million in 1992, with imports from China surpassing Malaysia's exports to it. The volume of trade between the two countries has increased from RM982 million in 1986 to more than RM3 billion in 1992.

Table 11.1: China and Malaysia: Directions of Trade
(in RM millions)

Year	Export	Growth Rate	Import	Growth Rate	Volume	Growth Rate
1980	499.1		551.3		1,050.4	
1981	221.5	(55.6)	631.6	14.6	853.1	(18.8)
1982	258.2	16.6	648.5	2.7	906.7	6.3
1983	364.4	41.1	625.8	(3.5)	990.1	9.2
1984	387.3	6.3	668.4	6.8	1,055.7	6.6
1985	398.5	2.9	621.4	(7.0)	1,020.0	(3.4)
1986	421.6	5.8	728.2	17.2	1,149.8	12.7
1987	702.8	66.7	946.3	30.0	1,649.1	43.4
1988	1,089.4	55.0	1,266.3	33.8	2,355.7	42.8
1989	1,302.0	19.5	1,650.0	30.3	2,952.1	25.3
1990	1,675.2	28.7	1,521.2	(7.8)	3,196.4	8.3
1991	1,760.7	5.1	2,212.9	45.5	3,973.6	24.3
1992	1,961.2	11.4	2,485.0	12.3	4,446.2	11.9

Source: *Trade Statistics*, Malaysia

Two general observations can be made with regard to the development of bilateral trade during the past five years. Firstly, two-way direct trade has increased. Based on official Malaysian statistics, Malaysia's exports to China has been increasing since 1981. A similar trend is found in its imports from China. The increases are quite impressive.

Secondly, with the rapid growth in trade, there comes the belief and hope, on both sides, that the potential for increased two-way trade would be large. In terms of direct trade, careful monitoring by Malaysian officials suggests that during the year 1993 the total volume of Malaysia's direct trade with China has reached the RM3 billion level. Malaysian officials are confident that the total volume of trade will soon exceed RM5 billion annually.

Malaysia's direct trade exports to China is still relatively simple in terms of its commodity composition. Diversification is important. In 1990, for example, on the basis of the statistics, Malaysia's direct exports to China were confined to only 10 items. On the other hand, China exported 200 items to Malaysia.

Malaysian Investments in China

Malaysian investors are considered latecomers to China when compared with the others, especially those from Singapore and Thailand. But by early 1993, Malaysian investors were ranked among the top ten. For example, in 1992, Malaysian companies invested about RM1.3 billion in China, making it the tenth largest investor in the Republic. According to the Malaysian Deputy Minister of International Trade and Industry, Chua Jui Meng, about 37 Malaysian investors have invested capital in China "since China opened its doors to foreign investment". He was quoted as saying, "Even though the exact number is not available, the government estimated total investment to be more than RM1.54 billion, in hotel, food processing and manufacturing industries."[15] With increased trade and investment, Malaysia is expected to move to the fifth spot as one of China's largest investors in 1993, with investment doubling to US$1 billion.

There are no complete official statistics on Malaysian investments in China, as a top official in the Malaysian government has acknowledged. Table 11.2 is merely a sample of some of the Malaysian firms and companies which have invested or are about to invest in China. In general, there are several features to note. First, Malaysian investments cover several sectors, including construction, services (restaurants, supermarkets, hotels, tourist spots), trading, banking and financial services, and information technology.

Second, Malaysian investments tend to be concentrated along the coastal regions which range from the Liadong Peninsula in the north to Hainan Island in the south. This is hardly surprising as the area China first opened to the world are the coasts and China has actively developed an outward-orientation in these areas. Third, Malaysian businessmen are increasingly inclined to invest directly in China without going through a third party. Previously, many Malaysian investors used their Hong Kong-based companies to invest in China. The trend is changing with the opening of China.

Table 11.2: Selected Malaysian Firms' Investment in China

Company	Areas	Investment (in RM millions)	Destination
Pembinaan Jayabumi	Waste water treatment	26	Fuzhou
Sungai Way Holding Bhd	Construction & property	25	near Beijing
Archwell Development Sdn Bhd	Construction, hotel, shopping complex	130	Guangzhou
Sembawang	Oil rig, fabrication, ship repair, infrastructure	103	Pearl River Delta
EKRAN Bhd	Beach resorts, golf course	290	Haikou, Hainan Island
SIG Holdings	Printing operations	2.8	Beijing
Daichung Sdn Bhd	Hotels	37.5	Fuzhou
Samanda	Adhesive tape, label stocks	5.3	Jilin
Arkitek MAA	Consultancy	n.a	n.a
Ceramica Indah Sdn Bhd	Tiles, ceramics	30	Shanghai
Kanzen	Spring mattresses	n.a	Tianjin, Shanghai, Xiamen
	Steel plant	n.a	Shanghai
KFC Holdings	Poultry, animal and aqua feeds	n.a	Beijing Tianjin
Kim Hin Industry	Tiles	30	Shanghai
Sateras	Construction (commercial & residential projects)	162.5	Anhui
Mamee-Double Decker	Food processing	10	Suzhou
Leader Universal Holdings	Cable facilities	n.a	Shantou
Mercury Industries	Poly putty	n.a	Hubei

Sources: *New Straits Times*, *Straits Times*, *Business Times*, *The Star*, *Utusan Malaysia*, and *Nanyang Siang Pau.*

Malaysian Chinese Investments in China: Economic Rationales and Political Sensitivities

Economic Rationales

Overseas Chinese remittances and investments in China are certainly not a recent phenomenon. As far back as the early 19th century, Chinese traders in Southeast Asia were already sending home gifts in cash and kind to their relatives. Others built schools and hospitals in their ancestral villages.[16] At the same time, the Imperial Chinese government attempted to recruit overseas Chinese businessmen to assist in the modernization of the Chinese economy.

> Beginning with the discovery of the plight of the coolie labourers in the 1860s, the Ch'ing dynasty shaped a policy which, in its final form, granted returning businessmen a major part in economic affairs. Gradually, the strategic emphasis shifted from the protection of workers to the encouragement of renewed contacts with the motherland to the outright exploitation of overseas experience and wealth.[17]

Since the 1980s, the political and economic orientations of overseas Chinese have undergone a major transformation – from being what one author called "a Peking tool"[18] to what is now the economic motif of China's modernization programmes. The assistance to China by the overseas Chinese has gone a full circle. Overseas Chinese investment once again is being recruited to help modernize the Chinese economy.

In Malaysia, the Chinese transformed themselves from being "China-centred" to "Malayan-centred" in the 1950s.[19] As far as investment in and remittances to China are concerned, they have always kept a low profile. They realized early on that a high profile would certainly invite questions about their allegiance and loyalty. Since their control of the indigenous economy was often perceived as a threat, they had to be extremely careful so as not to provoke further resentment among the local population.

The Malaysian Chinese business community found an unlikely partner in Prime Minister Mahathir in 1993. The open call by the prime minister to trade with China certainly boosted the morale of the Chinese business community, and this has given them the confidence to expand their trade with China. Although their allegiance and loyalty were still open to conjecture, this time it was the Malay opposition, not the government, that raised the question. This is a very significant difference as the Chinese community, in following the official policy of trading with China, can now openly defend itself.

Since 1986, the number of Malaysian Chinese going to China has increased tremendously. In 1991, with the easing of travel restrictions, Malaysian tourists to China doubled from the previous year. At the same time, business delegations from the PRC are also making frequent trips to Malaysia. Table 11.3 shows the number of delegations which have visited the Kuala Lumpur & Selangor Chinese Chamber of Commerce & Industry over the last decade. In 1991, the number of missions increased five-fold, and in 1992 the number doubled.

Table 11.3: Number of Chinese Missions to the Kuala Lumpur & Selangor Chinese Chamber of Commerce & Industry

Year	Number
1986	2
1987	4
1988	2
1989	5
1990	6
1991	26
1992	46

Source: The Kuala Lumpur & Selangor Chinese Chamber of Commerce & Industry

As far as investment in China is concerned, it is extremely difficult to distinguish between Chinese and Malay capital in Malaysia, especially after the implementation of the New Economic Policy (NEP) in 1971, which has made many Malay capitalists. It is argued that Malaysian Chinese businesses have many connections with the Malay political and business elites,[20] although the extent of this is still relatively unknown. What is certain is that increasingly Malay and Chinese capital have intermingled and have become harder to differentiate. However, despite these general observations, there are a few distinguished Chinese businesses which have substantial investment in China.

Malaysian hotel and commodities tycoon Robert Kuok is among the leading foreign investors in China, with his investments approved to date totalling about US$2.5 billion.[21] Most of Kuok's investments are carried out through his Hong Kong based company, Kerry's, and also his Singapore company, the Pacific Carrier Ltd (PCL), which has invested in China's Tylfull.[22] Projects in China which Robert Kuok is said to be involved in include manufacturing, a hotel and palm oil refineries.

In the mid-80s, the Malaysian government used to complain that China favoured private enterprises owned by overseas Chinese when doing business. Its officials criticized China for being partial to overseas Chinese, and ignoring non-Chinese businessmen. They wanted China to do business with Malaysia's state-owned enterprises, and subsequently set up PERNAS to perform the function of helping *bumiputera* businessmen to trade in China. While China defended its practice as being traditional, it nevertheless speeded up trading with *bumiputera* businesses to avoid the appearance of being biased or unfair to non-Chinese business groups.

Political Sensitivities: The Question of Loyalty

Two important political issues have always affected contemporary relations between China and the ASEAN countries: the issue of China's support of the Malayan Communist Party, and the divided loyalty of overseas Chinese communities.

For Malaysia, the first issue was resolved in 1989, but the second issue remains significant. The question of the Malaysian Chinese's loyalty has been there for a long time. Although the Chinese government has reiterated that ethnic Chinese are not allowed to hold dual nationality, there is serious and lingering apprehension about the mainland Chinese and Malaysian Chinese's cultural and emotional attachments to each other.[23] It is reported that Chinese bureaucrats would prefer to do business with Malaysian Chinese, and there is a great tendency for the Malaysian Chinese to invest in the mainland despite the need to do so in local soil. Indeed, Malaysian authorities have always been suspicious of the loyalty of citizens of Chinese origin.

The official position changed drastically in 1993 after Mahathir's visit to China. Questions on ethnic Chinese loyalty now came from the Malay opposition. Semangat '46 party chief Razaleigh openly questioned Malaysian Chinese loyalties to Malaysia. He was quoted as saying, "We are worried. If this trend (investment in China) continued, it will create doubts about their loyalties to Malaysia." Such an accusation brought a strong reaction from the Chinese community. Razaleigh's statements were censured not only by the the Malaysian Chinese Association (MCA) and the GERAKAN, which are in the Barisan government, but also by the opposition Democratic Action Party (DAP). Even Malay community leaders took the side of the Chinese investors. For example, the President of the Malay Chamber of Commerce and Industry, Tan Sri Wan Azmi Wan Hamzah, said the Malaysian Chinese investment was not one-sided but has proven to be a mutually beneficial relationship that can help boost the Malaysian economy.[24] As such, their loyalty to Malaysia should not be questioned.

Some Chinese politicians have suggested that one way to dampen or dispel the lingering doubts about ethnic Chinese loyalties is to establish Malay-Chinese joint ventures in China. For example, Deputy Speaker of the Parliament, Ong Ji Kit, appealed to local Chinese and Malay businesses to invest together in China. They could cooperate and make use of their expertise to help each other. Since the Chinese have the advantage of speaking the language, and the Malays are more experienced in dealing with government bureaucracies, it would work to their advantage if they established joint ventures in China.[25]

Probably the issue of ethnic Chinese loyalty to Malaysia obscures the important point. If any questions should be raised at all, it should not be about political loyalty but economic rationales. Chinese businessmen should be concerned that in their pursuit of individual profits, they might be inclined to overlook the economic welfare of the nation. If their interest in China becomes too great, they could become an interest group vulnerable to manipulation by the PRC government. Furthermore, if large investments are drained out by Malaysian producers, a "hollowing-out" of important segments of Malaysia's economy could result. In short, economic considerations are more compelling reasons to question the trend in the rapid volume of Malaysian, and Malaysian Chinese, investments in China.

Projects in the Pipeline and Potential Problem Areas

With economic trade ties developing at a rapid pace, there are several big projects in the pipeline. First, PETRONAS, Malaysia's national oil company, is set to export more crude petroleum and petrochemical-related products to China as well as to set up oil refineries in the future.[26] Second, Malaysian investors are also exploring gaming ventures for possible investment. Gaming ventures are a very profitable line of business, and have attracted many Malaysian businessmen. For example, Tan Sri Lim Goh Tong of the Genting Bhd Group is one of the persons reported to be involved. Also, T.K. Lim of the Magnum Corp Bhd, said that he has secured a lottery licence in the Guangdong province. At the same time Tan Sri Lim Geok Chan of Innovest Bhd was said to have landed a licence for a casino in Kunming city. Apparently all these licences were approved by the local governments, not the central authority. The Chinese government, however, still has a ban on gambling. So when these Malaysian businessmen announced that they had obtained licences from local governments to set up gaming businesses, many observers were sceptical.

Sino-Malaysian economic relations, however, were not problem-free. Several issues have hindered the development of these ties and they require attention from both sides. In early 1990, reports of difficulties encountered by Malaysian investors on the Chinese mainland began to appear in the Malaysian press. The first of these difficulties are the obvious discrepancies between the central and local governments in China. This has created a problem for investors, who are confused over which authority to deal with. These comments from one businessman are very illuminating:

> Some provincial governments look at the list of things that can be done and say, Everything mentioned in the list we will do, and anything not mentioned we will not do. Other provincial governments look at the list of things that cannot be done and say, Everything mentioned in this list, we will not do. Anything not mentioned in the list, we will do. So, the Yunnan and Guangdong provincial governments must have looked at the list of things that cannot be done, and found that gaming was not in it. So, they decide to carry out the business.[27]

Secondly, there seems to be a lack of guidance by the governments as far as investment regulations are concerned. It was reported that manufacturers in Perak were eager to explore the China market for investment, but are hesitant to do so due to a lack of guidance.[28] The availability of infrastructure and trade institution building are necessary if trade is to be promoted. At the moment, the absence of intergovernmental agreements on methods for resolving trade disputes have placed traders and investors in a difficult position. Likewise, there are few formal procedures or mechanisms to deal with trade problems.

Thirdly, there is an over-concentration of investments in a few areas. At one point, China Embassy Commercial Counsellor Cen Zhixiao warned that Malaysian businessmen had been focusing too much on consumer products and the manufacturing sector. They were advised to participate in banking, insurance, transportation, infrastructure and telecommunications projects.[29] China has opened out more sectors, which were previously closed to foreigners. These include agriculture, transport (including airlines, sea and river shipping), insurance, telecommunications, and raw material processing. The same advice was given by Deputy Minister of International Trade and Industry Chua Jui Meng after his unofficial visit to China in October 1992. He said there are a number of areas in which Malaysian entrepreneurs could seriously consider venturing into. These included the construction of houses and infrastructure, the services sector such as restaurants and supermarkets, trading, banking and financial services and information technology.

Fourthly, there have been continual complaints by overseas investors that Chinese workers do not work as hard as their counterparts in Southeast Asia. The work attitude of the Chinese labour force is very different. It is said that they are less efficient and lack motivation and initiative in their work.

Fifthly, Malaysian officials also complained that the Chinese government was only willing to do business with private enterprises owned by overseas Chinese. Government corporations are given lower priority in the dealings. The partiality of the Chinese government has been criticized. The PRC government explained that doing business with private enterprises owned by ethnic Chinese in Southeast Asia has been a traditional pattern. While such a tradition will continue, they have agreed to speed up dealings with government-owned enterprises.

Finally, Malaysia faces growing competition from other ASEAN states for China trade. At the moment, there is not much of competition from other ASEAN countries in promoting exports of primary commodities to China. But in the long run, stiff competition with Malaysia will be inevitable. Indeed, the Malaysian government will have to ensure and make an effort to attract and sustain Chinese corporation interests so that they do not go to other countries for their primary commodities. Indeed the government is already making this effort. Given the fact that 80% of Malaysian exports to China are made up of palm oil, timber, petroleum, plywood, cocoa, natural rubber and latex, and another 20% comprises wood products, fertilizers, iron and electrical machinery, the Malaysian government has decided to provide credit facilities for the export of palm oil to China.[30]

Conclusion: Implications and Future Trends

China's economic reform programmes and its opening to the outside world in 1979 has made the Chinese market increasingly attractive to its neighbouring economically booming states. Continued strong economic growth in the mainland, together with Deng Xiaoping's call for speeding up of economic reforms and opening to the outside, has drawn renewed interest from the ASEAN states. Malaysia's focus on China as an investment centre corresponds with the macro-trend to invest in China by the Southeast Asian countries. Although Malaysia is a relative latecomer as far as focusing on China as an investment centre is concerned, it is developing bilateral trade and relations with China rapidly. The changes that this policy will bring about are enormous. The question at this moment is: What are the implications and impact, both politically and economically?

From the political and security perspective, whether China still constitutes a threat to the Southeast Asian region is really a matter of perception. Southeast Asian leaders certainly are not in agreement as far as this issue is concerned. Even individual heads of states have changed their perception of the role of China over time. Malaysia's Prime Minister Mahathir is one example. In the early part of his career he saw China as a threat to the security of the country, but during his 1985 visit, his ideas about Sino-Malaysian relations changed drastically. Economics became the primary motif, and China was no longer looked upon as a military threat. Moreover, China has expressed support for Mahathir's proposal for the EAEC. The prime minister is well aware that the success of the EAEC would depend on the approval and support of the two economic giants in the region, China and Japan. In that regard, cooperation with China would certainly help to strengthen the bilateral ties between the two countries.

Domestically, the "Chineseness" factor, though much politically manipulated, is ever present and will continue to exert significant influence on politics. But in the past few years two factors seem to have contributed to its diminishing significance. Firstly, the merging of Malay and Chinese capital has made it increasingly difficult to distinguish between the two. When the Chinese community is accused of disloyalty for investing in China, they have the Malay capitalists who do the same on their side. Their defence is made stronger in that regard, though it is not altogether impregnable. It is undeniable that there exists an emotional and cultural bond to the Chinese mainland. But, as in international politics, for Malaysian Chinese businesses profit line would definitely come first as a consideration when deciding to invest.

Secondly, Malaysian Chinese investment in China has the open approval of the governing elites, which has made it less likely to be raked up as a sensitive issue. In Malaysian politics, unless an issue is approved by the administration for open discussion, it is politically sensitive and lies outside the limits of freedom of expression, or the proposer runs the risk of being labelled anti-nationalistic. Since the mending of Sino-Malaysian ties was initiated by Mahathir himself, it is likely to remain high on the policy agenda.

It is clear that, within the limits imposed from both sides, the rapid growth of trade and investment between China and Malaysia in the past six years was driven predominantly by economic considerations. Malaysian investment decisions in general were made in the expectation of making a profit. However, while economic benefits alone were sufficient to justify the efforts to promote Malaysian investment in China, Malaysian Chinese businessmen will have to be more sensitive to the local ethnic and nationalist sentiments in the multi-ethnic country. In that regard, Singapore's Senior Minister Lee Kuan Yew's warning that the ethnic Chinese in Southeast Asia "should take care that their investments in their own countries do not diminish as a result of their China investments"[31] is indeed timely and appropriate.

To sum up, it is reasonable to expect China to become an important trading partner of the ASEAN states in general in the years to come. Sino-Malaysian economic ties will become less ideological and more geared to the economic needs of both sides. The prospects for greater economic interactions will depend largely on how China's economic reforms continue to unfold in the post-Deng period and how Malaysia sustains its economic growth and copes with ethnic politics.

Endnotes

1 *The Star*, 22 June 1993.
2 Stephen Leong, "Malaysia and the People's Republic of China in the 1980s", *Asian Survey*, Vol. XXVII, No. 10, 1987, pp. 1109–1126.
3 As John Wong remarked: "The most remarkable feature about Sino-Malaysian trade is its tenacious and persistent character. For over two decades, trade activities between the two countries were conducted in the absence of a formal diplomatic framework. Each side was apparently contented with the ambiguous but pragmatic arrangements which had nonetheless proved to be quite effective in overcoming the mutual political vituperation and ideological antipathy that often cropped up in the heyday of the Cold War." John Wong, *The Political Economy of Malaysia's Trade Relations with China*, Singapore: Institute of Southeast Asian Studies, 1974, p. 2.
4 See, for example, Cheah Boon Kheng, "Malayan Chinese and the Citizenship Issue, 1945–48", *Review of Indonesian and Malayan Affairs*, Vol. 12, No. 2, 1978, pp. 108–117.
5 Leo Suryadinata, *China and the ASEAN States: The Ethnic Chinese Dimension*, Singapore: Singapore University Press, 1988, p. 103.
6 Robert L. Worden, et al. (eds.), *China: A Country Study*, 4th ed., Washington, D.C.: U.S., 1988, p. 345.
7 "China-Malaysia Joint Communique, 31 May 1974", in R.K. Jain (ed.), *China and Malaysia, 1949–1983*, New Delhi: Radiant Publishers, 1984, pp. 221–222.
8 Bruce Gale, *Politics and Public Enterprise in Malaysia*, Petaling Jaya, Malaysia: Eastern Universities Press, 1981, and Lo Guat Sim, "The Role of PERNAS in the Context of the Second Malaysia Plan", in Norris (ed.), *Case Studies in Malaysian Public Enterprises*, Vol. II, University of Malaya, 1974.

9 *Straits Times*, 14 July 1993.
10 *Straits Times*, 14 July 1993.
11 *New Straits Times*, 22 June 1993.
12 *New Straits Times*, 22 June 1993.
13 *Straits Times*, 27 July 1993.
14 *Star*, 26 April 1993.
15 *Straits Times*, 14 July, 1993.
16 See, for example, George Hicks (ed.), *Overseas Chinese Remittances from Southeast Asia 1910–1940*, Singapore: Select Books, 1993.
17 Michael Godley, *The Mandarin-capitalist from Nanyang: Overseas Chinese Enterprise in the Modernization of China 1893–1911*, Cambridge: Cambridge University Press, 1981, p. 3.
18 M.A. Andreyev, *Overseas Chinese Bourgeoisie – A Peking Tool in Southeast Asia*, Moscow: Progress Publishers, 1975.
19 Heng Pek Koon, *Chinese Politics in Malaysia*, Singapore: Oxford University Press, 1988.
20 Sieh Lee Mei Ling, "The Transformation of Malaysian Business Groups", in Ruth McVey (ed.), *Southeast Asian Capitalists*, Cornell: SEAP, 1992.
21 *Business Times*, 9 January 1993.
22 *Business Times*, 5 August 1991.
23 Shee Poon Kim, "Peking's Foreign Policies Towards Malaysia", *Issues and Studies*, Vol. 23, No. 8, 1987.
24 *New Straits Times*, 17 May 1993.
25 *Sin Chow Jit Poh*, 8 October 1992.
26 *Star*, 11 May 1993.
27 *Star*, 25 November 1992.
28 *Business Times*, 7 May 1993.
29 *Business Times*, 9 January 1993.
30 *Straits Times*, 29 July 1993.
31 Lee Kuan Yew, "Ethnic Chinese, Networking and Where Loyalties Lie", *Straits Times*, 23 November 1993. This is a speech given by Lee Kuan Yew at the Second World Entrepreneurs Convention in Hong Kong on 22 November 1993.

References

M.A. Andreyev, *Overseas Chinese Bourgeoisie – A Peking Tool in Southeast Asia*, Moscow: Progress Publishers, 1975.

Theresa Chong Carino, *China and the Overseas Chinese in Southeast Asia*, Quezon City: New Day Publishers, 1985.

Chang Pao-min, "China and Southeast Asia: The Problem of a Perception Gap", *Contemporary Southeast Asia*, Vol. 9, No. 3, December, 1987, pp. 181–193.

Fu Zhengluo, "Sino-Malaysian Economic Relations", in Chia Siow-Yue and Cheng Bifan (eds.), *ASEAN-China Economic Relations: Trends and Problems*, Singapore: Institute of Southeast Asian Studies, 1987.

Michael R. Godley, *The Mandarin-capitalists from Nanyang: Overseas Chinese Enterprise in the Modernization of China 1893–1911*, Cambridge: Cambridge University Press, 1981.

Richard L. Grant (ed.) *China and Southeast Asia. Into the Twenty-first Century*, Washington: Center for Strategic and International Studies, 1993.

Gary Hamilton (ed.), *Business Networks and Economic Development in East and Southeast Asia*, Hong Kong: Hong Kong University Press, 1991.

Fred Herschede, "Trade between China and ASEAN: The Impact of the Pacific Rim Era", *Pacific Affairs*, Vol. 64, No. 2, 1991.

George L. Hicks (ed), *Overseas Chinese Remittances from Southeast Asia 1910–1940*, Singapore: Select Books, 1993.

Ho Khai Leong, "The Changing Political Economy of Taiwan-Southeast Asia Relations", *The Pacific Review*, Vol. 6, No. 1, 1993, pp. 31–40.

R.K. Jain (ed.), *China and Malaysia 1949–1983*, New Delhi: Radiant Publishers, 1984.

Victor Simpao Limlingan, *The Overseas Chinese in ASEAN: Business Strategies and Management Practices*, Pasig, Metro Manila: Vita Development Corporation, 1986.

J.A.C. Mackie, "Changing Patterns of Chinese Big Business in Southeast Asia", Department of Economics, Research School of Pacific Studies, ANU, no date (mimeographed).

Richard Whitley, *Business Systems in East Asia: Firms, Markets and Society*, London: Sage, 1992.

J. Saravanamuttu, "Malaysia-China Ties, Pre and Post 1974: An Overview", in F. Loh Kok Wah, Phang Chung Nyap and J. Saravanamuttu, *The Chinese Community and Malaysia-China Ties: Elite Perspective*, Tokyo: Institute of Developing Economies, 1981.

Leo Suryadinata, *China and the ASEAN States: The Ethnic Chinese Dimension*, Singapore: Singapore University Press, 1985.

John Wong, *The Political Economy of Malaysia's Trade Relations with China*, Singapore: Institute of Southeast Asian Studies, 1974.

John Wong, *The Political Economy of China's Changing Relations with Southeast Asia*, New York: St. Martin's Press, 1984.

Yen Ching-hwang, *Coolies and Mandarins: China's Protection of Overseas Chinese during the Late Ch'ing Period (1851–1911)*, Singapore: Singapore University Press, 1985.

Straits Times, Singapore

New Straits Times, Malaysia

Star, Malaysia

Nanyang Siang Pau, Malaysia

Sin Chow Jit Poh, Malaysia

Utusan Malaysia, Malaysia

Business Times, Malaysia

12

Singapore's Investment in China

Yong Pow Ang

My paper outlines the pattern of Singapore's investment in China. I would suggest in my paper that the Singapore government plays an important role, first as a catalyst, and subsequently as an active player, in the investment in China. The other point I wish to make is that the Singapore government has been handling, and will continue to handle its neighbours sensitively when promoting investment in China.

For analytical purposes, Singapore's investment in China can be divided into three stages.

The first phase was between 1979 and 1984. This period started off with the setting up of four special economic zones and ended with the opening of 14 coastal zones for foreign investors. Lee Kuan Yew, the then prime minister of Singapore, made his first visit to China in 1976. This was a signal to Singapore businessmen that the hostile relationship between Singapore and China was set to change in the post-Cultural Revolution era. Moments after Lee's visit, a team of Chinese businessmen led by the president of the Singapore Chinese Chamber of Commerce and Industry Tan Keong Choon went on a trip to Beijing. (Tan is the nephew of prominent philanthropist Tan Kah Kee). It is perhaps no accident that Tan Keong Choon was among the first Singapore businessmen investing in China. One of his largest ventures in China, together with a group of Singapore Chinese businessmen, was a palm oil project in Hainan. It, however, failed miserably. Lee Kuan Yew made his second trip to China in 1980. A year later, China and Singapore set up Commercial Representative Offices.

Riding on the first investment wave were mainly Singapore businessmen in the private sector, who went in to test the waters. The Chinese official statistics suggested that the aggregate sum of investment from Singapore prior to 1985 was minuscule. I suspect most of the investments from private individuals during that time was channelled from Hong Kong. But the amount would be small.

Singapore's government-linked companies were a minor player during this period with the exception of two projects. One was the palm oil project which was started off by a group of Singapore businessmen including Tan Keong Choon. The other was an oil supply base. The investment in the oil supply base was made by a consortium of 10 Singapore companies. Such was the cautious or hands-off approach of the government companies towards investment in China.

The second wave started on the positive signal from both countries in 1985. Lee Kuan Yew made his third visit to the country. Immediately after the trip, the two countries signed several agreements, including the Investment Promotion and Protection Agreement, a Double Taxation Treaty, and a Tourism, Civil Aviation and Exhibitions Agreement. On 15 May the same year, Singapore Airlines made its inaugural flight to Beijing and Shanghai.

This period from 1985 till 1988 was marked by a China investment fever. Quite a few hotel projects were committed by Singapore companies at that time, especially in 1986. This period saw a sizeable number of public listed companies making inroads into China. Of course, private individuals continued their foray into China.

The overheated economy in 1988 and the Tiananmen incident in 1989 took its toll on foreign investment. Singapore's investment in China declined in 1989 and 1990.

The third wave of investment started from late 1991, especially after the landmark visit of Deng Xiaoping to Southern China in early 1992.

Singapore's investment commitment in China in 1992 was the sum total for the previous 13 years. This was a result of a confluence of factors both in China and Singapore.

In China, the most significant impetus came from Deng Xiaoping whose symbolic visit to Shenzhen had unleashed forces of change. Investor confidence, which was badly shaken by the Tiananmen incident, made a comeback as China opened up its domestic market and allowed the transfer of land-use rights, which was as good as land lease for the purpose of loan mortgage.

At home, the Singapore government was prodding its businessmen to spread their wings overseas and venture abroad to boost the external economy. The government-linked companies are increasingly under pressure to make a higher return on their reserves. Hence, there was a greater willingness to look for investment opportunities in the fast-growing countries, China being the major one.

The surge of Singapore's investment in China was in line with the general trends where foreign investors re-rated the country. Total investment commitment in China in 1992 was a record US$58 billion, which was equal to the sum total of the investment commitment between 1979 and 1991.

In fact, the growth of Singapore's investment in China pales in comparison with Hong Kong, Taiwan and South Korea. In sum, the increase in Singapore's investment in China is attributed largely to the pull factor, namely, the improvement of the investment climate in China.

The third wave, of which we have not seen the peak yet, is marked by a greater involvement of the Singapore government and its investment arms in China. There are two major factors contributing to the policy shift. Firstly, the substantial foreign reserves of Singapore traditionally invested in the properties and bonds in the developed economies, such as the United States, had yielded meagre returns as the West was gripped in recession. In contrast, the Asia-Pacific economies were developing at a high end of 8 to 10%. Lee Kuan Yew recently said Singapore would "buy into" the region by investing part of the national reserves. Secondly, Lee is bullish about the economic potential of China. He believes China will grow into a big power, both economically and perhaps militarily. Investing in China will bring in good returns. There could also be strategic or security considerations as China is seen to be growing as a major power in this region.

Lee felt that Singapore investors had a lot to catch up with in investing in China. In the mid-80s, Lee lamented that Singapore businessmen were not tapping fully into the reservoir of political goodwill between Singapore and China. He emphasized that it was up to the private sector to translate the political goodwill into tangible economic benefits. During a trip to China in October 1992, Lee again expressed his concerns that Singapore businessmen could miss out on the opportunities in a thriving economy. And putting his money where his mouth is, Lee has recently decided to take a more hands-on approach in regional investment.

Symbolic of such government involvement is the development of a 70-sq-km township in Suzhou. With a project of such scale, Singapore and China will work together for a long time to come. The stakes are high for this project, both financially and politically. So are the returns.

The regionalization move in Singapore has generated enormous interest in China. Singapore businessmen in the private sector, of course, could not have missed this signal.

In the past, Singapore Chinese businessmen went into China quietly for fear of political backlash. They were acutely aware of the geopolitics of Singapore, namely, a tiny island surrounded by a sea of Malays. At home, the last thing they wanted was to be labelled chauvinists. A chauvinist would court as much trouble in Singapore as a communist during the Cold War period.

The end of the Cold War, together with the changing threat perception in Southeast Asia, has helped ease the sensitivity of Singapore Chinese businessmen towards investing in China. But the agent of change is still the Singapore government, or more specifically, Lee Kuan Yew.

Now, businessmen cannot wait to announce any business deals in China, however preliminary they are, particularly when these announcements help push up the share price of the companies.

Another interesting trend of Singapore's investment in China is the growing strategic alliance between Singapore government-linked companies and local individuals and public companies on the one hand, and between Singapore companies and the ethnic Chinese companies in this region, such as Indonesia and Hong Kong. The strategic alliance helps spread risk. It also enables Singapore consortiums to take up larger projects, such as infrastructure developments which involve billions of dollars.

The strategic alliance goes beyond the ethnic Chinese businessmen in this region. The Sembawang group, a Singapore government-linked company, has teamed up with American Bechtel to look for investment opportunities in China. Singapore's government investment arm, Temasek Holdings, has joined hands with American Wing-Merrill to explore a power plant project in Henan province. It has now become fashionable for countries like Germany, the UK, France, Japan, and lately Taiwan and Malaysia to talk about forming strategic alliances with Singapore to invest in third countries, China being the main target.

Singapore's investment in China is set to grow further, so is its investment in this region. There will be more big-ticket items undertaken by government-linked companies, together with local or foreign investors.

This is made possible partly because the neighbouring countries are now adopting a business approach towards the investment in China. Malaysian Prime Minister Mahathir's recent trip to China with a large team of businessmen resulted in numerous business deals. Indonesian President Suharto also visited China.

But the drop of foreign investment in both Malaysia (by 52%) and Indonesia (by 22%) last year, in contrast to the sharp rise of ASEAN's foreign investment in China, was a cause of concern.

Table 12.1: Singapore's Investment in China by Value, 1979–1992

Year	No. of Projects	Contract Value (US$10,000)	Actual Sum Invested (US$10,000)
1979–82	n.a.	3,820	n.a.
1983	6	1,627	n.a.
1984	25	6,256	120
1985	62	7,551	1,013
1986	53	13,741	1,300
1987	53	6,979	2,163
1988	105	13,663	2,782
1989	78	11,113	8,414
1990	72	10,349	5,043
1991	169	15,521	5,821
1992	742	99,655	12,231
Total	**1,365**	**190,275**	**38,887**

Source: *Almanac of China's Foreign Economic Relations and Trade, 1984–1993* (various issues)

Table 12.2: ASEAN Investment in China by Contract Value

			US$10,000		
	Malaysia	Indonesia	Thailand	Philippines	Singapore
1984	37	76	2,328	210	6,256
1985	24	173	1,456	4,056	7,551
1986	24	—	1,321	381	13,741
1987	957	118	453	3,039	6,979
1988	522	205	3,767	730	13,663
1989	266	98	5,679	471	11,113
1990	320	34	4,173	1,078	10,349
1991	4,021	1,091	10,825	1,744	15,521
1992	20,910	12,141	72,342	27,316	99,655

Source: See Table 12.1

Table 12.3: ASEAN Investment in China by Actual Value

			US$10,000		
	Malaysia	Indonesia	Thailand	Philippines	Singapore
1984	57	—	445	229	120
1985	25	8	884	311	1,013
1986	41	49	910	108	1,300
1987	13	—	1,124	380	2,163
1988	130	32	610	363	2,782
1989	40	137	1,268	152	8,414
1990	64	100	672	167	5,043
1991	196	218	1,962	585	5,821
1992	2,467	2,017	8,303	1,628	12,231

Source: See Table 12.1

Lee Kuan Yew has urged the ethnic Chinese businessmen in this region to invest more in their home countries. He also suggested that China should, through the help of the ethnic Chinese businessmen, invest in Southeast Asia.

For Singapore, it is likely to diversify its investment in this region both for economic and strategic considerations. A stock brokering firm estimates that foreign income will contribute 2 to 3 percentage points to Singapore's GNP in a few years' time. The asset allocation by geographical region is likely to be directed by profit and strategic considerations. Singapore's investment in China will continue its uptrend. But its growth will not be at the expense of the investment in the region. The Singapore government is acutely aware of the fact that Singapore, at the end of the day, is in Southeast Asia. It has the capacity to diversify its investment geographically through its omnipresent and omnipotent government-linked companies and its investment arms.

List of Contributors

Azlan Bin Ghazali, M.A. Student, School of Accountancy and Business, Nanyang Technological University, Singapore.

Teresa Chong Carino, Director, Philippine-China Development Resource Centre, Manila, the Philippines.

Chew Soon Beng, Ph.D, Associate Professor, School of Accountancy and Business, Nanyang Technological University, Singapore.

Ho Khai Leong, Ph.D, Lecturer, Department of Political Science, National University of Singapore.

Huang Jianli, Ph.D, Lecturer, Department of History, National University of Singapore.

Jamie Mackie, Emeritus Professor, Department of Economics, Research School of Pacific Studies, Australian National University.

Leo Suryadinata, Ph.D, Associate Professor, Department of Political Science, National University of Singapore.

Wang Gungwu, Ph.D, Emeritus Professor, Vice-Chancellor of the University of Hong Kong.

Christianto Wibisono, Drs., Director, Indonesian Business Data Centre, Jakarta, Indonesia.

Wong Kan Seng, Singapore's Minister for Home Affairs.

Yen Ching-hwang, Ph.D, Reader, Department of History, University of Adelaide, Australia.

Yong Pow Ang was a senior journalist of *Business Times* (Singapore) and a fellow of the Institute of East Asian Political Economy, Singapore.

Yoshihara Kunio, Ph.D, Professor of Economics, Institute of Southeast Asian Studies, Kyoto University, Japan.

Index